# Madrid

# WORLD BIBLIOGRAPHICAL SERIES

General Editors:
Robert G. Neville (Executive Editor)
John J. Horton

Robert A. Myers                     Hans H. Wellisch
Ian Wallace                     Ralph Lee Woodward, Jr.

**John J. Horton** is Deputy Librarian of the University of Bradford and was formerly Chairman of its Academic Board of Studies in Social Sciences. He has maintained a longstanding interest in the discipline of area studies and its associated bibliographical problems, with special reference to European Studies. In particular he has published in the field of Icelandic and of Yugoslav studies, including the two relevant volumes in the World Bibliographical Series.

**Robert A. Myers** is Associate Professor of Anthropology in the Division of Social Sciences and Director of Study Abroad Programs at Alfred University, Alfred, New York. He has studied post-colonial island nations of the Caribbean and has spent two years in Nigeria on a Fulbright Lectureship. His interests include international public health, historical anthropology and developing societies. In addition to *Amerindians of the Lesser Antilles: a bibliography* (1981), *A Resource Guide to Dominica, 1493-1986* (1987) and numerous articles, he has compiled the World Bibliographical Series volumes on *Dominica* (1987), *Nigeria* (1989) and *Ghana* (1991).

**Ian Wallace** is Professor of German at the University of Bath. A graduate of Oxford in French and German, he also studied in Tübingen, Heidelberg and Lausanne before taking teaching posts at universities in the USA, Scotland and England. He specializes in contemporary German affairs, especially literature and culture, on which he has published numerous articles and books. In 1979 he founded the journal *GDR Monitor*, which he continues to edit under its new title *German Monitor*.

**Hans H. Wellisch** is Professor emeritus at the College of Library and Information Services, University of Maryland. He was President of the American Society of Indexers and was a member of the International Federation for Documentation. He is the author of numerous articles and several books on indexing and abstracting, and has published *The Conversion of Scripts and Indexing and Abstracting: an International Bibliography*, and *Indexing from A to Z*. He also contributes frequently to *Journal of the American Society for Information Science*, *The Indexer* and other professional journals.

**Ralph Lee Woodward, Jr.** is Professor of History at Tulane University, New Orleans. He is the author of *Central America, a Nation Divided*, 2nd ed. (1985), as well as several monographs and more than seventy scholarly articles on modern Latin America. He has also compiled volumes in the World Bibliographical Series on *Belize* (1980), *El Salvador* (1988), *Guatemala* (Rev. Ed.) (1992) and *Nicaragua* (Rev. Ed.) (1994). Dr. Woodward edited the Central American section of the *Research Guide to Central America and the Caribbean* (1985) and is currently associate editor of Scribner's *Encyclopedia of Latin American History*.

VOLUME 193

# Madrid

## Graham Shields

*Compiler*

CLIO PRESS

OXFORD, ENGLAND · SANTA BARBARA, CALIFORNIA
DENVER, COLORADO

© Copyright 1996 by ABC-CLIO Ltd.

British Library Cataloguing in Publication Data

Shields, Graham J. (Graham John), 1953-
Madrid. – (World bibliographical series; v. 193)
1. Madrid (Spain) – Bibliography
I. Title
016.9′4641

ISBN 1–85109–250–1

ABC-CLIO Ltd.,
Old Clarendon Ironworks,
35A Great Clarendon Street,
Oxford OX2 6AT, England.

———————

ABC-CLIO Inc.,
130 Cremona Drive,
Santa Barbara,
CA 93116, USA.

Designed by Bernard Crossland.
Typeset by Columns Design Ltd., Reading, England.
Printed and bound in Great Britain by Bookcraft (Bath) Ltd., Midsomer Norton.

# THE WORLD BIBLIOGRAPHICAL SERIES

This series, which is principally designed for the English speaker, will eventually cover every country (and many of the world's principal regions), each in a separate volume comprising annotated entries on works dealing with its history, geography, economy and politics; and with its people, their culture, customs, religion and social organization. Attention will also be paid to current living conditions – housing, education, newspapers, clothing, etc.– that are all too often ignored in standard bibliographies; and to those particular aspects relevant to individual countries. Each volume seeks to achieve, by use of careful selectivity and critical assessment of the literature, an expression of the country and an appreciation of its nature and national aspirations, to guide the reader towards an understanding of its importance. The keynote of the series is to provide, in a uniform format, an interpretation of each country that will express its culture, its place in the world, and the qualities and background that make it unique. The views expressed in individual volumes, however, are not necessarily those of the publisher.

## VOLUMES IN THE SERIES

*For my mother*

# Contents

# Contents

Contents

# Introduction

## Madrid: a brief historical background

Madrid is located almost exactly in the centre of the Iberian peninsula at an altitude of 2,100 feet (635 metres) above sea level on the undulating plateau of the *meseta* (from the Spanish, *mesa*, meaning 'table'). Built like Paris and Rome on seven hills, and lying on the banks of the Manzanares river (a tributary of the Tagus), it is Europe's highest capital and today the continent's third largest. Dominated by the Sierra de Guadarrama to the north, its thin, mountainous skies (acknowledged for their 'admirable purity' by Beaumarchais in 1764) allow temperatures to fall below freezing in winter and sometimes to rise to over 40°C in summer. But it was not for any compelling geographical, or even economic or military, reason that Philip II decided to establish his court at Madrid in 1561. His decision was intended to be permanent, despite the fact that Madrid would be the only major European capital not situated on a navigable river, and at that time had neither a printing press nor a cathedral. Indeed, it was the town's relative obscurity which, for Philip, guaranteed its political innocence and independence of all established power save that of the King himself.

Despite attempts to furnish Madrid with an ancient past, the embarrassing fact for Spaniards has always been that in reality it was founded by Moslems in 854, during the reign of Mohammed I. It comprised a small fortress which formed part of the outlying defences of Toledo, forty-three miles (seventy kilometres) to the south-west. The original Arabic name of Mayrit referred to its excellent water supply from underground streams within the rocky crag on which it stood (where the Palacio Real stands today), and its Alcázar represented one of a series of watchtowers used by the Moslems as a defence against the southward expansion of the Christian states. Attacked on numerous occasions by Christian armies, it withstood their advances until (aided by the disintegration of the Caliphate of Córdoba) it was captured by Alfonso VI of Castile in 1083. Over the next thirty years it continued to be in the front line, and in 1109 and again in 1197 was besieged by Moorish armies camped in the fields below the Alcázar, in the place which became known as the Campo del Moro (Field of the Moor). Madrid's patron saint, San Isidro, was a 12th-century peasant (believed to have died in 1172) who with his wife, Santa María de la Cabeza, was known for extreme piety, kindness to the poor and miraculous acts. In 1622 both were canonized and remain the only husband-and-wife saints in history.

By the beginning of the 13th century, the population of Christian Madrid had increased very slowly to around 3,000. In 1202 the town was given its *Fuero* (Royal Statutes) and in 1309 the *Cortes* (Parliament) met in Madrid for the first time. Mediaeval Castile was beset by a number of civil wars and social unrest, but Madrid began to gain popularity as a royal residence, and the Alcázar was improved to provide more comfortable accommodation for the monarchs who stayed there. Henry IV of Castile (1454-74) gave Madrid the title of 'muy noble y muy real' (very noble and very loyal). As the town grew into a thriving trading and agricultural community new quarters sprang up outside the old walls (*arrabales*) and new walls were constructed. Towards the end of the 15th century political stability was achieved in the region as a result of the marriage of Isabella of Castile and Ferdinand of Aragón, and the consequent union of the two crowns. Together, these two figures imposed their authority on the aristocracy and created a strong professional army. In 1516 their grandson, Charles I, succeeded to the throne and in 1519 was proclaimed Holy Roman Emperor. Much of his time was spent in and around Madrid (including hunting at El Pardo), and after recovering from a long illness there he gave Madrid its title, 'Villa Imperial y Coronada' (Imperial and Crowned Town), choosing the Alcázar as the royal residence for his son, the Crown Prince Philip.

After Charles' abdication, Philip II became Spain's second Habsburg monarch (1556-98). A deeply religious and austere man, personal and political factors led him to believe that Spain needed a permanent capital. In May, 1561 he sent a letter to the nobles who administered the town of Madrid, informing them that the royal household would shortly be coming to stay, and for centuries afterwards Madrid was referred to as *la Corte* (the Court). Having established his capital, Philip made little effort to enhance and upgrade its infrastructure. Although the Alcázar was refurbished and the walls of the town were extended (1566), little new building was undertaken. Instead his attention fixed upon the palace-monastery of San Lorenzo, which he had ordered built in 1562 at the village of El Escorial in honour of his victory over the French on San Lorenzo's day in 1558. His main impact on Madrid and its inhabitants was the founding of seventeen convents and monasteries and the forced conversion to Christianity, or exile, of the small Moslem population. However, as large numbers of lesser nobles and those aspiring to greatness began to flock to Madrid, hoping to attach themselves to wealthy or aristocratic patrons at Court, some new buildings were constructed to accommodate the huge influx. From around 20,000 in 1561, the population rose to approximately 55,000 by 1584, and approached 90,000 by 1600. Others attracted to the capital from the surrounding provinces did much to shape Madrid's future character and outlook. The town acted as a magnet, drawing in thousands of people from different ends of the social spectrum. It inevitably became a mecca for drifters, gamblers and prostitutes and was home to a great many of the very poor, who relied upon the charity of the city's numerous religious institutions. Travellers from northern Europe and Italy began to write about Madrid, usually in uncomplimentary terms, highlighting its 'filthy' streets, lack of drains and 'unbearable stench'. Hindered by the lack of a navigable river, the town produced almost nothing economically. Chronic unemployment made crime a way of life, and those traders that did develop were virtually all oriented towards the Court and the aristocracy. Nevertheless, to entertain the masses, permanent theatres began to be built in the 1570s, and the production of literature and drama became an important and thriving industry.

Philip II died in 1598 at El Escorial and was succeeded by his son, Philip III (1598-1621), who confirmed the establishment of the Court in Madrid and its status as capital ('sólo Madrid es Corte' – only Madrid is the Court) in 1606, despite the efforts of his first minister, the Duke of Lerma, to return the capital to Valladolid, having temporarily moved it there in 1601. Thereafter Madrid expanded rapidly, with builders, architects, painters and playwrights in particular migrating to the city. The Plaza Mayor was completed in 1619, followed within a few years by the Ayuntamiento (Town Hall) and the magnificent Palace of the Buen Retiro. Madrid's population during Philip IV's reign (1621-65) reached 175,000, making it the fifth-largest capital in Europe after Constantinople, Naples, London and Paris. Nevertheless, the Habsburgs built few squares and no grand avenues, and Madrid developed in a disorderly mix of shabby houses and large aristocratic palaces and places of worship. The city's fifth and final wall was completed in 1656, the enclosed area roughly encompassing the parts now designated 'old Madrid'. The surrounding woods were cut to allow expansion and although the climate remained dry the weather alternated between extremes of heat and cold. The famous saying about its climate, 'three months of winter, nine months of hell' was coined by European travellers to the city at this time.

# Introduction

Whilst 17th-century Madrid witnessed a prospering of the arts (in particular literature and painting), Spain generally was beginning to experience political and imperial decline. Even Madrid's population fell, so that by 1700 it had dropped to around 100,000. Under Charles II (1665-1700) Madrid's economy and administration continued to slide and the monarch's predisposition to serious ill-health did nothing to instil confidence in the Crown. With his death in 1700 the Spanish Habsburg dynasty came to an end. The new Bourbon king, Philip V (1700-46), brought with him new ideas, architects and painters from both France and Italy. Raised at Versailles, he was not overly saddened when the Alcázar burned down in 1734, and immediately commissioned a new Royal Palace. Other new religious buildings were constructed and the King's general reforming approach led to economic recovery and a growth in Madrid's population.

Fernando VI (1746-59), a popular king, died childless and was succeeded by his half-brother, Charles III (1759-88). Affectionately nicknamed *El Rey-Alcalde* (the 'King-Mayor'), Charles left an indelible mark on Madrid. Fascinated by the Enlightenment ideas of progress, he sought to improve from the top and became the very model of an enlightened despot as he strove to make Madrid a noble, modern capital. He challenged the privileges of the religious orders and in 1767 expelled the Jesuits from Spain. In Madrid great improvements were made to the city's infrastructure. In 1761 the dumping of waste in the streets was prohibited and the building of sewers and street lighting began. Houses were numbered and street-cleaning and refuse collection were introduced. New public buildings were erected (including the Post Office in the Puerta del Sol and the Puerta de Alcalà), and the beautiful Paseo del Prado was completed in 1782. Part of the gardens of the Palace of the Buen Retiro was opened to the public after the King moved from there to the recently completed Royal Palace in 1767. Reform and an improved economy created a feeling of well-being in late-18th-century Madrid, and although popular reaction at the time to the King's improvements was ambiguous, it is undeniably apparent that the quality of life in the city improved immeasurably under Charles III. His son and successor, Charles IV (1788-1808) was not endowed with his father's intelligence or energy, and was unable to ride the storm brought to Europe by the French Revolution. In 1808 an anti-French riot in Madrid proclaimed Charles IV's son, Ferdinand, as King (1808-33) in his place, and Napoleon subsequently sent troops to the city and made his brother, Joseph Bonaparte, King of Spain. The Peninsular War (or Spanish War of Independence) lasted until 1814, during which time Joseph effected some improvements in the city, including the construction of squares such as the Plaza de Oriente and the Plaza

Santa Ana. Nevertheless, great suffering and destruction was caused by the conflict, perfectly exemplified in Goya's *Disasters of War*. The misery of these events was compounded by a famine in 1812, which killed over 30,000 people.

During the remainder of the century the country swung between absolutism and constitutionalism. Despite Isabella II's (1833-68) relative weakness as monarch, urban reformers continued to improve the city's buildings and roads and the Puerta del Sol was rebuilt (1854-62). Up until this time Madrid had merely been an administrative capital, but once railways were laid in the 1840s it began to fulfil an economic and communication role. Similarly, with the completion of the Canal de Isabel II in 1858, the city was supplied with an adequate supply of fresh water for the first time in its history, and in 1860 a plan by Carlos María de Castro was approved for the general expansion (*ensanche*) of the city. Isabella's unpopularity and the scandal surrounding her court led in 1868 to another military revolt which overthrew the government and dethroned the Queen. Years of civil war followed, and after the abdication of King Amadeo I (1870-73) Spain became a Republic. Growing resistance from the Right and increased reliance on the army culminated in the installation of a military dictatorship in 1874, after which the Bourbon dynasty was restored in the form of Alfonso XII (1874-85), son of Isabella II.

During the 1870s and 1880s Madrid underwent a ten-year building boom with apartment blocks, financial and public buildings and the new Almudena Cathedral being planned and erected. Towards the close of the century immigration to Madrid increased dramatically, and the need for new housing and employment became economically and socially more important. At the same time reassessment and self-examination were taking place with regard to Spain's political, economic and industrial backwardness. 1898 saw the country defeated in a short war with the United States and Spain's subsequent loss of the last of her American possessions. Intellectual debate and much soul-searching ensued, and political changes were inevitable. The King, Alfonso XIII (1885-1931), through his arrogance, succeeded in alienating even his most staunchly right-wing allies, and became the object of several assassination attempts. After 1900 the speed of change quickened with the economy growing rapidly. Massive urbanization took place and the city's population doubled in only thirty years (to just under a million by 1930), although only forty per cent had been born in the city. Buildings sprang up everywhere and the Gran Vía (one of the city's main arteries) opened in 1910. Electricity also led to innovation with the electrification of the trams in 1898 and the opening of the first Metro line in 1919. At the same time the city began to attract intellectuals and professionals from around the country, and Madrid could boast a wealth of literary and artistic talent. Political events, however, changed the optimistic outlook of the city. In 1910 a Republican-Socialist coalition won local elections in Madrid for the first time, and constitutional reforms were demanded after the General Strike of 1917. In 1923 the Captain-General of Barcelona suspended the Constitution and declared himself Dictator under Alfonso XIII, thereby returning Spain to military rule. However, in 1930 he resigned and the government decided to hold municipal elections in April 1931. The results showed sweeping majorities for Republican candidates in all of Spain's cities.

The proclamation of the Second Republic led to the abdication of the King. The new government had plans for a *Gran Madrid* (Greater Madrid) and building work began to extend the Paseo de la Castellana and the Gran Vía. However, the pace of change was curtailed due to ever-deepening social and political crises. The economy declined and unemployment grew, and political parties became even more polarized. After new elections in February 1936, the Left, united once again as the *Frente Popular* (Popular Front), was victorious. Right-wing politicians called for military support to save the country from the Left, and on 9th November Franco's forces commenced their assault on Madrid: the siege of the city had begun. Although the capital suffered major bomb damage, Franco was unable to capture the city, despite besieging it for three years. The population suffered great hardships with severe shortages of food and fuel. Eventually, internal fighting broke out between those Communists committed to resistance and those who wanted to negotiate a peace with Franco. The city finally surrendered to the Nationalists on 28th March 1939. During the *años de hambre* (years of hunger), immediately after the war, recovery was slow. Hundreds of buildings lay in ruins and the city's spirit had been shattered. Franco's repressive régime treated Madrid as an occupied city and, surrounded by military bases, the city personified the most conservative aspects of his dictatorship. For a time, Madrid's loyalty to the Republic threatened its very capital status, but in the end economic and traditional arguments ensured that it remained as capital. The post-war years saw massive immigration to Madrid from the provinces and the city became the fastest-growing European capital this century. Between 1930 and 1970 the population increased from just under one million to over three million.

In the 1950s Spain's isolation dissipated as international recognition of the régime led to a cooperation and defence agreement with the United States in 1953, and Spain's membership of the United Nations in 1955. Multinational companies established themselves in the capital and Madrid's industry began to expand rapidly. The growth of mass tourism, American investment and sporting success (particularly through the Real Madrid football team) instilled some degree of optimism and economic success. At the same time Madrid's central location became increasingly important as road, rail and air transport networks developed. The city was transformed, but not always for the better: the dramatic increase in population and the manufacturing industry led to its suffering the modern urban consequences of congestion and pollution. Although certain areas of the city were conserved, whole neighbourhoods of architectural interest were demolished to make way for new office blocks and car parks. During the 1960s and 1970s shanty towns (*chabolas*), devoid of running water and plumbing, sprang up on the edge of the city. New roads cut into the banks of the Manzanares river and suburban development grew to the north and west of the city. Madrid began to look and feel like a big city.

On the political scene during these years opposition to Franco's régime revived. Labour and student unrest grew and regionalist protest and violence sprang up, culminating in 1973 with the assassination by ETA (Euskadi ta Askatasuna – Basque Homeland and Freedom), the Basque separatist group, of Admiral Luis Carrero Blanco, the first Prime Minister appointed by Franco. Rising unemployment and inflation, combined with the failing health of the Dictator, led to the democratic movement's aspirations focusing upon his nominated successor, Juan Carlos (grandson of Alfonso XIII). Following Franco's death in November 1975, the Bourbon monarchy was restored and the transition to democracy began. After years of repressive authoritarian rule, the pent-up desire for change propelled Madrid into a decade of frenetic activity and the *movida madrileña* (Madrid movement) emerged. Identified with art, creativity, counter-culture and nightlife, the *movida* was also associated with certain individuals, such as the artist, Ouka Lele, Martirio (with her outrageous costumes) and in particular Pedro Almodóvar, who began his film-making career in Madrid's nightclubs. The city's much-loved Socialist mayor, Enrique Tierno Galván (universally known as 'the old professor'), was widely recognized as the sponsor of Madrid's cultural revival. Rapid modernization accompanied socialist rule in the city. The sanitation system was renovated, pollution controls were inaugurated, squares and parks were cleaned up and the road network was improved. Nevertheless, political changes did not take place entirely unopposed. Although unsuccessful, the attempted military coup which took place in the capital in February 1981 demonstrated the fragility of democracy. The King's swift and decisive assurance to the country that the army had pledged him its allegiance proved a major factor in foiling the real threat of a return to military dictatorship. Spain's international recognition grew when the country joined NATO in 1982, the European Community in 1986 and the Western European Union in 1988. Rapid economic growth marked these years and by the end of the decade the country had the fastest-growing economy in Europe. Within a matter of years Madrid could boast Europe's fifth-largest Stock Exchange and the continent's third-busiest convention centre. In 1991 the city successfully hosted the opening round of the Middle East Peace Conference and in 1992, in recognition of the tremendous progress that the city had made in only fifteen years, it was chosen as Europe's cultural capital.

With a population approaching four million, the compact city of today suffers from serious overcrowding (with an average of 3.5 persons per dwelling) and the number of cars has doubled in the last ten years. Unlike the *ensanche* (expansion) of the 19th century, modern growth and development has generally been chaotic and savage. This has led to biting criticism of the city's architecture, and in a recent poll of Spanish architects Madrid was voted least architecturally interesting of the country's principal cities. Nonetheless, it is undeniable that Madrid contains a fascinating wealth and diversity of architectural styles, although the image of the city does not revolve solely around its built environment. It has a great deal more to offer, and much of its charm lies in its 'small-town' provincial character. For centuries Madrid was referred to as *Los Madriles* (The Madrids) as each district (*barrio*) or quarter had its own local traditions and character. It is this coexistence of the old and the new which particularly appeals to the city's visitors. Glass skyscrapers look down upon mediaeval churches and historic monuments, and the busy hustle and bustle of modern city life goes on alongside its tranquil old squares and expansive parks. The vibrant streets and noisy cafés of modern Madrid bear witness to the city's renowned vitality, and the restless, frenetic inhabitants proudly boast the nickname, *los gatos* (the cats), in recognition of their innate ability in past centuries to climb the city walls and in modern times to survive on minimal sleep.

Madrid continues to attract not only tourists and foreign visitors, but people from all corners of Spain, although most are second-generation Madrilenians at best, retaining strong provincial ties. Those who have fallen under its spell and adopted the city as their home are eager to embrace the popular saying, 'Ser español un orgullo, ser madrileño un título' (To be Spanish a pride, to be Madrilenian a title).

## The bibliography

This work represents the first full-scale, English-language bibliography on Madrid and contains 538 main entries together with over 600 subsidiary items. Although comprehensive in scope, it is by necessity selective in some areas. Books, chapters, periodical articles and theses are included and, as with all volumes in the *World Bibliographical Series*, emphasis is on English-language publications which are both up to date and generally available. However, in order to provide as expansive a study as possible, and to encompass the full range of subject headings, it was necessary to include a large number (comprising around half of the main entries) of standard or useful Spanish-language sources. The accessibility of these Spanish publications was a major consideration, and many of those cited are available from the British Library, the Library of Congress and British and American university libraries. Similarly, all can be found in the Biblioteca Nacional in Madrid and in the city's principal bookshops (see 'Useful Addresses'). Much has also been published in Spanish on the wider province and Autonomous Region of Madrid, and reference has been made to a number of these works where it was apparent that they also referred extensively to the city itself.

My aim has been to provide scholars, librarians and informed readers with a helpful and, at the same time, interesting reference guide to Madrid. Entries within each of the chapter headings have been arranged alphabetically by author, editor or compiler and, where none of these is apparent, by title. Critical and descriptive annotations accompany each item and, where appropriate, factual explanations or interpretations of the particular topic concerned. Extensive cross-references have been made between chapters. Separate alphabetically-ordered indexes to authors, titles and subjects should ensure the easy location of relevant items. In addition, the inclusion of the standard Spanish bibliography on Madrid, *Bibliografía de Madrid*, by Rodríguez and Martínez (La Librería, 1994), and a large number of works which contain substantial bibliographies should assist those looking to pursue a subject in more detail. No bibliography is ever complete, but I hope that this book will prove to be a valuable reference tool and guide which both provides answers to specific questions and stimulates further interest amongst readers.

## Acknowledgements

This work could not have reached fruition without the help and advice of a number of people. I am grateful to the University of Northumbria at Newcastle Research Section and the Department of Information and Library Management Research Committee for their awards which enabled me to undertake visits to libraries, research institutes and government offices in both London and Madrid. I would particularly like to thank Dick Hartley, Mike Heine and Ian Winkworth for their support in this respect. I would also like to acknowledge the efforts of the staff of the Inter-Library Loans Section of the University Library, especially Margaret Howie, Ann Johnston and Alison Darling. Invaluable assistance was also provided by Mayte Azorín and Matilde Javaloyes at the Instituto Cervantes library in London, José del Corral and staff at the Instituto de Estudios Madrileños in Madrid, and Manuel Rico at the Consejería de Educación y Cultura of the Comunidad de Madrid who was kind enough to donate his time as well as some useful material on the city. Finally, I would like to thank my wife for her constant advice and support, and in particular her assistance in both editing and typing the finished work.

*Graham J. Shields*
*Newcastle upon Tyne*
*August 1996*

# Chronology

| | |
|---|---|
| **854** | Madrid founded by Emir Mohammed I |
| **1085-86** | Alfonso VI of Castile conquers Emirate of Toledo, including Madrid |
| **1109** | Madrid besieged by Moorish army |
| **1202** | Alfonso VIII gives Madrid *Fuero* (Statutes) Population c. 3,000 |
| **1212** | Battle of Navas de Tolosa – decisive defeat of Moslems in Spain |
| **1309** | Ferdinand IV chooses Madrid as the meeting-place of the *Cortes* (parliament) |
| **1360** | King Pedro the Cruel rebuilds Madrid's Alcázar |
| **1476** | Isabella becomes Queen of Castile |
| **1478** | Establishment of the Inquisition |
| **1492** | Recapture of Granada (last Moorish stronghold) Expulsion of the Jews Discovery of the New World by Columbus |
| **1516** | Charles I succeeds to the throne |
| **1520-21** | Madrid joins the *Comuneros* revolt |
| **1547** | Birth of Cervantes in Alcalá de Henares |
| **1556** | Philip II ascends the throne |
| **1561** | Philip II declares Madrid seat of Court |
| **1562** | Lope de Vega born in Madrid |
| **1563-84** | Building of El Escorial |
| **1566** | Beginning of Dutch revolt |
| **1574** | First theatre in Madrid, the *Corral de la Pacheca* |
| **1588** | Defeat of the Spanish Armada by the English |
| **1598** | Philip III ascends the throne |
| **1599** | Birth of Velázquez |
| **1599-1600** | Plague and famine throughout Castile |
| **1601-06** | Court moved to Valladolid |

# Chronology

| | |
|---|---|
| **1605, 1615** | *Don Quijote* published in two parts |
| **1606** | Philip III officially declares Madrid the capital of Spain |
| **1609-14** | Expulsion of the Moriscos (christianized Moslems) |
| **1617-19** | Construction of the Plaza Mayor |
| **1621** | Philip IV ascends the throne |
| **1630-33** | Buen Retiro Palace built |
| | Population of Madrid c. 160,000 |
| **1635** | Death of Lope de Vega |
| **1660** | Death of Velázquez |
| **1665** | Charles II ascends the throne |
| **1700** | Death of Charles II without an heir – Philip V becomes first Bourbon King of Spain |
| **1700-14** | War of the Spanish Succession |
| **1734** | Alcázar destroyed by fire |
| **1735-64** | Construction of the Royal Palace |
| **1759-88** | Reign of Charles III, who does much to improve Madrid |
| **1761** | Waste-dumping banned in Madrid's streets |
| **1767** | Retiro Park partially opened to the public |
| **1775-82** | Paseo del Prado created |
| **1785-1808** | Construction of the Prado Museum |
| **1788** | Charles IV becomes King |
| **1800** | Population of Madrid c. 185,000 |
| **1808-13** | French occupation – Joseph Bonaparte becomes King of Spain |
| **1812** | *Cortes* of Cádiz proclaims the first Spanish Constitution |
| **1813** | Ferdinand VII restored to the throne |
| **1819** | Prado opened to the public |
| **1832** | Introduction of gas to the city |
| **1833** | Death of Ferdinand VII |
| | Beginning of Carlist Wars and reign of Isabella II |
| **1834** | Cholera epidemic |
| **1836** | University of Alcalá de Henares moves to Madrid |
| **1837** | Execution of the bandit, Luis Candelas |
| **1851** | Inauguration of railway line to Aranjuez |
| **1854-62** | Puerta del Sol rebuilt |
| **1858** | Inauguration of the Canal de Isabel II, bringing water from the Guadarrama mountains |
| **1860** | Plan for *Ensanche* (expansion) of Madrid approved |
| | Puerta del Sol opened to the public |

| | |
|---|---|
| **1868** | Revolution overthrows Isabella II |
| **1871** | Amadeo of Savoy becomes King |
| | Appearance of first public trams in Madrid, drawn by mules |
| **1872** | Population of Madrid 335,000 |
| **1873** | Amadeo abdicates |
| | First Republic declared |
| **1874** | Republic becomes a military dictatorship |
| | Alfonso XII declared King, thereby restoring Bourbon line |
| **1879** | Spanish Socialist Party (PSOE) founded in Casa Labra *taberna* |
| **1883** | Introduction of electric lighting to the city |
| **1884-91** | Construction of Bank of Spain |
| **1886** | Alfonso XIII becomes King |
| **1892** | Inauguration of Atocha railway station |
| **1896** | First film show in Madrid |
| **1898** | Spanish-American War (Spain loses last of American possessions) |
| | Madrid's tramlines are electrified |
| **1900** | Population of Madrid 540,000 |
| **1905** | *ABC* daily newspaper begins publication |
| **1907** | First registration of motor vehicles |
| **1909** | Tragic Week |
| **1910** | Building of Gran Vía begins |
| **1917** | General Strike throughout Spain |
| **1919** | First Metro line opened |
| **1920** | Death of Galdós |
| **1923-30** | Dictatorship of General Primo de Rivera |
| **1928** | Death of María Guerrero (actress) |
| **1929-31** | Barajas airport opened |
| **1930** | Fall of Primo de Rivera |
| | Population of Madrid c. 955,000 |
| **1931** | Second Republic proclaimed after Alfonso XIII's abdication |
| **1933** | First Madrid Book Fair |
| | *Gran Madrid* development plan approved |
| **1934** | General Strike |
| **1936-39** | Spanish Civil War |
| **1936-37** | Siege of Madrid |
| **1939** | Franco becomes Head of State |
| **1946-50** | UN imposes sanctions on Spain |
| **1950-60** | Population of Madrid rises to over two million |

# Chronology

| | |
|---|---|
| **1951** | Creation of Instituto de Estudios Madrileños (Institute of Madrid Studies) |
| **1953** | Signing of cooperation treaty with the United States |
| **1961** | First act of violence by ETA (Euskadi ta Askatasuna – Basque Homeland and Freedom) |
| **1962** | Publication of *Tiempo de silencio* |
| **1963** | Execution of Julián Grimau |
| **1965** | Student demonstrations |
| **1969** | Juan Carlos nominated as Franco's successor Population of Madrid 3,146,000 |
| **1972** | Madrid's zoo (in the Casa de Campo) opened |
| **1975** | Death of Franco – restoration of the Bourbon monarchy in King Juan Carlos I |
| **1977** | First democratic general election |
| **1978** | Spanish Constitution approved |
| **1979** | Enrique Tierno Galván becomes Mayor of Madrid |
| **1980** | First feature film of Pedro Almodóvar |
| **1982** | Socialist Party (under Felipe González) wins national elections |
| **1983** | Statute of Autonomy for the Community of Madrid approved |
| **1986** | Spain joins the European Community Death of Tierno Galván |
| **1989** | TeleMadrid begins to broadcast |
| **1991** | Popular Party (PP) wins power in Madrid city council Madrid hosts first Middle East Peace Conference |
| **1992** | Madrid designated European cultural capital First high-speed train (AVE) journey from Madrid to Seville Thyssen-Bornemisza Museum opened |
| **1995** | President Clinton visits Madrid to attend a meeting of the European Council |
| **1996** | José María Aznar becomes Prime Minister |

# Useful Addresses

**Government and Commerce**

British Chamber of Commerce
Plaza de Santa Bárbara 10, 1ª
28004 MADRID
Tel. 341 3081
Fax 341 4605

Spanish Chamber of Commerce in Britain
5 Cavendish Square
LONDON
W1M 0DP
Tel. 0171 637 9061
Fax 0171 436 7188

Spanish Embassy
39 Chesham Place
LONDON
SW1X 8SB
Tel. 0171 201 5522
Fax 0171 259 6487

Ayuntamiento de Madrid (Municipal Authority)
Oficina del Alcalde (Mayor's Office)
Plaza de la Villa, 4
MADRID
Tel. 248 1815

Cámara Oficial de Comercio e Industria de Madrid (Chamber of
    Commerce)
Calle Huertas, 13
28012 MADRID
Tel. 538 3500
Fax 538 3677

Oficina de Congresos de Madrid (Madrid Convention Bureau)
Calle Mayor, 69
28012 MADRID
Tel. 588 2900
Fax 588 2930

IMADE (Instituto Madrileño de Desarrollo Empresarial – Madrid
   Development Institute)
Calle García de Paredes, 92
28010 MADRID
Tel. 310 2063
Fax 319 4290

Institución Ferial de Madrid (IFEMA) (Madrid Trade Fairs
   Organization)
Avenida de Portugal
28011 MADRID
Tel. 470 1014
Fax 464 3326

INE (Instituto Nacional de Estadística) (National Statistics Institute)
Paseo de la Castellana, 183
28046 MADRID
Tel. 583 9301
Fax 583 9086

Oficina de Estadística del Ayuntamiento de Madrid (Statistics Office of
   Madrid City Council)
Calle Alcalá, 168
28071 MADRID
Tel. 580 2367

American Embassy
Calle Serrano, 75
28006 MADRID
Tel. 577 4000

British Embassy
Calle Fernando el Santo, 16
28010 MADRID
Tel. 319 0200/8

English-Speaking Helpline (any aspect of, or practical information on,
   Madrid)
Tel. 559 1393
(Mon. – Fri. 7-11 pm)

## Tourism and Transport

Spanish National Tourist Office
57-58 St. James Street
LONDON
SW1A 1LD
Tel. 0171 499 0901

Oficina Municipal de Turismo (City Tourist Office)
Plaza Mayor, 3
28012 MADRID
Tel. 366 5477/588 1636

Oficina de Turismo (Tourist Office)
Calle Princesa, 1
Edificio Torre de Madrid
28042 MADRID
Tel. 541 2325

Consorcio de Transportes de Madrid (Regional Transport Consortium)
Plaza Descubridor Diego de Ordás, 3
28003 MADRID
Tel. 580 4538/39
Fax 580 4634

Consejería de Transportes (Transport Council)
Comunidad de Madrid
Calle Orense, 60
28020 MADRID
Tel. 580 2865
Fax 580 2792

## Libraries, Museums, Archives and Research Institutes

Canning House Library
2 Belgrave Square
LONDON
SW1X 8PJ
Tel. 0171 235 2303
Fax 0171 235 3587

Biblioteca Nacional (National Library)
Paseo de Recoletos, 20
28071 MADRID
Tel. 580 7800
Fax 577 5634

## Useful Addresses

Biblioteca de la Universidad Complutense de Madrid (Library of the
   Complutense University)
Ciudad Universitaria
28040 MADRID
Tel. 544 6696
Fax 544 3131

British Council Libraries
Calle Almagro, 5                    Plaza de Santa Bárbara, 10
28004 MADRID                        28004 MADRID

Biblioteca del Palacio Real (Library of the Royal Palace)
Palacio Real
Calle Bailén s/n
28071 MADRID
Tel. 559 7404 Ext. 243
Fax 548 2691

Biblioteca Regional de la Comunidad de Madrid (Regional Library of
   the Community of Madrid)
Calle Azcona, 42, 4ª
28028 MADRID
Tel. 725 9800
Fax 361 0506

Biblioteca Histórica (History Library)
Ayuntamiento de Madrid
Calle Conde Duque, 9-11
28015 MADRID
Tel. 588 5723

Biblioteca del Senado (Senate Library)
Plaza de la Marina Española, 8
28013 MADRID
Tel. 538 1000

Biblioteca Municipal (City Library)
Calle Conde Duque, 11
28015 MADRID
Tel. 588 5724/44

Hemeroteca Municipal de Madrid (Municipal Newspaper Library)
Calle Conde Duque, 9-11
28015 MADRID
Tel. 588 5771

Museo Nacional del Prado (National Prado Museum)
Paseo del Prado
28014 MADRID
Tel. 420 2836
Fax 420 0794

Museo Nacional Centro de Arte Reina Sofía (National Queen Sofía
    Arts Centre Museum)
Calle Santa Isabel, 52
28012 MADRID
Tel. 467 5161
Fax 467 3163

Museo Thyssen-Bornemisza (Thyssen-Bornemisza Museum)
Paseo del Prado, 8
28014 MADRID
Tel. 420 3944
Fax 420 2780

Museo de la Real Academia de Bellas Artes de San Fernando (Museum
    of the San Fernando Royal Academy of Fine Arts)
Calle Alcalá, 13
28014 MADRID
Tel. 522 1491
Fax 523 1599

Museo Arqueológico Nacional (National Archaeological Museum)
Calle Serrano, 13
28001 MADRID
Tel. 577 7912
Fax 431 6840

Museo Municipal (City Museum)
Calle Fuencarral, 78
28004 MADRID
Tel. 521 6656
Fax 532 7620

Planetario de Madrid (Madrid Planetarium)
Parque Tierno Galván
28045 MADRID
Tel. 467 3461
Fax 468 1154

Centro Cultural de la Villa (Cultural Centre)
Jardines del Descubrimiento
28001 MADRID
Tel. 575 6080

**Useful Addresses**

Instituto Cervantes (Cervantes Institute)
22-23 Manchester Square
LONDON
W1M 5AP
Tel. (Library) 0171 935 1518
Fax 0171 935 6167

Instituto de Estudios Madrileños (Institute of Madrid Studies)
Calle Duque de Medinaceli, 6
28014 MADRID
Tel. 585 4830

Instituto de la Mujer (Women's Institute)
Calle Almagro, 36
28010 MADRID
Tel. 347 8000
Fax 347 7998

Fundación Amigos de Madrid (Friends of Madrid Foundation)
Calle Alcalá, 93, 2º
28009 MADRID
Tel. 431 9984
Fax 431 4502

**Bookshops**

El Avapiés
Calle Hermosilla, 20
MADRID
Tel. 575 9271

La Librería
Calle Santiago, 12
28013 MADRID
Tel. 541 7170
Fax 559 4249

El Corte Inglés (Libros)
Calle Preciados, 3
28013 MADRID
Tel. 556 2300

Librería de Mujeres
Calle San Cristóbal, 17
28012 MADRID
Tel. 521 7043

Librería del Ministerio de Cultura
Gran Vía, 51
28013 MADRID
Tel. 547 3312/547 2146

# Madrid and Its People

1 **A stroll through Madrid.**
Luis Carandell, Ramón Masats.    Barcelona, Spain: Lunwerg, 1995.
108p.
First published in Spanish in 1985, this beautifully produced work primarily presents a
photographic interpretation of the city, although the corresponding text emphasizes
important facts about Madrid and its people. The book as a whole reflects all that is
attractive about the city and is one of a number of collaborative works by this author
(Carandell) and photographer (Masats) which include: *Madrid from the sky*
(Barcelona, Spain: Lunwerg, 1988. 133p.), a coffee-table book full of aerial views of
the city; and *Madrid, Madrid, Madrid* with photographs by Ramón Masats and text by
Luis Carandell, Adrian Piera and Fernando Chueca Goitia (Barcelona, Spain:
Lunwerg, 1995. 285p.), another beautifully illustrated homage to Madrid, its buildings
and people.

2 **Curiosidades de Madrid.** (Curiosities of Madrid.)
José del Corral.    Madrid: El País; Aguilar, 1992. 191p. bibliog.
This lively and entertaining little book is written by one of Madrid's most prolific
writers and historians. He is also Director of the Institute of Madrid Studies, which
publishes widely on the history and culture of the city. His useful study encompasses
many aspects of the city including its streets, people, churches, saints, festivals and
buildings. It is well illustrated and indexed.

3 **Madrid.**
Nina Consuelo Epton.    London: Cassell, 1964. 205p.
Epton's book is a highly readable description and study of Madrid's history, social life
and customs. Written over thirty years ago, it is particularly evocative of Madrid
during the early 1960s. Accounts of her travels with her Aunt Nieves include
descriptions and historical details relating to the city's inhabitants, districts and
monuments, together with its distinctive features and customs. An introductory
chapter recounts memories of her first visit to Madrid as a girl of seven. Other topics

1

of interest are described, with particular emphasis placed on the Royal Palace, the literary quarter, the Puerta del Sol, the Retiro Park, San Isidro, gypsies and visits to Aranjuez, Segovia and La Granja. An index provides easy access to individual subjects, buildings and historical figures, and a number of illustrations are also included. One of the earliest and most interesting Spanish guides to Madrid is *Madrid y su provincia* (Madrid and its province) by José María Quadrado (Barcelona, Spain: El Albir, 1977. 398p.). First published in 1886 (Barcelona, Spain: Daniel Cortezo), it provides a full description of the city and province of Madrid during the 19th century.

4 **Imagen de Madrid.** (A picture of Madrid.)
Fernando Fernán-Gómez, photographs by Francisco Ontañón. Madrid: El País; Aguilar, 1992. 92p.

This work is principally a collection of colour photographs illustrating the people, places and life of contemporary Madrid. These, together with an apposite text, clearly evoke the ethos and verve of the city and its inhabitants. Francisco Ontañón also co-authored another book on Madrid, *Vivir en Madrid* (Living in Madrid) with Luis Carandell (Barcelona, Spain: Kairós, 1971. 176p.).

5 **Imágenes de/Pictures of Madrid.**
María Isabel Gea Ortigas, Javier Leralta García. Madrid: La Librería, 1995. 189p.

Beautifully illustrated and produced, this book is predominantly a photographic record of contemporary Madrid, its buildings and its people. Parallel English and Spanish texts provide the necessary factual detail and narrative to allow the reader to understand the make-up of modern-day Madrid and its rich cultural heritage.

6 **Madrid.**
David Gilmour. In: *Cities of Spain*. The Author. London: Pimlico, 1994, p. 179-97. bibliog.

Written by a highly respected historian and novelist, this short chapter presents an informative and impressionistic account of the city. Aspects of Spain's past are depicted through the author's presentation of Madrid's history and references to notable travellers' accounts. Gilmour also looks at specific areas of the city including their architectural highlights, social history and famous characters. His study concludes with a brief look at contemporary Madrid. Those interested in reading a concise, Spanish study of the city and its people should refer to the short article by Fernando Chueca Goitia, 'Carácter de Madrid y personalidad del madrileño' (The character of Madrid and personality of the madrilenian) (*Revista de Estudios Políticos*, vol. 75 [1954], p. 45-67). Despite being written over forty years ago, it is the work of one of the most prolific writers on Madrid and its history and still offers the reader a fascinating insight into the city and its inhabitants.

7 **Imágenes del Madrid antiguo: álbum fotográfico 1857-1939.** (Pictures of old Madrid: photographic album 1857-1939.)
Madrid: La Librería, 1994. 256p. bibliog.

This photographic guide to Madrid is published by one of the two principal bookshops and publishers (El Avapiés being the other) specializing in books on the city, its history and its culture. The 200 sepia photographs from the city's most important archives wonderfully evoke Madrid's past and include churches, buildings, monuments, the River Manzanares, people and Madrid at war. 1857 is the date of the first photograph of Madrid that the publisher could find. It was also the time when the future King Alfonso XII was born, when the Puerta del Sol was being rebuilt (1854-62, opened in 1860), and when the Canal de Isabél II (which brought water to the city from the Guadarrama mountains) was nearing completion.

8   **Madrid: sus gentes, calles y monumentos.** (Madrid: its people, streets and monuments.)
    Ramón Irigoyen.   Madrid: Prodhufi, 1993. 639p. (Tres de Cuatro Soles, 31).
The author is a well-known radio and television presenter, and in a series of short chapters he provides an interesting description of contemporary Madrid as seen through its streets, people and historic buildings.

9   **Madrid.**
    Robert W. Kern.   In: *The regions of Spain: a reference guide to history and culture.*   The Author.   Westport, Connecticut; London: Greenwood Press, 1995, p. 210-28. map. bibliog.
This is one of the most comprehensive English-language reference books on Spanish history, life and culture from prehistoric times up to the present day. Designed to provide students and interested readers with concise information on all these areas, it is easy to use and well produced and written. The chapter on Madrid gives useful statistical information and short sections describe the economy, history, literature, art, music, customs and society, historic sites and cuisine of the city, province and region.

10   **Madrid, sus cosas y sus gentes.** (Madrid, its stories and its people.)
     Aurora Lezcano, prologue by Gonzalo Fernández de la Mora.   Madrid: Prensa Española, 1976. 3rd ed. 261p.
Daughter of a famous painter (Carlos Lezcano), the author casts a nostalgic eye over Madrid and recounts memories of her childhood and life in the city. Short chapters cover a variety of aspects of the history, events and inhabitants of the city, including famous people, legends, and streets and buildings (e.g. *Casa de las Siete Chimeneas*/House of the Seven Chimneys). The book contains several black-and-white photographs of people and places.

11   **Well met in Madrid.**
     Archibald Lyall.   London: Putnam, 1960. 205p.
Lyall wrote several travel books (as well as writing satire and fiction) and in the present work he dissects '*los madriles*', or the several distinct areas of Madrid. After a brief introductory history, eleven chapters deal with various aspects of life in the city including: important buildings and monuments; restaurants and eating out; café culture; fiestas (including Holy Week and San Isidro celebrations); museums; city-centre nightlife; and the university city. Despite its age, this interesting book continues to offer the reader some fascinating historical details and insights.

12 **Madrid.**
In: *The new encyclopaedia Britannica*. Chicago; London:
Encyclopaedia Britannica, 1974, 15th ed. (vol. 23), p. 373-77. map.
bibliog.

Each year the 15th edition of this encyclopaedia is revised with a new printing. The section on Madrid, though short, provides a useful starting-point for the general reader for two reasons: firstly, everyone has access to the *Encyclopaedia Britannica* through their local libraries; and secondly, no matter which printing of the 15th edition one refers to (updating does not radically affect the general background information on Madrid) it is consistently clear and authoritative. The section provides information on Madrid's physical and human geography; the character of the city; the landscape; the people; the economy; administrative conditions; cultural life; and the city's history.

**Memorias de un setentón, natural y vecino de Madrid.** (Memoirs of a seventy-year-old, born and bred in Madrid.)
*See* item no. 118.

**Madrid.**
*See* item no. 314.

# Geography

13  **Geografía de España: tomo 7; Extremadura, Castilla-La Mancha, Madrid.** (A geography of Spain: vol. 7; Extremadura, Castile-La Mancha, Madrid.)
Edited by Joaquín Bosque Maurel.  Madrid: Planeta, 1991. 592p. maps. bibliog.

This volume of a standard and comprehensive work on the geography of Spain contains over 250 pages on the Autonomous Community and city of Madrid (p. 335-589). Maps, illustrations, graphs and statistics enhance an authoritative text written by a team of respected specialists.

14  **Estudios Geográficos.** (Geographical Studies.)
Madrid: Consejo Superior de Investigaciones Científicas, Instituto de Economía y Geografía Aplicadas, 1940- . quarterly.

Over the years numerous articles have been published in this prestigious journal, on various aspects of the geography of Madrid. The text of the articles is in Spanish, accompanied by summaries in English and French. Each year an annual index is produced, with a cumulative index appearing every ten years. In the area of human geography readers could usefully refer to Carmen Gavira's *Geografía humana de Madrid* (The human geography of Madrid) (Barcelona, Spain: Oikos-Tau, 1989. 84p.). Gavira also wrote *Guía de fuentes documentales para la historia urbana de Madrid, 1940-1980* (A guide to documentary sources for the urban history of Madrid, 1940-80) (Madrid: Instituto de Información y Documentación en Ciencias Sociales, 1984. 365p.) (q.v.).

15 **Aproximación a la geografía de la Comunidad de Madrid.** (An approach to the geography of the Community of Madrid.)
Miguel Angel Torremocha. Madrid: Comunidad, Dirección General de Madrid, 1992. 128p. maps. bibliog. (Colección Conocer la Comunidad de Madrid).

Although generally dealing with the Madrid region, much of this book is relevant to the city itself. Covering physical, human and economic aspects, it contains numerous maps, graphs, diagrams and statistical data and is particularly aimed at students and teachers of geography. For studies of Madrid's climate and geology readers should refer to two standard works in Spanish: *Notas para una climatología de Madrid* (Notes on the climatology of Madrid) by Antonia Roldán Fernández (Madrid: Instituto Nacional de Meteorología, 1985. 48p.); and *Madrid y sus terremotos* (Madrid and its earthquakes) by Juan Bautista Olaechea Labayen (Madrid: Ayuntamiento; Instituto de Estudios Madrileños, 1980. 45p.).

16 **Madrid, capital city and metropolitan region.**
Manuel Valenzuela, Ana Olivera Poll. *Nederlandse Geografische Studies*, no. 176 (1994), p. 51-68.

The authors consider various aspects of Madrid as Spain's capital city and as the wider metropolitan region. They argue that because Madrid was principally a political capital, the city's evolution reflected Spain's international situation as well as the changes in régime over the years. Due to the lack of urban and social planning, the city evolved in an unstructured way until the transition to democracy in 1975. Since then the growth of Madrid has shifted into a suburban 'ring' of more than twenty municipalities. After a very useful geographical and historical introduction, the article proceeds to describe various features including environment, urban development, population change and demographic trends, economy and finance, transport, housing, and culture and leisure activities. Enhanced by a number of maps, tables and statistical data, this article is an excellent starting-point for those requiring an accessible and concise survey of the city.

# Atlases and Maps

17 **Atlas de Madrid: guía de la ciudad.** (Atlas of Madrid: guide to the city.)
Madrid: Almax, 1996. 36th ed. 560p. Scale 1:10,000.
Almax is one of the leading publishers of maps and atlases in Spain, and this standard reference work on Madrid is updated annually. It includes street maps and plans together with all the street names, numbers and postal codes. An A-Z section provides general information on the city and there is also a separate folding map of Madrid (scale 1:75,000) and Metro plan (scale 1:20,000). Another useful atlas of the city was produced in 1992 to coincide with Madrid's status as European capital of culture, namely: *Atlas de la ciudad de Madrid* (Atlas of the city of Madrid), coordinated by Carlos Buero Rodríguez and compiled by Luis Alcalá del Olmo et al. (Madrid: Ideographis, 1992. 306p.). For a more wide-ranging work which encompasses the region of Madrid, readers should refer to the *Atlas de la Comunidad de Madrid* (Atlas of the Community of Madrid) edited by Rafael Mas Hernández (Madrid: Fundación Caja de Madrid; Consejería de Política Territorial, 1992. 88p.).

18 **Madrid.**
Berlin: GeoCenter, 1994. Scale 1:15,000. (Euro-City Map).
GeoCenter publishes a wide range of maps and pocket atlases on all countries. This map of Madrid is clear and detailed and includes a street index and tourist information on places of interest and hotel accommodation. It also contains a multilingual index to the tourist information relating to hotels, restaurants, museums and theatres.

19 **Madrid: city map.**
Bolzano, Italy: Freytag & Berndt, 1993. Scale 1:9,500.
Including information on places of interest and the surrounding area of the city, this is a standard map of Madrid which is available from most good bookshops. It also contains a map of the Metro system, although this is less clear than others.

20 **Madrid plano y callejero.** (Madrid map and street plan.)
Hamburg, Germany: Falk, 1993. 16th ed. 35p. Scale 1:8,000 and
1:14,000. (Falk Plan).

This detailed map and guide also includes an index of districts, street-names,
embassies, theatres, museums and other places of interest. Its clear fold-out map
contains a map of Madrid's city centre and another covering the areas around the city.

21 **Madrid y extrarradio.** (Madrid and outlying area.)
Madrid: Almax, 1995. Scale 1:15,000.

A standard street map of the city which includes general information and a Metro
plan. Almax also produces maps in a similar format for central Madrid, Madrid city,
historic buildings in Madrid, Madrid's transport system and an atlas guide to the city
(q.v.). All of these are available from bookshops in Madrid and specialist map shops
in Britain.

22 **Plano callejero de Madrid: plano del metro; plano de accesos y
salidas.** (Street plan of Madrid: Metro plan; plan of approaches and
exits.)
León, Spain: Everest, 1993. 2nd ed. Scale 1:14,000.

This clear, detailed street plan is a standard map for the tourist. The publishers also
produce a *Plano callejero de Madrid: centro urbano* (Street plan of Madrid: city
centre) (León, Spain: Everest, 1991. Scale 1:10,000). Two other similar maps for
tourists and visitors are the *Plano callejero de Madrid* maps published by Everest
(1995) and Anaya-Touring (Madrid, 1995).

23 **Plano de Madrid.** (Plan of Madrid.)
Madrid: El Corte Inglés, 1995.

Produced by the department store which is an institution in Spain, employing English-
speaking staff and providing tax-free shopping for tourists, this is one of the best and
most detailed fold-out plans of Madrid. It includes: a map of the city centre which
shows buildings three-dimensionally; a plan of Madrid's Metro system; an English-
language guide to the three principal art museums (Prado, Museo Nacional Centro de
Arte Reina Sofía, Museo Thyssen-Bornemisza); useful addresses; and, naturally,
promotional information on the store itself.

24 **Streetwise Madrid: central city.**
New York: Streetwise Maps, 1994.

This fold-out glossy map of central Madrid is clear and easy to carry and use. Besides
a street index, it also includes an index of *plazas* (squares), hotels and places of
interest, as well as providing a plan of the city's Metro system.

**Walks through Madrid.**
*See* item no. 43.

**Madrid walks.**
*See* item no. 50.

**Atlas de la industria en la Comunidad de Madrid.** (Atlas of industry in the Community of Madrid.)
*See* item no. 221.

**Atlas provisional lepidópteros de Madrid.** (Provisional atlas of the butterflies and moths of Madrid.)
*See* item no. 284.

**Artwise Madrid: the museum map.**
See item no. 363.

# Tourism

25 **Madrid, centro de atracción turística.** (Madrid, centre for tourism.)
José Díez Clavero. *Estudios Turísticos*, no. 125 (1995), p. 5-18.
bibliog.
Reprinted from a talk given by the author at the beginning of the academic year 1994-
95 at the Centre of Tourist Initiatives for Madrid, this interesting article surveys
Madrid's attraction as a tourist centre. Noting that after the Balearic Islands Madrid
ranks second in Spanish tourism importance, the author considers: the positive and
negative factors affecting tourism in Madrid; hotels and gastronomy; transport and
communications; Madrid as a business centre; and the activities of the Madrid
Chamber of Commerce in promoting the city's tourist trade. Emphasis is placed on
strategic planning, promoting the image of the city, increasing the number of trade
fairs and boosting cultural events in the city to increase the number of visitors. A
number of bibliographical references appear at the end of the article. An article of
related interest, which discusses a particular aspect of Madrid's attraction as a tourist
centre, appeared in an earlier issue of the same journal. Written by José Luis Bozal
and Nieves Serrano, 'La conservación del medio ambiente: aportación al patrimonio
prehistórico de Madrid; un futuro por conservar' (Protecting the environment: its
importance to the prehistoric heritage of Madrid: a future through conservation)
(*Estudios Turísticos*, no. 122 [1994], p. 41-51) examines the tourist boom in Madrid at
the end of the 1950s and during the 1960s, and the growth and urban development of
the city. The environmental and heritage problems are particularly emphasized in
relation to urban planning and tourism. The article concludes with a brief selection of
Madrid's tourist attractions and some suggestions for alternative or 'green' tourist
activities in and around the city.

**Reseña bibliográfica y documental en las áreas de trabajo, industria y
comercio en la Comunidad de Madrid.** (A bibliographical and documentary
report on the subjects of work, industry and trade in the Community of
Madrid.)
*See* item no. 528.

# Guidebooks

## General

26 **Guide to Madrid.**
Carmen Aguelo Radigales, Flora López Marsá, Celia Mas Mayoral.
Barcelona, Spain: Escudo del Oro, 1994. 2nd ed. 199p. 14 maps.
This is one of the best general guidebooks to Madrid, but it is only generally available
in Spain (bookshops and newspaper kiosks). It is particularly noted for its attractive
presentation, ease of use and its excellent maps and illustrations.

27 **Baedeker's Madrid.**
Basingstoke, England: Automobile Association, 1995. 4th ed.
171p. 12 maps.
The famous Baedeker guides have become standard works for travellers to countries,
regions and cities throughout the world. The new series updates the classic original
volumes. After initial sections which supply general background information on
Madrid, the principal places of interest (buildings, churches, streets and areas) are
listed in alphabetical order. This constitutes the largest section of the book and is
followed by another A-Z section providing practical information on topics such as art
galleries, emergencies, food and drink, hotels, museums, public transport, restaurants,
shopping and theatres. The guide also contains a list of useful telephone numbers, a
plan of the Metro system, 137 colour illustrations and a large pull-out map of Madrid
at the end of the book. Another series which has established itself as a standard
guidebook is the Blue Guides Series. Although delayed, their volume *Madrid*, edited
by Annie Bennett, is due to be published in April 1997 (London: A. & C. Black.
c.200p.). Following in the tradition of others in the series, the volume will be
particularly strong in its coverage of Madrid's art, architecture and history.

28 **Berlitz Madrid.**
Oxford: Berlitz, 1996. 14th ed. 128p. maps. (Berlitz Pocket Guides).

This is one of the most popular guides which offers succinct practical information in an easy-to-use format. The text is clear and enhanced by a wealth of colour illustrations and essential facts, ranging from places of interest to restaurants and shopping. Unfortunately, however, it lacks a map of Madrid's Metro system.

29 **Fodor's Madrid and Barcelona.**
Edited by Christopher Billy. New York: Fodor's Travel Publications, 1994. 13th ed. 194p. bibliog.

Fodor's guidebooks first appeared in 1936 when their founder, Eugene Fodor, published their first country guide. This particular volume constitutes reprinted sections from the 1994 edition of *Fodor's Spain* (New York: Fodor. 577p.), edited by Larry Peterson. Various sections provide information and advice including essential details on staying in Madrid, food and drink, the arts, nightlife and exploring around Madrid. A number of tours are also described for those wishing to visit places of interest both inside and outside the city. Highly detailed, accurate and reasonably easy to follow, this guide is one of the most popular available. Nonetheless it is unfortunate that, despite numerous maps and plans (including one of Madrid's Metro system), it does not include any photographs or illustrations. For a short cultural comparison of the cities of Madrid and Barcelona, readers should refer to Nigel Farndale and Michael Hall's article, 'Guide to Madrid and Barcelona' (*Country Life*, vol. 189, no. 22 [1 June 1995], p. 62-73), which covers cuisine, society, art, museums and architecture.

30 **The companion guide to Madrid and central Spain.**
Alastair Boyd. Woodbridge, England: Companion Guides, 1988.
3rd ed. 474p. maps. bibliog. (Companion Guides).

This classic guide was first published in 1974 with the aim of providing the visitor with a companion, in the person of the author, 'who knows intimately the places and people of whom he writes, and is able to communicate this knowledge and affection to his readers'. Boyd's highly enjoyable, well-written guide contains over eighty pages on Madrid and includes general and historical information together with specific sections covering the city (both old and new), the Prado and the Buen Retiro. A number of useful appendices provide: a chronological table of events; a glossary of architectural terms; a glossary of Spanish words; recommended hotels; practical information; feast days and fairs; and a short list of suggestions for further reading. A detailed index completes the work.

31 **City breaks in Madrid, Barcelona, Seville and Granada.**
Reg Butler. London: Settle Press, 1996. 140p. 3rd rev. ed. maps.
(Thomson City Breaks).

Inexpensive and basic, this city guide devotes around thirty pages to Madrid and provides a very brief overview of the city and its culture.

32 **Madrid.**
Camilo José Cela, illustrated by Juan Esplandíu. Madrid: Alfaguara, 1966. 79p.

This light-hearted guidebook (in Spanish), by one of Spain's greatest writers, offers the reader over thirty snapshots of various aspects of the city to illustrate its history, culture and people. Each section includes a colour illustration to enhance the text. Cela's aim was to provide basic facts and information on famous Madrid institutions and landmarks in order to promote a better understanding of the city. Subjects covered include: San Isidro (Madrid's patron saint); Convento de la Encarnación (Convent of the Incarnation); Real Monasterio de las Descalzas Reales (Monastery of the Royal Barefoot Nuns); Palacio Real (Royal Palace); El Rastro (Flea market); Plaza Mayor; El Retiro (Retiro Park); plaza de toros (bullring); las Cortes (Parliament buildings); Real Academia Española (Spanish Royal Academy); Puerta del Sol; Casa de Campo (Casa de Campo Park); and the Gran Vía. Of particular interest to children and visitors, it is generally only available now in libraries.

33 **Madrid and Toledo.**
Fernando Chueca Goitia, translated by Monica Threlfall and Suzanne Sale, special photography by Mario Carrieri. London: Thames & Hudson, 1972. 288p. maps. (World Cultural Guides).

Despite its age, this has become a standard reference guide to Madrid and is particularly noteworthy for its wealth of illustrations. The main text provides a chronological survey of the two cities' cultural histories, supported by illustrations of paintings, sculpture, architecture and general views. Sections also cover El Escorial, Alcalá de Henares and the royal residences. Appendices deal with specific areas of interest to the tourist, including museums and galleries, historic buildings and churches, and painters, sculptors and architects (together with biographical details). Maps and plans are also included, but unfortunately the book lacks a bibliography and index. Although particularly useful for its coverage of the arts and culture in Madrid, those looking for tourist information should use the book in conjunction with up-to-date guidebooks. Chueca Goitia wrote prolifically on Madrid, its history and culture, including *Madrid, ciudad con vocación de capital* (Madrid: city with a vocation as capital) (Santiago de Compostela, Spain: Pico Sacro, 1974. 405p.) and *Royal Palace of Madrid* (Madrid: Everest, 1993. 80p.), a colourfully-illustrated English-language guide to the palace.

34 **Madrid and Castile.**
Catherine Clancy. Swindon, England: Crowood Press, 1991. 351p. maps. (Crowood Travel Guides).

This is a colourful and easy-to-use guide to Madrid and central Spain. It includes a section which provides practical information for the traveller (accommodation, money, restaurants, shopping etc.), detailed and clear advice and descriptions, and a large number of colour plates and illustrations. It also describes the principal aspects of the city's history and culture, and, in addition, contains a number of useful addresses and a full index.

35 **Essential Madrid.**
Basingstoke, England: Automobile Association, 1996. 2nd rev. ed.
128p. maps. (Essential Travel Guides).

Illustrated by renowned travel photographers, this guide is characterized by its conciseness and clarity. The essential information it provides includes sections on star ratings of sights and visits, shopping, eating out, nightlife, things to do for children, accommodation and an A-Z of practical information. This good, basic guide also contains an index and some excellent illustrations and maps.

36 **Madrid.**
Edited by Lucinda Evans, photographs by Bill Wassman. Singapore:
APA, 1992. 288p. maps. bibliog. (Insight City Guides).

This award-winning series boasts an experienced team of writers and excellent photographic illustrations, which in combination provide an attractive colour guide to all aspects of the city. The valuable information and feature sections offer practical facts and advice relating to sightseeing, sports, nightlife, accommodation and shopping. Other general sections cover the city's history and culture and useful tips for the tourist. The same publisher also produces the pocket guide, *Madrid*, by Vicky Hayward (Basingstoke, England: APA, 1996. 100p. maps. bibliog.) in their Insight Pocket Guides series. It presents a distillation of the principal points and information given in the city guide and also contains suggested excursions and itineraries for the short-stay visitor. Both guides are widely available in bookshops as they are distributed in the United Kingdom by GeoCenter International (Basingstoke) and in the United States by Houghton Mifflin (Boston, Massachusetts).

37 **Guía de Madrid: manual del madrileño y del forastero.** (Guide to
Madrid: handbook for residents and visitors.)
Angel Fernández de los Ríos. Madrid: Monterrey Ediciones, 1982. 813p.

First published in 1876 (Madrid: Oficina de la Ilustración Española y Americana), this classic work was one of the first and most detailed guidebooks ever written on the city. In his introduction to the original the author noted how Madrid was 'until recently the European capital least visited by foreigners'. Although limited in its usefulness for the contemporary traveller, it remains a mine of fascinating information and detail. Readers could also usefully refer to José Pamias Morato's *Guía urbana de Madrid* (Guide to Madrid) (Madrid: Pamias, 1995. 3 vols.), which contains information on Madrid's 13,000 streets and squares.

38 **Madrid.**
Alejandro Fernández Pombo et al. Madrid: Planeta, 1992. 127p.
2 maps. (Guías Planeta).

Well laid out and easy to use, this standard Spanish-language guide to the city contains a wealth of colourful illustrations and photographs, and full descriptions of every aspect of the sights and attractions of Madrid. Written by a number of specialists, there are five sections: the first provides a short history of the city; the second and principal section covers all the main places of interest in a single alphabetical sequence, including addresses, hours of opening, map coordinates and other details; the smaller third section suggests places to visit for particular historical periods of the city's evolution, such as Habsburg Madrid or the Madrid of the

Bourbons; the fourth analyses the character of the city and its people, its customs, festivals and gastronomy; and the final chapter recommends some walks for those wishing to experience the variety of ambiences in Madrid. An index of buildings and topics completes the work. A plan of the Metro system, together with a note of the nearest stations to each place of interest, would have been a helpful addition for tourists.

### 39 Madrid, Spain.
Aurora Fernández Vegue, translated by Vicky Howard. Madrid: Turespaña, Secretaría General de Turismo, 1993. 35p. maps.

This is a standard guide for English-speaking visitors and is widely available from all Spanish tourist offices. Reprinted and revised every few years, it obviously promotes all that is positive and exciting about the capital and succeeds in encouraging new and prospective visitors through its careful use of succinct text, colour photographs and excellent maps. It includes sections on Madrid's history, architecture, parks and gardens, museums, culture, nightlife and shopping. In addition, maps highlight the principal places of interest and there is a list of useful addresses and a plan of the Metro system. A similar guide, again available from Spanish tourist offices, is *Madrid and its surroundings* (Madrid: Turespaña, Secretaría General de Turismo, 1993. 20p.) which includes brief details of Madrid's main tourist attractions, a good map of the city centre and short guides to the principal places of interest around the capital.

### 40 Guía azul: Madrid. (Blue guide: Madrid.)
Madrid: Gaesa, 1996. 669p. maps. (Guías Azules de España).

Thorough and well written, this book is a standard Spanish-language guide to the city. Various sections look at different aspects of Madrid from its history, culture and gastronomy to its areas, restaurants, sights and transport. It also includes excellent maps, plans and colour illustrations, together with a detailed index. Other standard guides to Madrid, published in Spain, include: *Guía de Madrid* (Guide to Madrid) by José del Corral (Madrid: El País; Aguilar, 1992. 2nd ed. 287p.); *Madrid* (Madrid: Escudo de Oro, 1995. 64p.), a colourful guide generally available from newspaper kiosks in the city; *Guía de hoy Madrid* (Guide to today's Madrid) by Javier Martínez Reverte and Ignacio Medina, translated by Nigel Williams (Madrid: Anaya, 1991. 175p. maps.), a well-illustrated guide with information on where to go, what to see, food and drink, festivals, activities for children, and sport, along with useful addresses and an index of buildings and monuments; and *El mejor Madrid – the best of Madrid* (Madrid: Eurolex, 1995. 645p. maps. bibliog.), an illustrated and comprehensive guidebook which includes itineraries, timetables and a list of useful addresses.

### 41 Madrid inside out: an insider's guide for living, working and studying in the Spanish capital.
Arthur Howard, Victoria Montero, edited by David Applefield.
Vincennes, France: Frank Books, 1992. 231p. maps. bibliog.

Aimed at all categories of visitors including those spending extended time in Madrid, this useful book offers a wide variety of information. Initial chapters describe the basic facts about getting to the city, with notes on its history and culture, followed by sections supplying details on banking, shopping, health services, neighbourhoods and nightlife. Although illustrations would have enhanced the text, and it is now in need of updating, this still remains a helpful guidebook in that it provides information which many other guides do not cover.

42 **Madrid: architecture, history, art.**
Michael Jacobs, photographs by James Strachan. London: George
Philip, 1992. 192p. maps. bibliog. (Philip's City Guides).

Represents a well-written, beautifully photographed and highly detailed guidebook to
Madrid, its art, architecture and history. Jacobs is a prominent art historian and travel
writer, whilst this was Strachan's (a highly acclaimed photographer) first book. What
stands out in particular is the clarity of text and illustration throughout the seven
chapters, each representing a carefully planned thematic or chronological route
through the city. Jacobs describes in detail the famous buildings and monuments as
well as some lesser-known places/sights of artistic value or historical significance.
Thus there is ample coverage of the Prado Museum, the Retiro Park, the Puerta del Sol
and the Royal Palace as well as the university city, the hunting ground of El Pardo, the
17th- and 18th-century heart of the city and the districts of Salamanca and Chamberí.
Extensive appendices provide easy reference to rulers, major events in Madrid and
Spain's history, the artists who worked in the city, and the opening times of important
buildings. This reasonably-priced coffee-table guide is a must for those wanting to
delve more deeply into Madrid's history and culture. A revised edition of this work,
with the title *Madrid explored*, is due to be published in late 1996.

43 **Walks through Madrid.**
Bert Lief, L. M. Keely. New York: VLE Ltd., 1994. 3rd ed. (Walks
Through Europe).

This illustrated fold-out map tries a different approach to guiding tourists around the
centre and principal sights of Madrid. Through illustrations and photographs readers
are able to see what lies ahead of them as they explore a particular route from a choice
of four. Reading from the bottom of the page, they are directed to the appropriate
street for commencing the walk, after which points of interest along the way are
described, as well as other noteworthy sights in proximity and the streets which lead
to them. This reader did not find the guide particularly easy to use.

44 **Barcelona, Madrid and Seville.**
Herbert Bailey Livesey. London: Mitchell Beazley, 1993. 279p. maps.
(American Express Travel Guides).

Aimed at independent travellers on holiday or away on business, the American
Express Travel Guides are widely accepted as one of the most authoritative and
comprehensive series available. Sections are included on accommodation, sightseeing,
food and drink, entertainment, shopping, history, architecture, the arts, language and
bullfighting. The guide also includes a number of maps and plans, but is otherwise
sparsely illustrated. An extensive index completes the work.

45 **Madrid.**
Lorenzo López Sancho, translated by Susan Gosling. León, Spain:
Editorial Everest, 1992. 192p. maps.

This is a standard pocket guidebook, written by Madrid's official historian and
produced by a long-established publisher of guidebooks for Spain (available in
English, French and Spanish). It includes nearly 200 colour plates, street maps and
plans as well as a wealth of general background information. Despite the occasional
grammatical error, the book has generally been well translated and includes sections
on: old Madrid; Madrid under the Habsburg and Bourbon dynasties (with emphasis on

the architecture and history of the most important buildings); the Prado Museum, together with other principal museums in the city; and contemporary Madrid. The book also contains facts and advice relating to transport, places of interest, hotels, food and drink, sport, fairs and festivals, shopping and nightlife. A basic index completes the work, but unfortunately it only includes places and people and does not cover general topics of interest. Readers may also like to refer to *Madrid, Alcalá, Aranjuez, El Escorial* (Madrid: Museum Line, 1994. 96p. maps.), an illustrated guide to Madrid and its neighbouring towns for the tourist; and *Travellers' Guide Madrid* (Barcelona, Spain: Plaza & Janés, 1992- ), an annual publication for the tourist which contains clear maps and likewise deals not only with Madrid but with other towns and cities in the Community.

46 **Window on Madrid: a newcomer's guide.**
Diana Nicholson, assisted by Joan Elms. Madrid: British Ladies Association, 1987. 112p.
Although somewhat dated now, and readers may find some difficulty in locating a copy, this is still an interesting guide to the city. Similarly, *Bare facts about Madrid* (Madrid: The American Women's Club of Madrid, 1987. 157p.) includes some fascinating information but is not readily available in bookshops (although several libraries in Madrid have copies). The latter also contains a 'services and shopping guide'. Also available in Madrid is a guide to excursions from the city, *Itineraries from Madrid*, translated by James Cerne (Madrid: Anaya, 1992. 192p. maps.), which is the work of a team of writers and provides an illustrated guide to eight 'classic' trips around the capital (including Toledo, Aranjuez, Alcalá de Henares, Salamanca and Valladolid).

47 **Frommer's comprehensive travel guide, Madrid & the Costa del Sol.**
Darwin Porter, assisted by Danforth Prince. New York: MacMillan Travel, 1995. 2nd ed. 324p. maps. bibliog. (Frommer City Guide).
Extremely popular with American tourists, Frommer guides are easy to use and highlight the best travel deals in all price ranges. The information in the present guide essentially represents an expanded version of the relevant areas in their guide to Spain. Various fact-packed sections cover the general history and culture of Madrid; planning a trip; getting to know Madrid; accommodation and restaurants; places to see; walks; shopping; nightlife; and excursions. The book also contains numerous helpful tips for the first-time visitor to the city, a glossary of useful Spanish terms, maps and an index. Unfortunately, it lacks illustrations which might have relieved an often dense text. Frommer also produce an up-to-date pocket-sized guide, *Madrid '94- '95 on $50 a day*, by F. Lisa Beebe (New York; London: Prentice Hall Travel, 1994. 178p. maps. bibliog.), which provides information on living inexpensively in the city. As well as information on accommodation and restaurants, there is plenty of advice on where to go, what to see, how to save money and other useful hints. More recently they have also published *Spain's favourite cities: Madrid, Barcelona & Seville* (New York; London: Macmillan Travel, 1995), a small pocket-guide which highlights the principal points of interest in each city.

## 48 Time Out Madrid guide.
Edited by Nick Rider. London: Penguin Books, 1995. 282p. maps. bibliog.

Currently the best and most comprehensive guide to Madrid on the market, this work has been exhaustively researched and compiled by resident *madrileños*. Not only is it packed with up-to-date information, but the writers also provide a critical survey of the various aspects of the city, thus enabling the visitor to make a more informed choice. There are sections on history; Madrid by area; food and drink; nightlife; shopping; galleries and museums; arts and entertainment; gay Madrid; women's Madrid; and trips out of town. An extensive index is also included. What sets this book above other guides is the insight and informed insiders' views it offers on contemporary Madrid. Excellently produced, clearly written (often with humour) and crammed with interesting illustrations, it sets the standard for travel guides and is an indispensable tool for discovering the real Madrid.

## 49 Madrid.
Managing editor Michael Schichor. London: Kuperard, 1995. 214p. maps. (Michael's Guides).

Described as the complete travellers' guide to Madrid, this guidebook follows the pattern of surveying areas of Madrid in a primarily geographical sequence. An introductory chapter discusses general topics (historical background, geography, culture, customs, accommodation, transportation and other practical information) and is followed by thirteen tour routes. Street by street, the visitor follows maps which highlight the principal sights along the routes and a text which surveys their history and importance. Following this section there are chapters covering excursions and 'making the most of your stay' (food and drink, entertainment, sport, trade fairs and congresses, shopping and important addresses), and the book is completed with an index of all the major sights. Despite its clear maps and simply-written text, this guidebook is not as easy to use as some. The need to keep referring back to each map in order to orientate oneself means that it is sometimes difficult to follow the descriptions of sights successfully. However, it is up to date and full of colour illustrations and useful facts (albeit with the occasional factual or typographical error) and will be of particular use to first-time visitors to Madrid. Future editions would benefit from the inclusion of a plan of the Metro system, a bibliography of further reading and a more extensive index to include subjects and names. Likewise, it would also be helpful to include a glossary or dictionary of phrases which, although listed in the contents of the current edition, is missing from the actual text.

## 50 Madrid walks.
George Semler, photographs by Matthew P. Semler. New York: Henry Holt & Co., 1993. 284p. maps. bibliog. (An Owl Book).

This interesting pocket-format work presents five self-guided walking tours relating to the most culturally and historically rich aspects of Madrid. These include mediaeval and Christian Madrid; the Habsburg city; literary Madrid; the *barrios bajos* (working-class districts) of the Rastro and Lavapiés; and Goya's Madrid. Other sections include information and advice on Madrid's history, gastronomy and restaurants, accommodation, shops and museums. Aimed at those visitors who want to learn about the city in depth, its lively text (with anecdotes) has been written by a knowledgeable author who has lived in Madrid for nearly quarter of a century. Also of interest might be the Spanish Tourist Office's English-language map guide entitled *Walks in Madrid* (Madrid: Turespaña, 1995).

51 **Madrid: a travellers' companion.**
Selected and introduced by Hugh Thomas. London: Constable, 1988.
464p. maps. bibliog. (The Travellers' Companion Series).

Aimed at the discerning traveller, this excellent guide provides a wonderful evocation of Madrid through the centuries, with its enthralling anthology of writings on the city from the Middle Ages to the 1930s by authors as varied as St Teresa of Avila, Casanova, Buñuel and the Duke of Wellington. It contains more than 200 extracts from diaries, letters, memoirs and novels covering a range of topics such as: general impressions; Madrid's streets; the Puerta del Sol; the Plaza Mayor; hotels and cafés; palaces (including the Royal Palace); the Prado; prison; customs and manners; dress; the Church; processions and fiestas; the bullfight; and theatres. Hugh Thomas (author of the classic work, *The Spanish Civil War* [London: Penguin, 1986. 3rd rev. ed. 1,115p.]) prefaces the book with a thoroughly interesting and entertaining history of Madrid from 1561 when the city became the capital. Maps and historical prints and illustrations complement this delightful work, and a useful index is also included.

52 **Vip Madrid: guide for the business visitor.**
Madrid: Madrid Tourist Board; Madrid Chamber of Commerce and Industry; IFEMA, 1993. 360p.

This detailed guide is a practical and helpful directory of information on Madrid which particularly emphasizes the services connected with business, the financial markets and company activities. After an introduction to the capital and its history, various sections provide essential information on a range of topics including: daily life in Madrid; mass media; Madrid as an economic and financial centre; culture; administration; commerce; academic and professional life; fairs and congresses; accommodation; gastronomy; shopping; sports and recreation; nightlife; customs and folklore; and business and health services. The strength of the guide is its extensive listings of useful addresses and telephone numbers. Unfortunately, it does not contain an index but the contents pages are very detailed. One of the co-publishers, IFEMA (Madrid Trade Fair Organization), also publishes an annual *Guía Ferial de Madrid* (Trade Fair Guide to Madrid) (Madrid: IFEMA, 1990- ), which details all the trade fairs and congresses being held in the city.

**Atlas de Madrid: guía de la ciudad.** (Atlas of Madrid: guide to the city.)
*See* item no. 17.

**Madrid: an historical description and handbook of the Spanish capital.**
*See* item no. 87.

**Guía de Madrid: nueva arquitectura.** (Guide to Madrid: new architecture.)
*See* item no. 293.

**En Madrid.** (In Madrid.)
*See* item no. 494.

**Enjoy Madrid.**
*See* item no. 495.

**Guía de Madrid.** (Guide to Madrid.)
*See* item no. 496.

**Guía del Ocio.** (Leisure Guide.)
*See* item no. 497.

# Children's

**53  Madrid para la escuela.** (Madrid for schools.)
Carlos Arnaiz et al.   Madrid: Acción Educativa, 1990. 192p.

This clear and simple guide provides schoolchildren with a description and survey of the city, its history, buildings and culture.

**54  Madrid para niños.** (Madrid for children.)
Teresa Avellanosa.   Madrid: La Librería, 1993. 128p.

Produced in collaboration with the Friends of Madrid Foundation (Fundación Amigos de Madrid), this attractive little book invites young children to explore and learn about the history, charm and secrets of Madrid. It is written in a simple and entertaining style by the author of several children's books and other works on Spain's *plazas* and *paradores* (state-owned hotels). The cover of the present work depicts the '*oso y madroño*' (bear and strawberry tree) which is the symbol of the city, a statue of which forms a focal point and meeting place in the Puerta del Sol.

**55  Madrid visto por los niños.** (Madrid through the eyes of children.)
Clemente Herrero Fabregat.   Madrid: Centro Madrileño de Investigaciones Pedagógicas, 1992. 123p.

This survey of children's views on Madrid describes and analyses their opinions on various aspects of the city. The author also wrote some short educational guides to Madrid: *El Madrid actual* (Contemporary Madrid) (Madrid: Ayuntamiento, Servicio de Educación, 1991. 43p.); and *El Madrid medieval* (Mediaeval Madrid) (Madrid: Ayuntamiento, Servicio de Educación, 1991. 32p.). Two other works of interest relating to children and Madrid are: *Madrid para los niños* (Madrid for children) (Madrid: Ayuntamiento, 1982. 42p.); and *El niño y la ciudad* (The child and the city) by Adriana Bisquert (Madrid: Colegio Oficial de Arquitectos, Servicio de Publicaciones, 1982. 103p.).

**56  Living in Madrid.**
Elena Sainz.   Hove, England: Wayland, 1981. 52p. map. bibliog.
(Living in Famous Cities).

Despite the fact that much of this work is now out of date, parts of it can still be used to provide schoolchildren with an introduction to daily life in the Spanish capital. Sections look at homes and families, festivals, food and drink, transport, school life, shopping and the Prado amongst other topics. The volume includes numerous illustrations, a glossary and a simple index.

# Specific features

57 **Diccionario de Madrid: las calles, sus nombres, historia, y ambiente.**
(Dictionary of Madrid: the streets, their names, history and
surroundings.)
Juan Antonio Cabezas. Madrid: El Avapiés, 1989. 3rd ed. 479p.

First published in 1968 (Madrid: Compañía Bibliográfica Española), this classic work
on Madrid is an excellent source of fascinating information on Madrid's streets and
squares and their history. A wealth of biographical data is also provided for those
famous Spaniards after whom many of the streets are named. Cabezas limited himself
to including the streets within the boundaries of the 1860 urban expansion programme
(*ensanche*) for Madrid, designed by the engineer Carlos María de Castro. However,
entries not only include historical facts but also present-day details. Organized in a
single A-Z sequence, it also contains numerous illustrations. Another useful work is
the *Diccionario general de Madrid: historia, personajes, monumentos . . .* (Dictionary
of Madrid: history, people, monuments . . .) by José Montero Alonso, Francisco
Azorín García and José Montero Padilla (Madrid: Méndez y Molina, 1990. 586p.). It
covers a whole range of subjects including history, biographies, art, legends,
literature, theatres, cinema, historic buildings, institutions and food and drink. Its
3,000 terms are ordered in one alphabetical sequence and the annotations are
impressively clear and detailed. Of related interest are Manuel Montero Vallejo's
*Origen de las calles de Madrid* (Origins of the streets of Madrid) (Madrid: El Avapiés,
1989. 192p.) and *Madrid callejero* (Madrid street guide) by José Gutiérrez Solana,
edited by Teodoro Santurino Sanchís (Madrid: Castalia, 1995. 179p.), a classic
illustrated work which was first published in 1923.

58 **Cementerios de Madrid.** (Cemeteries of Madrid.)
Carlos Carrasco Muñoz de Vera. Madrid: Poniente, 1984. 47p.

This short illustrated work provides an interesting survey of and guide to Madrid's
cemeteries. Other works on this fascinating subject include: *Cementerios de Madrid*
(Madrid: Empresa de Servicios Funerarios, 1986. 46p.); *Los cementerios de Madrid*
(Madrid: Empresa de Servicios Funerarios y Cementerios del Ayuntamiento, 1986.
165p.); and *Cementerios en Madrid: mesa redonda* (Cemeteries of Madrid: round
table), edited by J. A. Cano Lasso (Madrid: Colegio Oficial de Arquitectos, 1977.
24p.).

59 **Guía de la Casa de Campo.** (Guide to the Casa de Campo.)
Carlos Carrasco Muñoz de Vera. Madrid: The Author, 1986. 31p.
map.

Covering nearly 4,500 acres, this huge expanse of greenery and open spaces is
Madrid's largest park. The property of the monarchs of Spain from 1562, it became a
public park under the Second Republic in 1931. It boasts a great number and variety
of trees and a large lake which has been extended to allow *madrileños* a place to
practise water sports. The park houses numerous other sports facilities, including
public tennis courts and swimming pools, and also has a youth hostel. It is home of the
zoo and funfair (*parque de atracciones*) and the *teleférico* cable car between the park
and the *Parque del Oeste*. At night the Casa de Campo becomes a more sinister place
and prostitutes line many of the park roads, particularly close to the Lago Metro

station. Traffic restrictions have been proposed and ecologists support these proposals for their own reasons. This short guide provides a useful illustrated tour of the park and its attractions and facilities.

60   **La Plaza Mayor de Madrid.** (The Plaza Mayor of Madrid.)
José del Corral.   Madrid: Méndez & Molina, 1987. 216p.

First built in the 15th century as the Plaza del Arrabal (square outside the walls), work began on converting it into a modern square in 1617 when Juan Gómez de Mora (Philip III's architect) drew up plans for its redevelopment. By 1619 it was completed and it remains a formidable example of town planning under the Habsburgs. The square was officially inaugurated in 1622 with festivities marking the canonization of St Isidro, the patron saint of Madrid. Its two most prominent buildings still retain their old names: the *Panadería* (bakery) and *Carnicería* (meat market). In 1847, thanks to the initiative of Ramón Mesonero Romanos, a bronze statue of Philip III on horseback (designed by the sculptor, Giambologna, and his pupil, Petro Tacca) was erected in the centre of the square where it stands today. Nowadays, the *plaza* can be enjoyed in different ways at different times. Weekday mornings are quiet and a good time to admire the square's architecture or take breakfast in the attractive but expensive cafés, whereas on Sunday mornings the square is busy with a stamp and coin market. It is useful to note that there is a tourist office located in the square which provides information and sells a number of helpful guidebooks on various aspects of Madrid's history, culture and architecture. Corral's excellent work presents a full historical survey and guide to the square, although smaller and glossier guides in various languages are also available from the tourist offices.

61   **De Madrid al cielo: Planetario de Madrid.** (From Madrid to the heavens: Madrid's Planetarium.)
Madrid: Ayuntamiento, 1986. 16p.

This brief guide covers the history and role of Madrid's planetarium, situated in the Tierno Galván park south of Atocha railway station (the park named after Madrid's much-loved socialist mayor [1979-86], who was hailed as the sponsor of the *movida madrileña* [Madrid Movement] and supporter of various progressive causes and projects). The planetarium's display is modern but explanations are in Spanish only, and can even be too daunting, wordy and dull for Spanish children. Many regard the pleasant playground outside as its best feature. The title of this booklet derives from a much-quoted saying about Madrid which refers to the city as the gateway to the heavens.

62   **El Observatorio Astronómico de Madrid: Juan de Villanueva, arquitecto.** (The Astronomical Observatory of Madrid: Juan de Villanueva, architect.)
Antonio Fernández Alba.   Bilbao, Spain: Xarait, 1979. 119p.

Situated at the southern end of the Retiro Park, the Observatory was one of Charles III's scientific institutions, but was only completed after his death in 1790. With its beautiful proportions, it is considered by many to be one of the finest neoclassical buildings in Madrid. It still contains a working telescope and one room is also open to the public as a museum. Designed by Juan de Villanueva, it was partly destroyed during the Peninsular War (1808-14). Work to restore it was completed in 1848, but it was only in 1974 that its original elegance was re-established through careful renovation and repairs. The present guide gives a historical and architectural survey of the building whilst concentrating on its architectural development and importance. Two other works which are useful bicentenary studies of the Observatory are: *Bicentenario del Observatorio Astronómico de Madrid, 1790-1990* (Bicentenary of the Astronomical Observatory of Madrid, 1790-1990) (Madrid: Instituto Geográfico Nacional, 1990. 35p.); and *Doscientos años del Observatorio Astronómico de Madrid* (Two hundred years of the Astronomical Observatory of Madrid) (Madrid: Asociación de Amigos del Observatorio Astronómico, 1992. 168p.).

63   **Guía del Rastro.** (Guide to the Rastro.)
Ramón Gómez de la Serna.   Madrid: Taurus, 1961. 218p.
This has become a standard work on the Rastro's history and place in Madrid society. Thought to date back five centuries, Madrid's open-air flea market begins at the Plaza de Cascorro and the stalls then ramble their way down the sloping Calle Ribera de Curtidores. It is particularly busy on Sunday mornings between noon and two o'clock. Many literary works and histories have made reference to the Rastro and its atmosphere and character; Arturo Barea, in his *Forging of a rebel* (q.v.), notes how he visited it frequently as a child in the years leading up to the First World War. Other relevant studies of the Rastro include: Antonio Corral Fernández' photographic guidebook, *El Rastro* (Barcelona, Spain: Ediciones 505, 1984. 93p.); *Conocer el Rastro* (Get to know the Rastro) by Félix Moneo Santamaría (Madrid: The Author, 1985. 229p.); and 'El Rastro de Madrid' by M. Herrero García (*Revista de la Biblioteca, Archivo y Museo [Madrid]*, vol. 9 [1932], p. 381-92).

64   **Madrid: the Royal Palace.**
Ramón Guerra de la Vega.   Madrid: The Author, 1995. 31p.
Aimed at tourists, this short, glossy guide to the Royal Palace is written by one of the most prolific writers on the architecture of Madrid. It provides a brief history and a plan of its layout, and some beautiful colour photographs accompany the text. The guide should be available at tourist offices and the larger bookshops in Madrid. The palace is known both as the Palacio Real (Royal Palace) and rather incongruously as the Palacio de Oriente (East Palace) as it lies to the west of the city. This name derived from its proximity to the Plaza de Oriente (East Square), although the latter is equally misnamed. Notwithstanding its name, the palace is a massive and hugely imposing edifice in Italian baroque style, occupying the spot where the *Alcázar* stood from Moorish times, which later became home to the Habsburg monarchs. Philip V, the first Bourbon monarch of Spain, was used to French refinements, and when in 1734 a fire destroyed the *Alcázar* he and his second wife, Isabel Farnese, commissioned the Sicilian architect, Filippo Juvara, to rebuild the palace. Initially, Juvara planned a building four times its eventual size, but this would have involved moving its site, something the king would not countenance. When Juvara died in 1736 his disciple, Giovanni Battista Sacchetti, and several Spanish architects (including Ventura Rodríguez) continued with the planning and construction. Work began in 1738 and was completed in 1764 when Charles III became the first king to take up residence. It cost a fortune to build and everything about it is on a grand scale. Containing over 3,000 rooms, the palace is full of art treasures and surrounded by majestic gardens. It is also the setting for Pérez Galdós' novel, *La de Bringas* (The spendthrifts) (q.v.).

65 **Madrid en sus plazas, parques y jardines.** (Madrid's squares, parks and gardens.)
Margarita Jiménez. Madrid: Abaco, 1977. 476p.

Madrid is one of the greenest cities in Europe, with numerous parks and gardens covering huge expanses of land including the Campo del Moro, Casa de Campo, Jardín Botánico, Parque Juan Carlos I, Parque Tierno Galván, Parque del Retiro, Parque del Oeste and Parque de las Vistillas. Similarly, the city has hundreds of squares ranging from small areas which hardly merit the title to the magnificent Plaza Mayor and the Plaza de la Armería adjacent to the Royal Palace. This book provides an extensive survey of these three important facets of Madrid's character and architecture, and their place in its society. Jiménez also wrote *La realidad de Madrid* (The reality of Madrid) (Madrid: The Author, 1991. 3 vols.); and *Madrid y provincia en sus plazas mayores* (The main squares of Madrid and its province) (Madrid: Abaco, 1979. 514p.).

66 **Fuentes de Madrid.** (Fountains of Madrid.)
Agustín Francisco Martínez Carbajo, Pedro Francisco García Gutiérrez.
Madrid: El Avapiés, 1994. 258p. bibliog.

This up-to-date study contains a fascinating, illustrated guide to, and history of, Madrid's fountains. The most famous of these are situated on the Paseo del Prado and were designed by Ventura Rodríguez (1717-85), from Cibeles (the Greco-Roman goddess of fertility and symbol of natural abundance) on a chariot drawn by lions at the most northern point, to Apollo, Neptune and finally the Four Seasons in front of the Prado Museum. Other relevant historical and artistic works which may be of interest include: *La Cibeles, Nuestra Señora de Madrid* (Cibeles, Our Lady of Madrid) by Pilar González Serrano (Madrid: Ayuntamiento, 1990. 254p.); and *Fuentes artísticas madrileñas del siglo XVII* (Madrid's 17th-century artistic fountains) by Miguel Molina Campuzano (Madrid: Ayuntamiento; Instituto de Estudios Madrileños, 1970. 51p.) which contains a number of illustrations.

67 **Templo de Debod.** (Temple of Debod.)
María del Carmen Priego Fernández del Campo, Alfonso Martín Flores.
Madrid: Museos Municipales, 1992. 67p.

Situated in the Parque del Oeste, the Templo de Debod is a genuine Egyptian temple from the 4th century BC. It was presented to Spain in 1968 by the Egyptian government as a gesture of thanks for the efforts of Spanish archaeologists in preserving a number of monuments threatened by the lake created by the Aswan Dam. Other useful studies of the temple are: Martín Almagro Basch's *El templo de Debod* (Madrid: Ayuntamiento; Instituto de Estudios Madrileños, 1971. 29p.); and his more extensive work of the same title (Madrid: Instituto de Estudios Madrileños, 1971. 88p.).

68 **Las calles de Madrid.** (The streets of Madrid.)
Pedro de Répide, compiled by Federico Romero. Madrid: La Librería, 1995. 805p.

Alongside Larra and Mesonero Romanos, Répide (1882-1948) ranks as one of Madrid's foremost chroniclers and historians. From 1921 until 1925 he published a series of articles, entitled *Guía de Madrid* (Guide to Madrid), in the daily newspaper, *La Libertad* (Freedom). These articles provided, in alphabetical order, a description and history of every street in Madrid. First published in 1971, this illustrated dictionary represents a compilation of all these articles in one alphabetical sequence. It offers a fascinating study of the city's streets, and in Répide's inimitable style includes not only description and history but also tradition and legend. The current edition also contains an appendix of streets which have changed their names since 1971. Répide was also a writer of novels on life in Madrid and although his quaint style, with its archaic terms, quickly went out of date, a collection of his *Novelas madrileñas* (Madrid novels) appeared in 1951 (Madrid: Afrodisio Aguado). For other standard works providing interesting studies of Madrid's streets, readers should refer to: Juan Antonio Cabeza's *Diccionario de Madrid* (q.v.); *Las calles de Madrid* by Hilario Peñasco de la Puente and Carlos Cambronero (Madrid: Plaza del Amo, 1990. 571p.); *Las calles de Madrid* by Antoni de Capmany i de Montpalau (Madrid: Plaza del Amo, 1990. 430p.); *Los nombres de las calles de Madrid* (The names of the streets of Madrid) by María Isabel Gea Ortigas (Madrid: La Librería, 1993. 288p.), part of a pocket-guide to Madrid series which provides a clear, well-presented history; and the long-established study by Luís Martínez-Kleiser, *Los nombres de las antiguas calles de Madrid* (The names of the old streets of Madrid) (Madrid: Tip. de A. Fontana, 1927. 32p.).

69 **Historia de la Puerta del Sol.** (History of the Puerta del Sol.)
Javier M. Tomé Bona. Madrid: La Librería, 1993. 293p. bibliog.
(Madrid de Bolsillo, no. 5).

The Puerta del Sol (Gate of the Sun) lies at the heart of Madrid, and comprises a semi-circular 'square' from which three of the city's principal streets branch out: the Calle Alcalá towards the Puerta de Alcalá, and the Calles Arenal and Mayor which lead away to the Plaza Mayor. In all, ten streets converge on the Puerta which literally stands at the centre of Spain, for in front of the square's most prominent building, the Casa de Correos (Post Office – now home of the regional government), lies 'kilometre zero', the point from which all distances in Spain are measured. During the 15th century this was the location of the easternmost gate of Madrid. A castle which bore a decorative motif of the sun also lay on this site, but was demolished in 1522. The Puerta del Sol became a popular meeting place in the 17th century and Joseph Bonaparte completed the enlargement of the area in 1862. Subsequently, numerous cafés grew up around it, reinforcing its reputation as a *mentidero* (gossip shop). The area has a fascinating past, one which reflects the history of Madrid. It has been the scene of many disturbances and uprisings but also the focus for innovations in the city. It was here in 1830 that gas lighting was used in Spain for the first time, followed four years later by the introduction of raised pavements; drains became a new feature in 1861, and electric lighting first appeared in 1875. In 1906 the first arc lamps were erected in the Puerta del Sol to celebrate Alfonso XIII's wedding, and in 1919 it became the terminus and centre of Madrid's newly-inaugurated Metro system. It was given a face-lift in 1986 when some renovation work was carried out, and it remains a focal point for *madrileños*. Traditionally, on the 31st December each year, a crowd gathers beneath the clock-tower of the Casa de Correos awaiting the twelve chimes and eating twelve grapes for good luck in the new year. Tomé Bona's book considers all aspects of the square, its buildings, personalities, legends and traditions throughout the centuries. Even in its pre-Civil War days, the square evoked such enthusiasm for Román Gómez de la Serna (Madrid's outstanding chronicler and historian) that he too devoted an entire book to it which is still well worth reading: *Historia de la Puerta del Sol* (Madrid: Méndez y Molina, 1987. 110p.).

**The new Plaza Mayor of 1620 and its reflections in the literature of the time.**
*See* item no. 105.

**El Manzanares: río de Madrid.** (The Manzanares: river of Madrid.)
*See* item no. 269.

**El Retiro: sus orígenes y todo lo demás (1460-1988).** (The Retiro: its origins and other matters [1460-1988].)
*See* item no. 280.

**Jardines históricos de Madrid.** (Historic gardens of Madrid.)
*See* item no. 281.

**El Parque Zoológico de Madrid 1774-1994.** (The Zoological Park of Madrid 1774-1994.)
*See* item no. 285.

**Parque Tecnológico de Madrid (P.T.M.).** (The Science Park of Madrid.)
*See* item no. 311.

**Madrid arts guide.**
*See* item no. 351.

**El Ateneo científico, literario y artístico de Madrid (1835-1885).** (The scientific, literary and artistic Athenaeum of Madrid [1835-85].)
*See* item no. 352.

**Boulevard of the arts: Madrid's great museums, Prado, Thyssen, Reina Sofía.**
*See* item no. 365.

**Museos de Madrid: guía de Madrid y región.** (Museums of Madrid: a guide to Madrid and its region.)
*See* item no. 369.

**Museums of Madrid: volume 1, the Prado Museum.**
*See* item no. 370.

**The Prado, Madrid.**
*See* item no. 372.

**Guide to the Prado.**
*See* item no. 373.

**Prado, Madrid.**
*See* item no. 376.

**Guide Prado Museum.**
*See* item no. 377.

**A basic guide to the Prado.**
*See* item no. 379.

**The Prado.**
*See* item no. 380.

**Royal palaces of Spain: a historical and descriptive account of the seven principal palaces of the Spanish kings with 164 illustrations.**
*See* item no. 384.

# Travellers' Accounts

70　**The Bible in Spain.**
　　George Borrow, with an introduction by Walter F. Starkie.　London:
　　Dent; New York: E. P. Dutton, 1961. 510p. map. bibliog. (Everyman's
　　Library, no. 151: Travel and Topography).

George Borrow's (1808-81) now classic work was originally published in 1843 in
three volumes (London: John Murray). The book represents an engrossing account of
Borrow's travels around Spain (including his time spent in Madrid) as an agent of the
British and Foreign Bible Society between 1835 and 1839. Based upon the letters and
diaries he wrote during this period, it is full of reminiscences and colourful anecdotes,
and evokes a fascinating picture of Spain during the years of the First Carlist War
(1833-39). In Madrid he made elaborate plans for printing the New Testament in
Spanish, but the time was not right for such a venture, and he was even imprisoned
there for a short time in 1838. Despite this, Borrow became quite a legend in various
parts of Spain and was affectionately known as 'Don Jorgito el inglés'. On his return
home he found it difficult to settle, having experienced such adventure, and always
maintained that the years he spent in Spain represented the happiest days of his life.

71　**The bumpkin capital – Madrid.**
　　Jimmy Burns.　In: *Spain: a literary companion*.　London: John
　　Murray, 1994, p. 22-37.

Burns was born in Madrid and worked there as a correspondent for the *Financial
Times*. This lively and entertaining chapter contains a variety of tales about historical
figures and travellers in Madrid over the centuries. Madrid is referred to as the
bumpkin capital because for centuries it was the antithesis of a capital city. Compared
to other European capitals, it lacked splendour, architectural beauty and a major river.
It was in fact a dirty and smelly place until Charles III implemented reforms in the
18th century.

72  A hand-book for travellers in Spain and readers at home:
describing the country and cities, the natives and their manners;
the antiquities, religion, legends, fine arts, literature, sports, and
gastronomy: with notices on Spanish history.
Richard Ford.   London: Centaur Press, 1966. 3 vols. 2 maps. bibliog.
(Centaur Classics).
First published in 1845, this timeless work is still a rich mine of information. Ford
travelled over 2,000 miles throughout Spain on horseback during a three-year period
in the 1830s and recorded the scenery through which he passed in a series of sketches
and paintings. His writings provide a fascinating and comprehensive evocation of the
Spain of that era, and volume three includes a wonderful description of Madrid
(p. 1,073-191) and excursions around the city, including El Escorial (p. 1,191-235).
One can immediately discern that Ford was not too impressed with Madrid from his
opening description: 'Madrid is built on several mangy hills that hang over the
Manzanares, which being often dry in summer, scarcely can be called a river'
(p. 1,075). Even the Prado comes in for some criticism in relation to its lack of
gardens and unlandscaped setting. Nevertheless, readers will find it a rewarding
experience to turn back the clock and immerse themselves in Ford's descriptions of
Madrid's streets, buildings and people as they appeared over a century and a half ago.

73  **The cities of Spain.**
Edward Hutton.   London: Methuen, 1906. 324p.
This work recounts the author's travels through Spain in 1904 and, in particular, the
major cities. Three chapters are devoted to Madrid (p. 97-164), in which Hutton
describes historical and travellers' accounts of the capital whilst devoting most of his
time to the Prado and the works of El Greco, Ribera, Velázquez, Goya and the Italian
Schools. Although a great deal of city detail will not be found here, the chapters
nevertheless provide fascinating insights into various aspects of Madrid's history, and
are supported by both colour and black-and-white illustrations.

74  **Reminiscences of an excursion to Madrid across the Pyrenees in
1834.**
Josias Henry Stracey.   Leamington, England: Edward Foden, 1847. 36p.
A short, yet fascinating account of Stracey's (1771-1855) journey to Madrid during
the reign of Isabel II. An expanded edition of this work was published in 1850
(Chichester, England: G. Pullinger. 90p.).

75  **Viajeros impenitentes: Madrid visto por los viajeros extranjeros en
los siglos XVII, XVIII y XIX.** (Unrepentant travellers: Madrid as seen
by foreign travellers in the 17th, 18th and 19th centuries.)
Madrid: Comunidad de Madrid, Consejería de Cultura, Secretaría
General Técnica, 1989. 98p. bibliog.
Beautifully illustrated, this work represents the catalogue of an exhibition organized
by the Community's Council for Culture during the seventh International Book
Exhibition in Madrid in June 1989. Short introductory sections discuss the history of
travel writings concerning Spain and Madrid, and also consider the importance of the
influence of travel writings on people's views of the city. These are followed by an
anthology of selections from a wide range of writings, from the general to extracts

describing Madrid's streets, climate, parks, theatres, squares, prisons, institutions, museums, cafés, customs, culture and, of course, its people. The famous writers represented include Giacomo Casanova, Henry Swinburne, George Borrow, Richard Cobden, Alexandre Dumas, Richard Ford, Théophile Gautier, Louisa Tenison and Lucien Vigneron. The 'unrepentant' of the title refers to the fact that most visitors to Madrid during the 17th, 18th and 19th centuries were highly critical of its physical condition and its inhabitants. Another work of related interest is Luciana Gentilli's *Fiestas y diversiones en Madrid: la segunda mitad del siglo XVII – relatos de viajeros europeos* (Festivals and entertainments in Madrid during the second half of the 17th century: European travellers' accounts) (Rome: Bulzoni, 1989. 73p.). Similarly, readers might find it worthwhile consulting Catalina Buezo's anthropological study, *El carnaval y otras procesiones del viejo Madrid* (The carnival and other processions in old Madrid) (Madrid: Avapiés, 1992. 185p.).

**Madrid.**
*See* item no. 3.

**Madrid.**
*See* item no. 6.

**Madrid: a travellers' companion.**
*See* item no. 51.

**Art and politics: nineteenth-century Madrid and Barcelona.**
*See* item no. 115.

**Europeos en Madrid.** (Europeans in Madrid.)
*See* item no. 324.

# Archaeology and Prehistory

76 **Prehistoria madrileña.** (Prehistory of Madrid.)
Martín Almagro Gorbea. Madrid: Ayuntamiento; Instituto de Estudios Madrileños, 1987. 29p.

The area around Madrid, and particularly around the banks of the Manzanares and Jarama rivers, has one of the longest histories of continuous settlement of anywhere in Europe, and is rich in prehistoric remains. This short study provides a brief overview of the Palaeolithic (300,000-200,000 BC), Neolithic (4,000 BC), Bronze (2,000 BC) and Iron (500 BC) Age periods of Madrid's prehistory.

77 **Anuario de prehistoria madrileña.** (Yearbook of Madrid prehistory.)
Madrid: Ayuntamiento, 1930-36. 6 vols.

First published in 1930 with volume one, and ceasing publication with volume six (for 1935) in 1936, this work would doubtless have continued to appear had it not been for the outbreak of the Civil War. Nevertheless, the six volumes contain a wealth of interesting facts and details.

78 **Arqueología urbana: Madrid medieval y moderno.** (Urban archaeology: mediaeval and modern Madrid.)
Luis Caballero Zoreda. *Revista de Arqueología*, no. 34 (1984), p. 56-65.

Brief but interesting, this article examines Madrid's archaeological remains relating to the mediaeval and modern periods.

79 **Ciento treinta años de arqueología madrileña: catálogo de la exposición.** (One hundred and thirty years of Madrid archaeology: exhibition catalogue.)
Madrid: Comunidad de Madrid; Real Academia de Bellas Artes de San Fernando, 1987. 237p.

This profusely illustrated catalogue reflects the exhibition displayed in the San Fernando Royal Academy of Fine Arts in 1987. It offers a panoramic guide to the artefacts which have been uncovered in and around Madrid from the 1850s onwards. The Royal Academy was founded in 1794 and is Madrid's oldest art institution, containing numerous prized and valuable works of art and rare books. Of related interest is *Madrid antes del hombre* (Madrid before man) (Madrid: Comunidad de Madrid, 1993. 52p.), a catalogue of an exhibition held at the Museo Nacional de Ciencias Naturales (National Museum of Natural Sciences) from March to July 1993. Fully illustrated, it disseminates the palaeontological studies which have recently been undertaken in the city and includes photographs of the life-size models of extinct animals, fossils and dinosaurs of prehistoric Madrid.

80 **Estudios de Prehistoria y Arqueología Madrileñas.** (Studies in the Prehistory and Archaeology of Madrid.)
Madrid: Museo Municipal, 1982- . annual.

This journal is the standard source of information on Madrid's prehistory and archaeology. Each year various aspects of these subjects are investigated. For example, in the 1983 volume an extensive study was made of the old walls of the city by Luis Caballero Zoreda and Hortensia Larren Izquierdo, entitled 'Las murallas de Madrid: excavaciones y estudios arqueológicos' (The walls of Madrid: excavations and archaeological studies) (p. 9-182). Another periodical which often contains articles relating to the archaeology of Madrid is the *Revista de Arqueología* (Archaeological Review) (Madrid: Zugarto Ediciones, vol. 1- , 1980- . monthly).

81 **Prehistoria y edad antigua en el área de Madrid.** (Prehistory and ancient times in the Madrid area.)
María del Carmen Priego Fernández del Campo et al.  In: *Madrid hasta 1875: testimonios de su historia: 1979 enero-febrero 1980.*
Madrid: Museo Municipal, 1979, p. 46-81.

Based upon exhibitions (at the Museo Municipal) of archaeological findings from excavations in the Madrid area, this book includes a wealth of fascinating detail regarding Madrid's past. This particular chapter presents an interesting overview of the prehistory of Madrid and the surrounding area. The museum collection, opened in 1929, traces the history of the settlement and growth of Spain's capital from the prehistoric age to the 19th century and includes such interesting items as maps, manuscripts, paintings and other relics. Many other prehistoric artefacts can be seen in the Museo Arqueológico Nacional (National Archaeological Museum) in Calle Serrano. Established in 1867, its holdings trace the development of human cultures from prehistoric times right up to the 15th century. Many of its most interesting relics come from the area around Madrid itself (e.g. 4,000-year-old Neolithic pottery bowls found south of the city at Ciempozuelos).

82   **El Neolítico y la Edad del Bronce en la región de Madrid.** (The
Neolithic and Bronze Age in the Madrid region.)
José Sánchez Meseguer et al.   Madrid: Diputación Provincial de
Madrid, 1983. 94p.

This academic study is a standard work on the prehistory of the province of Madrid,
and features a number of illustrations of examples of artefacts found in the area,
relating to the Neolithic and Bronze Age periods.

83   **Maŷrit: estudios de arqueología medieval madrileña.** (Maŷrit:
studies in the mediaeval archaeology of Madrid.)
Edited by Fernando Valdés.   Madrid: Polifemo, 1992. 220p.
(Biblioteca de Arqueología Medieval Hispánica, no. 1).

Madrid's original Arabic name was Maŷrit or Magerit, meaning 'place of many
springs'. The small settlement and fortress was built high above the Manzanares river
in c. 856 to defend the important lines of communication between Toledo and Aragón.
In 1086 Alfonso VI of Castile conquered Toledo, and with it Madrid, and although it
was again besieged by a Moorish army in 1109 it remained in Christian hands,
developing slowly until Philip II decided to establish Madrid as the permanent seat of
the Spanish court in May 1561. The present collection of studies provides a detailed
archaeological survey of mediaeval Madrid. Well illustrated, it benefits from the fact
that all the contributors are experts in the field of mediaeval archaeology. Valdés also
edited another interesting study of Madrid under the Moors: *Madrid castillo famoso:
diez trabajos sobre el Madrid árabe* (Madrid, famous castle: ten studies of Moorish
Madrid) (Madrid: Pefemar, 1990. 197p.).

**Boletín del Museo Arqueológico Nacional.** (Bulletin of the National Archaeological Museum.)
*See* item no. 503.

# History

## General

84 **Historia de la villa y corte de Madrid.** (History of the town and court
of Madrid.)
José Amador de los Ríos.    Madrid: Plaza del Amo, 1990. 4 vols.

For centuries after being designated capital in 1561, Madrid was commonly referred to
in Spain as *la corte* (the court) and never as a city in its own right. In 1606, after its
definitive establishment as capital, Philip III reiterated that '*sólo Madrid es corte*'
(only Madrid is the court). Originally published between 1861 and 1864 (Madrid: J.
Ferrá de Mena. 4 vols.), this is one of the standard histories of the city. Despite
emphasizing Madrid's role as capital, it spans all the centuries of its history and
describes every important event up to the middle of the 19th century. Another
standard multi-volume chronological history is Pedro Montoliú Camps' *Madrid, villa
y corte* (Madrid, town and court) (Madrid: Sílex, 1987. 3 vols.). Well illustrated, it
also relates the history of the city during the 20th century, and volume three contains a
number of plans and drawings. Some other useful one-volume studies include:
*Madrid: historia, arte, vida* (Madrid: history, art, life) by Luis Manuel Aubersón
Marrón et al. (Madrid: El Consultor de los Ayuntamientos, 1991. 402p.) which, in
addition, provides a history of Madrid's artistic and cultural heritage; Fernando
Aznar's *Madrid, una historia en comunidad* (Madrid: a community history) (Madrid:
Consejería de Cultura y Deportes, 1987. 321p.); and Montserrat del Amo's *Historia
mínima de Madrid* (A short history of Madrid) (Madrid: El Avapiés, 1985. 160p.).

85 **Anales del Instituto de Estudios Madrileños.** (Annals of the Institute
of Madrid Studies.)
Madrid: Consejo Superior de Investigaciones Científicas, 1966- . annual.

One of the best sources for information on all aspects of the city, these excellent
annual publications contain a wealth of detail and analyses on Madrid society and
culture. Each chapter considers, from a historical standpoint, a wide variety of themes

and topics including art, geography, literature, music and urban development. The work as a whole is aimed at anyone interested in the history and development of Madrid in general.

86 **Historia de Madrid: desde los orígenes de la ciudad hasta el 13 de septiembre de 1923, advenimiento del directorio del general Primo de Rivera.** (History of Madrid: from its origins to the 13th September 1923, the beginning of the Primo de Rivera dictatorship.)
Federico Bravo Morata. Madrid: Fenicia, 1986. 23 vols.

As the title denotes, this undertaking was originally intended to end at 1923 and Primo de Rivera's dictatorship. However, the author changed his plans and after the original four volumes he continued to chart Madrid's history in a chronological sequence, with each subsequent volume spanning two- or three-year periods. The complete illustrated work has now become a classic and standard history, with Bravo Morata himself recognized as one of the city's most prominent historians. Some other relevant works of his include: *Historia de Madrid* (History of Madrid) (Madrid: Fenicia, 1966. 4 vols.); *¿Por qué es Madrid la capital de España?* (Why is Madrid capital of Spain?) (Madrid: Fenicia, 1972. 189p.); and *Los nombres de las calles de Madrid* (Madrid street-names) (Madrid: Fenicia, 1984. 647p.).

87 **Madrid: an historical description and handbook of the Spanish capital.**
Albert F. Calvert. London: John Lane, The Bodley Head, 1909. 622p. map. (The Spanish Series, no. 9).

Written at a time when Madrid was coming into its own as an accessible and prosperous capital city of Europe, Calvert's work captures the essence and vitality of Madrid at the turn of the century. Only 169 of its pages are text; the rest are made up of 453 black-and-white illustrations which provide a fascinating pictorial record of Madrid's history, art, buildings and customs (including many on the bullfight and the new Plaza de Toros de Las Ventas which was still under construction). Calvert's fondness for Madrid is apparent throughout, and he has approached his book from the standpoint of a resident writing for visitors. Chapters cover the city's history; court and society; art, literature and drama; churches and public buildings; the bullfight and the art of the bullfighter; and café life. A separate chapter discusses the old university town of Alcalá de Henares (twenty miles east of Madrid): when its Complutense University was moved to Madrid in 1836, the town entered into decline, but a new university was opened there in 1977 in an effort to restore the town's importance and some of its former glory.

88 **Madrid: the circumstances of its growth.**
P. P. Courtenay. *Geography*, vol. 44 (1959), p. 22-34. maps. bibliog.

This brief review of the geography and history of Madrid discusses the historical development of the capital and attempts to indicate those factors which have been most significant in its rise to supremacy in Spain. It includes sections on the site of Madrid and its environment; its early development from prehistoric times; its choice as the capital of Spain in 1561; its growth up to 1800; and its development in the 19th and 20th centuries. Several maps and references are also included. Whilst ideal for those interested in a potted history of the city from earliest times, this piece obviously has its limitations as regards coverage of the 20th century, due to its age.

89 **Madrid past and present.**
Beatrice Steuart Erskine. London: Bodley Head, 1922. 295p.

Despite its age, this remains a highly readable and fascinating description of Madrid which mixes historical fact with surveys of various aspects of the city's artistic and cultural greatness. Erskine, author of biographical and historical works as well as novels, aimed to 'give some account of the attractions of the capital and of some of the places of interest that are not mentioned in guide-books'. At the time the book was written, Madrid was a city little-known to non-Spaniards despite its artistic treasures. The twenty-nine chapters include richly detailed descriptions of the Puerta del Sol, Royal Palace, Plaza Mayor, Rastro (flea market), Prado Museum (with studies of El Greco, Velázquez and Goya), the national museums, the theatre, churches and convents, El Escorial and daily life in the capital. All of these are complemented by a number of black-and-white illustrations and a helpful index.

90 **Historia de Madrid.** (History of Madrid.)
Antonio Fernández García et al. Madrid: Complutense, 1994. 737p. bibliog.

Together with the volume by Santos Juliá (q.v.), this is the most authoritative and up-to-date study of Madrid's history. It boasts numerous compilers, all of whom are respected and prominent academics and specialists in the field. Scholarly, though still accessible to general readers, it provides a detailed survey of Madrid, including its economy, society, politics, urban development and culture. The author also wrote a number of other interesting works on Madrid including: *La prensa madrileña ante el nacimiento de la Segunda República* (The Madrid press before the coming of the Second Republic) (Madrid: Ayuntamiento; Instituto de Estudios Madrileños, 1984. 38p.); *El cólera de 1885 en Madrid* (The cholera epidemic of 1885 in Madrid) (Madrid: Ayuntamiento; Instituto de Estudios Madrileños, 1982. 47p.); and *Epidemias y sociedad en Madrid* (Epidemics and society in Madrid) (Barcelona, Spain: Vicens Vives, 1985. 273p.).

91 **El ayer de Madrid, el Madrid de hoy.** (The Madrid of yesteryear, Madrid today.)
Reyes García, Ana María Ecija, Benjamín Larrea. Madrid: La Librería, 1995. 127p. bibliog.

This beautiful photographic study juxtaposes pictures of Madrid's old buildings with those of the modern city. The corresponding text carefully highlights the historical and architectural significance of each building. A similar work has been produced by María Isabel Gea Ortigas, entitled *El Madrid desaparecido* (Bygone Madrid) (Madrid: La Librería, 1992. 224p.), although this concentrates on how Madrid used to look and comprises a collection of illustrations and descriptions of those buildings which fell victim to the various plans for reforming the city over the years. Gea Ortigas also wrote: *Curiosidades y anécdotas de Madrid* (Sights and sounds of Madrid) (Madrid: La Librería, 1994. 192p.); and *Casas, casos y cosas de Madrid* (Madrid: people, places and things) (Madrid: Kaydeda, 1989. 175p.).

92 **Madrid: historia de una capital.** (Madrid: history of a capital city.)
Santos Juliá Díaz, David Ringrose, Cristina Segura. Madrid: Alianza,
1994. 486p. maps. bibliog.

Lavishly produced and containing some wonderful illustrations and photographs, this book is the most up-to-date and comprehensive general history of Madrid in Spanish. Its authors are respected historians who have published widely on Madrid, and in this study each writer covers a particular period in the city's history. Segura describes Madrid during the Middle Ages and its genesis as a capital (873-1561); Ringrose considers the city as the capital of imperial Spain (1561-1833); and Juliá's final section looks at Madrid's history and role as state capital between 1833 and 1993. The authors provide detailed surveys and interpretations of the different stages of the city's development, and have written with non-specialist readers particularly in mind. A useful chronology and short bibliographical essays are included, but it is a pity that no index is provided. The book has subsequently been published in a paperback edition which excludes many of the illustrations contained in the original (Alianza, 1995. 630p.).

93 **Madrid: villa y comunidad.** (Madrid: town and community.)
*Revista de Occidente,* nos. 27/28 (Aug.-Sep. 1983). 251p. maps. bibliog.

The whole of this special issue of the journal is devoted to various aspects of Madrid's role as a capital city and as an Autonomous Community. The 1978 Constitution created new regional structures for the political and administrative running of the country. Between 1978 and 1983 seventeen so-called Autonomous Communities came into being, endowed with their own presidents and parliaments. A number of highly respected writers (including David Ringrose, Santos Juliá Díaz and Enrique Tierno Galván) collaborated in the work, and particular topics covered include: the history of Madrid province; Madrid and its economy; Madrid as Spain's most liberal city, 1900-14; elections in Madrid; Madrid in the 1940s and 1950s; landscape and countryside in the province; urban growth and planning in Madrid; traditions and customs; and art in Madrid. Of related interest is *Madrid, villa, tierra y fuero* (Madrid: town, region and province) by Enrique Díaz y Sanz et al. (Madrid: El Avapiés, 1989. 243p.), which ranges across the centuries from earliest records to present-day Madrid. It is clearly organized and written, and contains illustrations, a chapter on music and dance, and a bibliography.

94 **Historia del nombre 'Madrid'.** (History of the name 'Madrid'.)
Jaime Oliver Asín. Madrid: Consejo Superior de Investigaciones
Científicas, 1959. 412p. maps. bibliog.

The origin of the name of Spain's capital city has continued to interest and intrigue historians over the past fifty years. In the 1940s two of Spain's most famous writers and historians, Ramón Menéndez Pidal and Manuel Gómez Moreno, offered distinct theories on the question. Nowadays, it is generally accepted that the word derives from the arabic 'Maŷrit', meaning 'well' or 'spring', after a Moorish fortress had been established in 856 on the bluff overlooking the River Manzanares (where the Royal Palace now stands). Asín's illustrated study has deservedly become a standard text on the subject. Exhaustive in coverage and meticulous in detail, it carefully analyses every possible derivation of the name. The work also contains several appendices and maps, and a number of indexes.

95 **Madrid: crónica y guía de una ciudad sin par.** (Madrid: chronicle and guide to a city without equal.)
Federico Carlos Sainz de Robles. Madrid: Espasa-Calpe, 1962. 747p. map.

Sainz de Robles is one of the most prolific writers on Madrid, and this illustrated history of the city has become a standard work. Many other books by him have also found their place amongst the classic histories and descriptions of the city and its culture, including: *Breve historia de Madrid* (A brief history of Madrid) (Madrid: Espasa-Calpe, 1970. 205p.); *Madrid: autobiografía* (Madrid: autobiography) (Madrid: Aguilar, 1949. 1,299p.); *Madrid: teatro del mundo* (Madrid: theatre of the world) (Madrid: Emiliano Escolar, 1981. 357p.); and his excellent study of Madrid's history and role as a capital city, first published in 1961, entitled *Por qué es Madrid capital de España: tema de interpretación histórica* (Why Madrid is capital of Spain: subject of historical interpretation) (Madrid: Maeva, 1987. 205p.).

96 **Toledo and Madrid: their records and romances.**
Leonard Williams. London: Cassell, 1903. 256p.

Formerly *The Times* correspondent in Madrid, Williams here presents a fascinating and painstaking study of the city covering nearly one hundred pages and illustrated with turn-of-the-century photographs. Written in a clear and often amusing style, it is a work which will appeal to all. The book generally covers Madrid from Moorish times up to the beginning of the 20th century, but specific incidents in the city's history, its folklore and customs are also included. Two final chapters detail the history and highlights of the Escorial and the university town of Alcalá de Henares.

**Madrid and Toledo.**
*See* item no. 33.

**Diccionario de Madrid: las calles, sus nombres, historia, y ambiente.**
(Dictionary of Madrid: the streets, their names, history and surroundings.)
*See* item no. 57.

**Policía municipal de Madrid: siete siglos de historia, 1202-1987.**
(Madrid's local police force: seven centuries of history, 1202-1987.)
*See* item no. 190.

**Tiendas de Madrid.** (Shops of Madrid.)
*See* item no. 218.

**La industria de Madrid.** (The industry of Madrid.)
*See* item no. 225.

**Iglesias de Madrid.** (Churches of Madrid.)
*See* item no. 292.

**Guía de Madrid: nueva arquitectura.** (Guide to Madrid: new architecture.)
*See* item no. 293.

**Trilogía de Madrid: memorias.** (Madrid trilogy: memoirs.)
*See* item no. 346.

**Leyendas de Madrid: mentidero de la villa.** (Legends of Madrid: gossip shop of the town.)
*See* item no. 427.

**Leyendas y misterios de Madrid.** (Legends and mysteries of Madrid.)
*See* item no. 429.

**Fiestas y tradiciones madrileñas.** (Festivals and traditions of Madrid.)
*See* item no. 430.

**Madrid: tabernas, botillerías y cafés, 1476-1991.** (Madrid: taverns, refreshment stalls and cafés, 1476-1991.)
*See* item no. 437.

**Guía de fuentes documentales para la historia urbana de Madrid: 1940-1980.** (A guide to documentary sources on the urban history of Madrid: 1940-80.)
*See* item no. 525.

**Contribuciones documentales a la historia de Madrid.** (Documentary contributions to the history of Madrid.)
*See* item no. 527.

**Fuentes para la historia de Madrid y su provincia: tomo 1, textos impresos de los siglos XVI y XVII.** (Sources for the history of Madrid and its province: volume 1, printed texts of the 16th and 17th centuries.)
*See* item no. 529.

**Colección de documentos sobre Madrid.** (A collection of documents on Madrid.)
*See* item no. 536.

# Mediaeval

97    **El Madrid de los Reyes Católicos.** (The Madrid of the Catholic
       Monarchs.)
       José Manuel Castellanos.    Madrid: El Avapiés, 1988. 161p. bibliog.
       (Colección Avapiés; no. 26).

The author describes daily life in Madrid at the time of the Catholic Monarchs (1479-1504), before the city was established as capital. Concentrating on the final years of the 15th century, he discusses a variety of topics including councils, tradesmen, customs, public order, the state of the streets and the inhabitants' 'peculiar vocabulary and way of speaking'. Entertainingly written and fascinating in its detail, the text is enhanced with a number of woodcut illustrations of the period. For a full range of books in Spanish covering different periods of Madrid's history, readers should refer to *Bibliografía de Madrid* (Bibliography of Madrid) by María Teresa Rodríguez and

María Luisa Martínez Conde (Madrid: La Librería, 1994) (q.v.); and also to the regularly updated catalogues of the two publishing houses which specialize in producing books about Madrid, namely El Avapiés and La Librería (for their addresses, refer to the 'Useful Addresses' section at the front of this book). In respect of mediaeval Madrid, two other publications are worth noting: *El Madrid medieval* (Mediaeval Madrid) by Manuel Montero Vallejo (Madrid: El Avapiés, 1987. 324p.); and *Madrid musulmán, cristiano y bajomedieval* (Moslem, Christian and late mediaeval Madrid), again written by Montero Vallejo (Madrid: El Avapiés, 1990. 202p.), and presenting a detailed, illustrated study of the period.

98 **El Madrid medieval.** (Mediaeval Madrid.)
   Ramón Hidalgo Monteagudo, Rosalía Ramos Guarido, Fidel Revilla
   González.   Madrid: La Librería, 1986. 67p. (Historia Breve de
   Madrid).

This offers a concise introduction to the history of mediaeval Madrid. The authors collaborated on a number of volumes in the same series (published 1986-91) covering different eras of Madrid's history including the Habsburg, Bourbon, baroque and neoclassical periods. Two other volumes in the series describe the areas of Cuatro Caminos and La Castellana in the city.

99 **Caminos y caminantes por las tierras del Madrid medieval.** (Tracks
   and travellers through the lands of mediaeval Madrid.)
   Edited by Cristina Segura Graíño.   Madrid: Asociación Cultural
   Al-Mudayna, 1994. 367p. bibliog. (Laya; no. 12).

The author is a noted specialist on mediaeval Madrid and in this pioneering study gathers together the most up-to-date information and latest research on this fascinating area of the city's mediaeval history. Each chapter analyses the importance of different aspects of Madrid's early communication links. The routes and tracks to, and from, the city during the Middle Ages are discussed, including military roads, communication routes and the economic and geographical significance of these links in the transportation of food and other supplies to the population. Expertly written and extremely detailed, it also sheds a great deal of light on the internal migration trends to, and through, mediaeval Madrid. Segura Graíño also wrote a very useful study of another important aspect of Madrid society during this period, entitled *Espacios femeninos en el Madrid medieval* (Women in mediaeval Madrid society) (Madrid: Horas y Horas, 1993) (q.v.).

**La comunidad mudéjar de Madrid: un modelo de análisis de aljamas mudéjares castellanas.** (The *mudéjar* community of Madrid: a model for analysing Castilian *mudéjar* communities.)
*See* item no. 145.

**Una ciudad ante el hecho religioso: Madrid en la Edad Media.** (Religion in the city: Madrid in the Middle Ages.)
*See* item no. 154.

# Habsburgs

### 100 The Spanish match, or Charles Stuart at Madrid.
William Harrison Ainsworth. Leipzig, Germany: Tauchnitz, 1865.
2 vols.

In 1623, before succeeding to the throne as Charles I of Great Britain, Charles Stuart, accompanied by the Duke of Buckingham, made a visit to Madrid under the alias of 'Tom Smith' in order to attempt to negotiate a marriage with the daughter of King Philip III. Lavish entertainments were staged, but the mission failed largely because of the Duke's arrogance and the Spanish court's insistence that Charles become a Roman Catholic. Ainsworth's fascinating work (which could prove difficult to obtain) not only describes the events of the visit, but also contains a wealth of detail on daily life in Habsburg Madrid.

### 101 El nacimiento de una capital europea: Madrid entre 1561 y 1606.
(The birth of a European capital: Madrid between 1561 and 1606.)
Alfredo Alvar Ezquerra. Madrid: Turner Libros; Ayuntamiento de
Madrid, 1989. 340p. maps. bibliog.

The author has written a number of important studies on Madrid during the 16th and 17th centuries, and is one of the leading authorities on Madrid during the reign of Philip II (1556-98). Many books have appeared on this period of the city's history, which covers the time of its establishment as capital and seat of government in 1561 to its re-establishment as such in 1606 after a five-year hiatus when the court was transferred to Valladolid. However, the present work is the first to provide a detailed survey of Madrid's population, food supply and sanitary conditions. Excellently produced in A4 format, the book contains a wealth of demographic information on migratory movements, illnesses and mortality; food costs and supply; and urban development related to sanitary conditions and attempts to clean up the city. Packed with statistical detail, it also includes a number of fascinating maps, plans and illustrations, together with several appendices and an extensive bibliography. Despite detailed contents pages, it lacks a proper index. Another work covering the same period, which considers the administration of Madrid, is Ana Guerrero Mayllo's *El gobierno municipal de Madrid 1560-1606* (The municipal government of Madrid 1560-1606) (Madrid: Instituto de Estudios Madrileños, 1993. 296p.).

### 102 The vulgar sort: common people in 'siglo de oro' Madrid.
Charles Lawrence Carlson. PhD thesis, University of California,
Berkeley, 1977. 315p. bibliog.

Carlson's thesis provides an in-depth analysis of the hierarchy of Madrid society during the 'Golden Age' (*siglo de oro*) of Spanish history (16th and 17th centuries). Sections consider various topics such as the court, poverty and morality, and the political economy of social life. In particular, the make-up of Spanish society, with its *hidalgos* (nobles), *gente principal* (better people or sort) and *gente vulgar* (common people or the vulgar sort), is extensively investigated and related to Madrid's social, economic and political structure generally. The study also looks at various aspects of how the common people lived and their integration into society, as well as the extent of their participation and power at a time when Madrid was seen as 'an encampment for the court'.

103 **El Madrid de los Austrias.** (Madrid under the Habsburgs.)
José del Corral.    Madrid: El Avapiés, 1992. 166p. bibliog.

First published in 1983, this work considers Madrid from the establishment of the court there in 1561 up to the advent of the Bourbon régime in 1700. Corral looks at all aspects of Madrid society including daily life, fashion, customs, gastronomy and the buildings which were constructed during the Habsburg era. He is also author of *Madrid 1561, la capitalidad* (Madrid 1561; its status as capital) (Madrid: La Librería, 1990. 111p.). Another work, by José Deleito y Piñuela, entitled *Sólo Madrid es corte: la capital de dos mundos bajo Felipe IV* (Only Madrid is the court: the capital of two worlds under Philip IV) (Madrid: Espasa-Calpe, 1953. 268p.) and first published in 1942, describes Madrid during Philip IV's reign (1621-65) and considers the city's role as capital of both Spain and a huge (but threatened) empire. For an anecdotal and well-illustrated account of the city during the 17th century, see Nestor Luján's *Madrid de los últimos Austrias* (Late Habsburg Madrid) (Barcelona, Spain: Planeta, 1989. 176p.).

104 **Madrid, capital de los Austrias.** (Madrid, Habsburg capital.)
Elena A. Fernández Arriba.    Madrid: La Librería, 1991. 24p.
(Cuadernos de Visitas).

Written to provide a general overview of Madrid under Habsburg rule, this work also considers its newly-acquired status as capital of Spain. The author also wrote an interesting account of society and daily life in Madrid at this time as part of the same series, entitled *Vida cotidiana en el Madrid de los Austrias* (Daily life in Habsburg Madrid) (Madrid: La Librería, 1991. 24p.).

105 **The new Plaza Mayor of 1620 and its reflections in the literature of the time.**
Ruth Lee Kennedy.    *Hispanic Review,* vol. 12 (1944), p. 49-57.

First built during the 15th century, Madrid's main square was in those days a simple market square, which was called the Plaza de Arrabal (meaning the square outside the walls). Juan de Herrera, Philip II's favourite architect, drew up plans for it to be rebuilt after the court was moved to Madrid in 1561. The only part which was built immediately was the Casa de la Panadería (the bakery), dominating the square with its two pinnacle towers, and completed in 1590. The remainder of the *plaza* was completed by Juan Gómez de Mora in 1619, during the reign of Philip III. After a fire in 1790 much of the square had to be rebuilt, and afterwards bullfights, carnivals and all the major festivals and ceremonies were held there. At the centre of the square is the 1616 statue of Philip III on horseback (by Giambologna and Pietro Tacca). Kennedy's short but interesting article discusses writings about the construction of the new square and other buildings in Madrid at the time. Over the past twelve years the façade of the Panadería has been decorated with some eye-catching frescoes, which have not met with universal approval.

106 **The impact of a new capital city: Madrid, Toledo, and New Castile, 1560-1660.**
David R. Ringrose.    *Journal of Economic History,* vol. 33, no. 4
(Dec. 1973), p. 761-91.

Ringrose, a highly respected economic historian, considers the economic relationship between Madrid, Toledo and New Castile generally, once Madrid was made the permanent capital of Spain by Philip II in 1561. The rapid growth of Madrid during the century being considered was matched with the equally spectacular decline of Toledo, which was the largest urban centre in the region until 1600. Besides considering the economic and geographical contexts of urban growth, Ringrose also discusses population distribution and trends together with industrial activity. His detailed, academic analysis helps to explain the effects Madrid's growth and its interaction with Toledo had on the economic crisis which Spain experienced in the 17th century. Ringrose also expanded upon the subject to produce his book, *Madrid and the Spanish economy, 1560-1850* (Berkeley, California: University of California Press, 1983) (q.v.).

107    **The invention of a capital: Philip II and the first reform of Madrid.**
       Claudia W. Sieber.    PhD thesis, Johns Hopkins University, 1985.
       487p. maps. bibliog.

This work examines the first forty years of Madrid's role as capital city of Spain, between 1561, when Philip II and his government arrived, and 1601 when Philip III removed his court to Valladolid for economic and social (overcrowding) reasons (although the court returned in 1606 after the failure of the Valladolid experiment). Sieber considers Madrid's expansion and the huge population growth which took place during the forty years and analyses the reasons behind them. Illustrations, tables and a glossary are also included. Other works, in Spanish, which consider Madrid's capital status include two short studies by a prolific writer on Habsburg Spain, Manuel Fernández Alvarez: *El establecimiento de la capitalidad de España en Madrid* (The establishment of Madrid as capital of Spain) (Madrid: Instituto de Estudios Madrileños, 1960. 28p.); and *El Madrid de Felipe II: en torno a una teoría sobre la capitalidad* (Madrid under Philip II: a theory about its capital status) (Madrid: Real Academia de la Historia, 1987. 56p.).

**La población de la villa de Madrid: desde finales del siglo XVI hasta mediadas del siglo XIX.** (The population of the town of Madrid: from the end of the 16th century to the middle of the 19th.)
*See* item no. 138.

**Mujeres del Madrid barroco: voces testimoniales.** (Women in baroque Madrid: testifying voices.)
*See* item no. 157.

**Delincuencia y seguridad en el Madrid de Carlos II.** (Criminality and security in Charles II's Madrid.)
*See* item no. 184.

**Las cárceles de Madrid en el siglo XVII.** (The prisons of Madrid in the 17th century.)
*See* item no. 197.

**Madrid and the Spanish economy, 1560-1850.**
*See* item no. 213.

**El Retiro: sus orígenes y todo lo demás (1460-1988).** (The Retiro: its origins and other matters [1460-1988].)
*See* item no. 280.

**A palace for a king: the Buen Retiro and the court of Philip IV.**
*See* item no. 383.

**Philip IV and the 'Golden House' of the Buen Retiro: in the tradition of Caesar.**
*See* item no. 388.

**From Madrid to purgatory: the art and craft of dying in sixteenth-century Spain.**
*See* item no. 425.

# Bourbons

108 **Tradition and change in the Madrid bourgeoisie, 1900-1914.**
Aviva Aviv. DPhil thesis, Oxford University, 1981. 344p. bibliog.

The Restoration régime in Spain was long-lasting (1875-1923) and was attacked by the Right as weak and tolerant towards revolutionary parties, while the Left regarded the system as corrupt and unrepresentative of the 'real Spain'. During the same period Madrid was criticized for being at the heart of Spain's over-centralized political system and home to its 'parasitic bureaucracy'. Aviv's thesis analyses Madrid's bourgeoisie during a crucial period at the beginning of the 20th century. It was also a time of dramatic change and great political debate and an important point in the evolution of Spanish liberalism. A full social history of Madrid's middle classes is combined with a description of the city, its demography, its economy and its social structure.

109 **La sociedad madrileña durante la restauración 1876-1931.** (Madrid society during the Restoration 1876-1931.)
Edited by Angel Bahamonde Magro, Luis Enrique Otero Carvajal.
Madrid: Comunidad de Madrid, Consejería de Cultura, 1989. 2 vols.
(Coloquios de Historia Madrileña).

Spain's Restoration period was a turbulent but exciting era in Madrid's history. At the end of 1874 the army decided to restore the Bourbon dynasty in the shape of Alfonso XII (1874-85). However, the architect of the Restoration régime was a civilian politician, Antonio Cánovas del Castillo. Through his system of *turno pacífico* (peaceful alternation), power was shared between a Conservative party, led by him, and a Liberal party made up of former progressives. This extensive survey of the period in Madrid presents a highly-detailed analysis of all aspects of government and society. Volume one includes sections dealing with population and territory; Madrid as an economic centre; and the middle classes and nobility. Volume two covers the political system; culture; public opinion and the dissemination of information; and social conflict and the working class. Both volumes contain a wealth of statistical data.

110 **Revolutionary wars and public finances: the Madrid treasury, 1784-1807.**
Jacques A. Barbier, Herbert S. Klein. *Journal of Economic History*, vol. 41, no. 2 (June 1981), p. 315-39.
This study of the Bourbon financial structure is based on the manuscript accounts for the Madrid treasury for 1784-1807. A scholarly and detailed analysis is made of colonial revenues and the stability of traditional income sources. The article confirms the facts of steady descent into bankruptcy, and also tries to explain why this situation arose. Ensuring that Spain's hard-won resources were ultimately exhausted was the constant need to finance wars and the limited means at the country's disposal. The authors provide a vast array of economic data to support their arguments, including numerous graphs and tables, and conclude that the régime's bankruptcy was primarily due to its inability or unwillingness to deal seriously with the restrictive economic structures which it employed.

111 **El Madrid de los Borbones.** (Madrid under the Bourbons.)
José del Corral. Madrid: El Avapiés, 1985. 168p. bibliog.
This standard text continues the history of Madrid which the author started in his earlier volume on the Habsburgs (q.v.). His succinct survey spans the 18th and 19th centuries and the first thirty years of the 20th century. The author describes and discusses various aspects of life in Madrid at this time, including buildings, urban reform, fashion, customs, and gastronomy. Corral also wrote *El Madrid de Alfonso XII* (Madrid under Alfonso XII) (Madrid: La Librería, 1992. 178p.), which spans the last quarter of the 19th century and Alfonso's reign (1874-85).

112 **Gentlemen, bourgeois, and revolutionaries: Madrid and the formation of the Spanish bourgeoisie, 1750-1850.**
Jesús Cruz. PhD thesis, University of California, San Diego, 1992. 475p. bibliog.
Cruz argues that a national bourgeoisie did not exist before the second half of the 19th century. In particular he looks at economic strategies, personal wealth and the social composition of Madrid's dominant groups. The second part of the study focuses on sociocultural developments and social relations in Madrid. Extensive tables and statistical data support the text.

113 **El Madrid de Primo de Rivera (1928).** (The Madrid of Primo de Rivera [1928].)
Juan de Dios Vallarín. Madrid: Nova, 1979. 234p. bibliog.
After a general strike in 1917, tensions rose as the country demanded sweeping constitutional reform. In 1923, the Captain-General of Barcelona, General Primo de Rivera, suspended the Constitution and declared himself Dictator under the King (Alfonso XIII), thereby returning Spain to military rule. Initially greeted with indifference in Madrid, a widespread feeling of discontent eventually evolved during the 1920s. In 1930 Primo de Rivera resigned and the following year republican candidates won sweeping majorities in the municipal elections. Vallarín's book details the effects on Madrid and the population's reaction to Primo de Rivera's dictatorship. A shorter, related study considers the city during the period when Primo de Rivera's son, José Antonio (1903-36), was establishing Spain's fascist party (the Falange) in

1933: *El Madrid de José Antonio* (The Madrid of José Antonio) by Tomás Borrás Bermejo (Madrid: Instituto de Estudios Madrileños, 1953. 49p.).

114  **Carlos III, Madrid y la ilustración: contradicciones de un proyecto reformista.** (Charles III, Madrid and the Enlightenment: contradictions of a reformist project.)
Equipo Madrid de Estudios Históricos.   Madrid: Siglo Veintiuno, 1988. 417p.

Charles III (1759-88) set out to improve the architecture and living conditions in Madrid, and was so active in his mission that he became known as Madrid's *Rey-Alcalde* ('King-Mayor'). Fascinated by the Enlightenment ideas of science and progress, he sought to improve and reform from the top, as the model of an enlightened despot. Other reforms were undertaken in the bureaucracy and armed forces, and he strongly challenged the privileges of the religious orders. The present study can be highly recommended as it contains valuable information on the reign of Charles III and summaries from recent research. Other works of related interest include: *Carlos III, alcalde de Madrid* (Charles III, mayor of Madrid) (Madrid: Ayuntamiento, 1988. 705p.); *El Madrid de Carlos III* (Madrid under Charles III) (Madrid: Consejería de Cultura, 1988. 331p.); and a short account by Pilar Tenorio Gómez, *El Madrid de Carlos III* (Madrid: Asociación Cultural Al-Mudayna; La Librería, 1992. 23p.).

115  **Art and politics: nineteenth-century Madrid and Barcelona.**
Adam Hopkins.   In: *Spanish journeys: a portrait of Spain.*   The Author.   Harmondsworth, England: Penguin Books, 1993, p. 243-84. bibliog.

In a series of evocative journeys the author, a seasoned travel writer, not only recounts his own experiences but provides a detailed account of Spanish history alongside his impressions and reflections on the literary and artistic life of Spain. This chapter on Madrid relates its 19th-century story using the streets of the city as a symbolic guide to the period. The book as a whole presents a vivid and personal portrait of Spain which is enhanced with maps and illustrations.

116  **Life and manners in Madrid, 1750-1800.**
Charles E. Kany.   Berkeley, California: University of California Press, 1932. 483p. maps. bibliog.

Reprinted in 1970 (New York: AMS Press), Kany's book has become a standard work on Madrid during the second half of the 18th century. A great deal of research went into the publication, and the huge output of Don Ramón de la Cruz's (1731-94) '*sainetes*' (playlets) (filled with vivid sketches of life in Madrid in the late 18th century) was Kany's starting-point before he moved on 'to more objective and reliable sources'. Contemporary newspapers, particularly the *Diario de Madrid*, accounts of travellers in Spain, royal decrees and laws, and the works of many Spanish writers of the time were all productive sources of information for him. Three kinds of material then are contained in his finished work: objective facts taken from municipal records and decrees; facts as seen by travellers or others resident in Madrid at the time; and illustrative material taken from de la Cruz's and other writers' works. Kany emphasizes the importance of Charles III's reign (1759-88), when most of the reforms were undertaken and many changes were wrought in Madrid's physical layout and appearance. Fascinatingly detailed, his coverage is comprehensive and illuminates all aspects of life in Madrid, ranging from court life, social types and dress to food and furniture, theatre, culture and religion, and specific parts of the city (Puerta del Sol, Plaza Mayor and the Plaza de la Cebada). It includes numerous plans and illustrations of the time, an extensive bibliography and a full index of people and subjects.

117 **Madrid: audiencia, provincia, intendencia, vicaría, partido y villa.**
(Madrid: court, province, government, vicariate, district and town.)
Pascual Madoz, edited by José Ramón Aguado.    Madrid: Abaco,
1981. 648p. (Mentidero de Madrid).

Originally published in 1848, at first glance this work may seem a little dry. But for those with a general interest in the history of Madrid's role in government, religion and culture, particularly during the Bourbon period, it represents a rich mine of information. The book covers all aspects of the city, including its buildings, economy, culture and administration, and is particularly well illustrated with fascinating prints of the places and people of Madrid.

118 **Memorias de un setentón, natural y vecino de Madrid.** (Memoirs of
a seventy-year-old, born and bred in Madrid.)
Ramón de Mesonero Romanos.    Madrid: Castalia, 1994. 632p.
(Clásicos Madrileños; no. 5).

Also published in three volumes (Madrid: La Librería, 1995) in the 'Madrid de Bolsillo' series, this classic work by Madrid's great 19th-century observer and chronicler was originally published in 1880 (Madrid: Oficinas de la Ilustración Española y Americana). Mesonero Romanos (1803-82) was the first of the true *madrileñistas* (experts on Madrid) and devoted his entire literary output to recording every aspect of his beloved city. Nostalgia permeates this excellent autobiography, as he recounts the daily episodes of life in Madrid between 1808 and 1850. His many works on Madrid are all worth reading for their evocative history, description and characterization of the city. Some of the best of these, and ones which are invaluable for providing details on the social history of Madrid during the 19th century, are: *Manual de Madrid: descripción de la corte y villa* (Guide to Madrid: description of the court and town) (Madrid: Imp. de M. Burgos, 1831. 368p.; later edition – Madrid: Plaza del Amo, 1990. 502p.), a painstakingly researched guidebook of which there are many later editions; *El antiguo Madrid . . .* (Old Madrid . . .) (Madrid: Est. Tip. de F. P. Mellado, 1861. 399p.), a work which concentrates principally on describing the streets and houses of the city (latest available edition – Madrid: Abaco, 1976); *Escenas matritenses* (Madrid scenes) (Madrid: Gaspar y Roig, 1851. 382p.; later edition available, edited by Leonardo Romero Tobar, selection and prologue by Ramón Gómez de la Serna, Madrid: Austral, 1986. 5th ed.), which contains personal anecdotes, descriptions of his friends, *tertulias* (intellectual/literary get-togethers) and a wealth of material on Madrid during the first half of the 19th century; *Escenas y tipos matritenses* (Scenes and characters of Madrid) edited by Enrique Rubio Cremades (Madrid: Cátedra, 1993. 511p.), a compilation of some of his most popular autobiographical and anecdotal material; *Manual histórico, topográfico, administrativo y artístico de Madrid* (Historical, topographical, administrative and artistic guide to Madrid) (Madrid: Imp. de Antonio Yenes, 1844. 514p.; later edition – Madrid: Abaco, 1977. 514p.); and *El Madrid de Mesonero Romanos* (The Madrid of Mesonero Romanos) (Madrid: Taurus, 1964. 158p.).

119  **Madrid: city of the Enlightenment.**
Charles C. Noel.   *History Today*, vol. 45, no. 10 (Oct. 1995), p. 26-32.
bibliog.

Noel's highly readable article provides an interesting overview of the importance of
Charles III (1759-88) for the remodelling and improvement of the Spanish capital. He
illustrates how the King set about transforming Madrid's buildings and roads in order
to clean the city up and also provide it with architecture corresponding to its status as
capital of Spain. The creation of new plans, roads (including the Calle de Alcalá, the
Paseo del Prado and the Paseo de Recoletos), buildings and institutions are all
discussed by the author. Well illustrated and clearly written, the article emphasizes
how the development of Madrid under Charles III reflected the new philosophical and
cultural concerns of the enlightened 'Age of Reason'.

120  **Madrid en la sociedad del siglo XIX.** (Madrid in 19th-century
society.)
Edited by Luis Enrique Otero Carvajal, Angel Bahamonde Magro.
Madrid: Comunidad de Madrid, Consejería de Cultura; Alfoz, 1986.
2 vols. (Coloquios de Historia Madrileña).

Based on one of a series of conferences which are held every two years on Madrid's
history, this is a lavishly produced and thorough study of all aspects of Madrid society
during the 1800s. Volume one considers the city and its surrounding area, its role as
the centre of political power, together with its economy and local élites. Volume two
discusses social conflict, population trends, food provision, living conditions, and
culture and ideas. Another useful study of the period is the book by Federico José
Ponte Chamorro, *Demografía y sociedad en el Madrid decimonónico (1787-1857)*
(Population and society in 19th-century Madrid) (q.v.).

121  **Madrid in 1835: sketches of the metropolis of Spain and its
inhabitants, and of society and manners in the peninsula.**
By a Resident Officer.   London: Saunders & Otley, 1836. 2 vols.

This fascinating work provides a detailed description and study of all aspects of
Madrid as it was in 1835. Written by a British army officer, its interesting style is
noteworthy not least for the many unflattering remarks made about the city. Volume
one (398 pages) describes: the appearance of Madrid; its hotels; the markets; the
Puerta del Sol; the Post Office; the Prado; the theatres; *tertulias* (intellectual/literary
get-togethers); masked balls; bullfights; and Christmas and New Year celebrations.
Volume two (410 pages) continues with the author's descriptive and critical comments
upon: the government; the grandees; the monasteries; convents; hospitals; prisons;
beggars; the Retiro Park; and recollections of the year 1834 (dominated by a cholera
epidemic). Subjective and full of detail, the work not only recounts memories of daily
events but is invaluable for shedding light on the minutest aspects of Madrid life and
society during the period when the First Carlist War (1833-39) was still raging in
Spain.

## 122 The riots of 1766 in Madrid.
Laura Rodríguez. *European Studies Review*, vol. 3, no. 3 (July 1973), p. 223-42.

Charles III (1759-88), formerly King of Naples and fascinated by the Enlightenment, sought to reform and improve Spanish society from the very top. In particular, he challenged the privileges of the clergy in general and the Jesuits specifically. However, the riots of Madrid in 1766 were occasioned by an event of apparent insignificance, when on 10th March posters appeared (issued by a decree of Charles's Italian minister, the Marqués de Esquilache) prohibiting Madrid's inhabitants from wearing the long capes and broad-brimmed hats which they traditionally wore. The edict was justified by the argument that these garments were being used by criminals to conceal both weapons and identities. Rodríguez's interesting article analyses whether the riots which ensued were truly 'popular' revolts or in fact part of a conspiracy organized by the Jesuits, with the purpose of bringing about the downfall of Esquilache and the King's confessor, and replacing them with someone more sympathetic to their Order. She concludes that no conclusive evidence exists to prove that the Church, or any section of it, was responsible for their organization. In the end the edict was repealed, Esquilache fled Spain (ironically, in disguise!), and the King stayed away from Madrid for nine months (at Aranjuez). Nevertheless, the policies of reform pursued by Esquilache were actually reinforced over the following years by these incidents, and in 1767 the Jesuits were expelled from Spain.

## 123 Dos décadas en la biografía de Madrid (1910-1930). (Two decades in the life of Madrid [1910-30].)
Federico Carlos Sainz de Robles. Madrid: Ayuntamiento: Instituto de Estudios Madrileños, 1984. 30p.

This short pamphlet provides a succinct overview of twenty years of the Restoration period, when Alfonso XIII (1885-1931) was King. During this time the building of the Gran Vía was initiated (1910) and the first Metro line was opened (1919).

**The Bible in Spain.**
*See* item no. 70.

**A hand-book for travellers in Spain and readers at home.**
*See* item no. 72.

**Viajeros impenitentes: Madrid visto por los viajeros extranjeros en los siglos XVII, XVIII y XIX.** (Unrepentant travellers: Madrid as seen by foreign travellers in the 17th, 18th and 19th centuries.)
*See* item no. 75.

**La población de la villa de Madrid: desde finales del siglo XVI hasta mediadas del siglo XIX.** (The population of the town of Madrid: from the end of the 16th century to the middle of the 19th.)
*See* item no. 138.

**Demografía y sociedad en el Madrid decimonómico (1787-1857).** (Population and society in 19th-century Madrid [1787-1857].)
*See* item no. 141.

**Guía diocesana de Madrid y los pueblos de su provincia.** (Diocesan guide to Madrid and its provincial towns.)
*See* item no. 150.

**Madrid: judíos, herejes y brujas: el Tribunal de Corte (1650-1820).** (Madrid: Jews, heretics and witches: the Court Tribunal, 1650-1820.)
*See* item no. 151.

**Madrid bajo el punto de vista médico-social.** (Madrid from a medico-social point of view.)
*See* item no. 164.

**Poverty in eighteenth-century Spain: the women and children of the Inclusa.**
*See* item no. 186.

**La Cámara de Comercio e Industria de Madrid, 1887-1987.** (The Madrid Chamber of Commerce and Industry, 1887-1987.)
*See* item no. 209.

**Madrid and the Spanish economy, 1560-1850.**
*See* item no. 213.

**Los primeros cien años del Canal de Isabel II.** (The first hundred years of the Canal of Isabella II.)
*See* item no. 266.

**El Parque Zoológico de Madrid 1774-1994.** (The Zoological Park of Madrid 1774-1994.)
*See* item no. 285.

**Arquitectura y arquitectos madrileños del siglo XIX.** (Nineteenth-century architecture and architects of Madrid.)
*See* item no. 295.

**La educación de la mujer en el Madrid de Isabel II.** (The education of women in Madrid during the reign of Isabella II.)
*See* item no. 303.

**La enseñanza privada seglar de grado medio en Madrid (1820-1868).** (Private lay education at college level in Madrid [1820-68].)
*See* item no. 304.

**Primeros pasos de la luz eléctrica en Madrid y otros acontecimientos.** (The arrival of electric lighting in Madrid and other events.)
*See* item no. 308.

**The Madrid writer in Spanish society: 1833-1843.**
*See* item no. 318.

**Trilogía de Madrid: memorias.** (Madrid trilogy: memoirs.)
*See* item no. 346.

**Postales antiguas de Madrid.** (Old postcards of Madrid.)
*See* item no. 348.

**El Ateneo científico, literario y artístico de Madrid (1835-1885).** (The scientific, literary and artistic Athenaeum of Madrid [1835-85].)
*See* item no. 352.

**Recalling the Golden Age: collections and taste in Madrid, 1833-1868.**
*See* item no. 353.

**A royal patrimony: the Prado Museum and Spanish history.**
*See* item no. 378.

**Historia del Casino de Madrid y su época.** (A history of the Madrid Casino and its era.)
*See* item no. 444.

**The book trade in Ibarra's Madrid.**
*See* item no. 458.

**Pedro Rodríguez and the wooden printing press in Madrid.**
*See* item no. 459.

**The Royal Company of Printers and Booksellers of Spain: 1763-1794.**
*See* item no. 460.

**Madrid newspapers 1661-1870: a computerized handbook based on the work of Eugenio Hartzenbusch.**
*See* item no. 466.

# Second Republic and Civil War

**124   The clash.**
   Arturo Barea, translated by Ilsa Barea.   London: Fontana, 1984. 396p.

This represents the third part of Barea's powerful autobiographical trilogy, *The forging of a rebel*, which was published in an omnibus edition by Davis-Poynter (London) in 1972. The first volume, *The forge*, describes his childhood and youth; and the second, *The track*, takes him from the age of twenty to twenty-eight years, a period spent as a conscript soldier in Spanish Morocco. The present volume is a most vivid account of what life was like in Madrid during the Spanish Civil War (1936-39). Born in Madrid in 1897, Barea lived in England from 1939 until his death in 1957, having worked for the BBC during the Second World War. In *The clash* he describes the horrors of the Civil War and his own part in the struggle against the nationalist forces of General Franco. For most of the time he was the head of the Foreign Press and Censorship Bureau of the Republican government in the capital and was also the radio broadcaster who became internationally famous as the 'Unknown Voice of Madrid'. What this book achieves that academic histories of the war cannot is to give the reader a personal and vivid understanding of what daily life was like in a city under siege.

The work is full of poignancy and evocative descriptions of people, places and events. A line from its review in *The Times* upon its publication sums up its lasting value and influence: 'It achieves that rare quality, partisanship without intellectual dishonesty or the distortion of the truth'. *The clash* was first published in English by Faber & Faber (London) in 1946 (before its publication in Spanish in 1951).

125   **The last days of Madrid: the end of the Second Spanish Republic.**
      Colonel Segismundo Casado, translated with an introduction by Rupert
      Croft-Cooke.   London: Peter Davies, 1939. 302p.

The author of this book (1893-1968) was Commander of the Republican Central Army during the Civil War, and was also responsible for the coup in March 1939 which set up a National Council of Defence, after which Juan Negrín (1892-1956) (prime minister of the Republic from 1937 to 1939) fled Spain in the last months of the war. At the same time he challenged the power of the PCE (Spanish Communist Party) in Madrid and that of its leader, Dolores Ibarruri, 'La Pasionaria' (1895-1989). It was her publication of an article signed 'La Pasionaria' (Passion flower), during Easter week 1918, which gave her the name by which she is best known. Casado also entered into secret negotiations with Franco, hoping to extract from him, as one military man to another, a conciliatory peace. In this he failed, and after the Republic's collapse and surrender Casado fled to London. His book presents a narrative account from a Republican soldier's point of view, yet it is clearly written from the heart, including throughout pleas for justice and democracy. The political and military events which unfolded during the final weeks of the war are recounted, and in particular those which took place in Madrid. In his introduction Croft-Cooke comments that 'Casado saved hundreds of thousands of lives and prevented the destruction of Madrid and many other cities', and although there were those at the time who disputed this, it certainly is an undisputed fact that by 1939 the population of Madrid had had enough of fighting and the terrible food shortages. Fascinating in its detail, Casado's book retains the immediacy of events and will be of interest to both scholar and general reader alike. The Spanish edition, which was published a number of years later, contains some interesting discrepancies with the English edition. Two other works written by, or about, protagonists on the Republican side are also worthy of mention here: *Así fue la defensa de Madrid* (Thus was the defence of Madrid) by General Vicente Rojo Lluch (Madrid: Gabinete del Presidente, 1987. 265p.) offers a methodical explanation of the battles, the terrain, the men and also the weapons in the struggle for Madrid; whilst Antonio López Fernández's *El general Miaja: defensor de Madrid* (General Miaja: defender of Madrid) (Madrid: G. del Toro, 1975. 334p.) presents a biographical study of the most famous of the Republican army's leaders.

126   **The struggle for Madrid: the central epic of the Spanish conflict
      (1936-37).**
      Robert Garland Colodny.   New York: Paine-Whitman, 1958. 256p.
      maps. bibliog.

Adapted from the author's PhD thesis, 'The campaign for Madrid: October, 1936 – April, 1937' (University of California, Berkeley, 1951), this is the best English-language study of the battle for Madrid during the Civil War. Although many other works on the subject have appeared (many of which have had the benefit of access to archival and other historical material which became available in the years after Colodny's book was published), none represents such a conscientious and detailed military study of the battles, both on a personal level and on the level of the strategic importance of Madrid to both sides. Extensive notes accompany the main text. Other works on the battle for Madrid include *La marcha sobre Madrid* (The march on Madrid) by José Manuel Martínez Bande, a prolific writer on the Civil War (Madrid: San Martín, 1982. 2nd ed. 213p.); *La lucha en torno a Madrid en el invierno de 1936-1937* (The struggle for Madrid in the winter of 1936-37), also written by Martínez Bande (Madrid: San Martín, 1984. 2nd ed. 338p.); and *Madrid, capital republicana* (Madrid, Republican capital) by David Jato Miranda (Barcelona, Spain: Acerbo, 1976. 716p.).

127  **Defence of Madrid.**
Geoffrey Cox.  London: Victor Gollancz, 1937. 221p.

The battle for Madrid in the winter of 1936-37 represented one of the most dramatic episodes of the Civil War. Many, according to Cox, saw it as 'one of the finest chapters in the history of the common people of the world' with the Republicans portrayed as the defenders of democracy against the onslaught of fascism. Franco had launched a full-scale frontal offensive against Madrid in October 1936, expecting a quick victory. His troops made advances and forced Largo Caballero's government to abandon the capital and continue to direct the war from Valencia. Madrid, however, did not fall. The reorganized Republican army, reinforced by the recently arrived International Brigades, fought fiercely during the crucial month of November, and the Nationalist advance was halted. The Republic had gained its first military victory, albeit a defensive one. The repercussions were enormous, for what appeared destined to be a short war would now become a protracted one. Madrid remained the centre of military operations over the next four months as the Nationalist army attempted to take the city through a series of flanking manoeuvres. In February 1937 they launched a heavy offensive in the Jarama valley (south-east of Madrid). The bloody battle which ensued lasted for three weeks and involved the American Abraham Lincoln Brigade in its first action. Casualties were very heavy on both sides but the Republican defence of Madrid held firm. Having failed to capture the city either by frontal or flanking attacks, Franco gave up hope of a rapid victory and instead set about the piecemeal destruction of the Republic. Cox, who was the *News Chronicle* correspondent in Madrid between October and December 1936, presents an enthralling account of events which excels in evoking both the fear and excitement of battle, and in extolling the virtues and heroism of the Republican defenders.

128  **Red terror in Madrid: an eye-witness record of the first six months of the Civil War.**
Luis de Fonteriz, with a foreword by Don Pedro de Zulueta.  London; New York: Longmans, 1937. 99p.

Written under a pseudonym, this short book presents a scathing indictment of the Popular Front government of Spain. The author singles out the government and trade unions (the eponymous 'red terror') in particular as guilty of war crimes and acts against humanity. Chapters detail the writer's experiences of life in Madrid over the first six months of the war and describe conditions ('murder-gone-mad') on the streets, reprisals and arrests, Madrid's prisons and the bombardment of the city. Hard-hitting and earnestly written, by one with 'no political axe to grind', it provides a useful counterpoint to the many works which detail the crimes committed by the Nationalist side.

129 **The battle for Madrid.**
George Hills. London: Vantage Books, 1976; New York: St. Martin's
Press, 1977. 192p. maps. bibliog.

Author of several books on Spain and a military man himself during the Second World
War, Hills presents a political and military history of the battle for Madrid. Based
upon research undertaken during the 1960s, he had the opportunity to interview
several of the then surviving principal figures, as well as gain access to a wealth of
documentary and archival material. The battle for Madrid, like the Spanish Civil War
itself, was the product of ideas and events dating back to long before November 1936,
when the Nationalist army laid siege to the city. It was in fact a series of battles, and
Hills' book is particularly helpful in detailing the military operations on the
battlefields and also the influence on them of political ideas, decisions and events.
Packed with maps, illustrations and fascinating contemporary photographs, the book is
accessible to the non-specialist and general reader interested in military history.
Interestingly, the term 'fifth column' was coined in 1936 when the Nationalist army
was advancing on Madrid in four columns: one of Franco's generals, General Mola,
stated that as soon as these columns entered the city a secret 'fifth column' would rise
up to complete the city's capture.

130 **Economic crisis, social conflict and the Popular Front: Madrid
1931-6.**
Santos Juliá Díaz. In: *Revolution and war in Spain 1931-1939*.
Edited by Paul Preston. London; New York: Routledge, 1993,
p. 137-58. bibliog.

First published in 1984 (London; New York: Methuen, 299p.), the book is a reprinted
edition of the original text. Juliá Díaz's chapter on Madrid examines the urban
development of the capital, the consequent changes in its demographic structure and
the growing militancy of unemployed youths and their relationship to the class war
which erupted in 1936. He emphasizes the importance of economic crisis, strikes and
rampant unemployment in raising the awareness amongst workers (particularly the
young) of class interests and inequalities. Well argued, clearly and succinctly written,
this chapter is an important source of information on industry and society in Madrid
during the period leading up to the Civil War, and highlights how tensions grew and
parties polarized to such an extent that political solutions became impossible to
achieve. Juliá Díaz (a professor of sociology at the Universidad Nacional de
Educación a Distancia, Madrid) is also author of the standard Spanish text which
analyses the class struggle in Madrid during the same period: *Madrid, 1931-1934: de
la fiesta popular a la lucha de clases* (Madrid, 1931-34: from popular celebration to
class conflict) (Madrid: Siglo Veintiuno España, 1984. 509p.). In it he minutely
dissects the various aspects of Madrid's social conditions and classes, and considers
the role of trade unions and employers in a situation which eventually led in 1934 to
confrontation and strikes.

131 **Miracle of November: Madrid's epic stand 1936.**
Dan Kurzman. New York: Putnam, 1980. 352p. maps. bibliog.

Kurzman's interesting study of the siege of Madrid during the Civil War is the fruit of
over two years' intensive research in a number of countries and interviews with
hundreds of people, many of whom were combatants during the battles for the capital.
Aimed at the general reader, it presents a clear and objective account of the siege and

as such is a perfect foil to some of the more subjective and academic studies on the subject. Notes on sources for each chapter and an extensive bibliography are also included. Two other useful works on the siege and battle for Madrid are: *La guerra civil en Madrid* (Civil War in Madrid) by Matilde Vázquez and Javier Valero (Madrid: Tebas, 1978. 926p.); and a recent French study, *Madrid, 1936-1939: un peuple en résistance ou l'épopée ambiguë* (Madrid, 1936-39: a people's resistance or the ambiguous epic), edited by Carlos Serrano (Paris: Autremont, 1991. 285p.).

132  **Murder in Madrid.**
London: International Brigade Association, 1963. 15p.

The dramatic title of this pamphlet refers to the execution by firing squad, in 1963, of Julian Grimau, a member of the Central Committee of the Spanish Communist Party. His treatment in captivity and subsequent death provoked an international outcry; six months prior to his killing he had apparently been thrown from an upper window of the police headquarters building in the Puerta del Sol, in an attempt to simulate suicide. The International Brigade Association, set up in 1938 by British volunteers who had fought in the Spanish Civil War, campaigned for a free and democratic Spain and an end to Franco's repression. Although the first few pages of this work detail the case of Grimau, the rest comprises a short history of the Spanish Civil War and the attempts of the Republicans to free Spain from fascist domination, and includes a description of the workers' strikes and student protests of 1962. The study is powerfully and passionately written and it concluded by urging British workers to support their Spanish counterparts in their struggle against the repressive measures of the Franco government.

133  **The defence of Madrid: mysterious generals, red front fighters, and the International Brigades.**
R. Dan Richardson. *Military Affairs*, vol. 43, no. 4 (Dec. 1979), p. 178-85.

This short article represents a useful counterpoint to Cox's work (q.v.) with Richardson disputing the view that the International Brigades saved Madrid from being taken by the Nationalist forces. Instead, he argues that the fact Madrid was successfully defended 'must be attributed chiefly to the organizational ability, the determination, the leadership, the professional and technical expertise, and the material support of the Soviet-Comintern apparatus'. Three years later he took his argument further in his book, *Comintern army: the International Brigades and the Spanish Civil War* (Lexington, Kentucky: University of Kentucky Press, 1982. 232p.). In it he propounds the view that 'the Brigades were, from beginning to end, an integral part of that interlocking directorate which was the Soviet-Comintern apparatus in Spain, largely sponsored, recruited and controlled by the Communist International for its own purposes'. Whether one agrees or disagrees, the article presents an interesting study of the battle for Madrid and contains a large number of supporting references. The recently published book, *Madrid 1937: letters of the Abraham Lincoln Brigade from the Spanish Civil War*, edited by Cary Nelson and Jefferson Hendricks (London: Routledge, 1996. 624p.), chronicles the experiences of the 2,800 American soldiers of the Brigade.

134 **Dancer in Madrid.**
Janet Riesenfeld, drawings by Lyle Justis. London: George G.
Harrap, 1938. 272p.

Born in New York and trained as a Spanish dancer, Janet Riesenfeld fell in love with
Jaime Castanys, a Catalan, whilst in Hollywood in the early 1930s when she was only
fifteen. Six years later she travelled from California to Madrid to be reunited with him,
and this book provides an evocative account of life in the city at the height of the Civil
War. Her personal anecdotes intermingle with her accounts of historical events such as
the rousing speeches of Dolores Ibarruri ('La Pasionaria'), to the defenders of Madrid,
and the destruction wrought by the bombings of the city. Riesenfeld returned to the
United States six months later, after Jaime had been killed.

135 **Individualisms in Madrid during the Spanish Civil War.**
Michael Seidman. *The Journal of Modern History*, vol. 68, no. 1
(March 1996), p. 63-83.

The author considers the role of individuals who asserted their own interests against
the demands of various causes and collectivities during the battle for Madrid.
Although many workers were willing to make huge sacrifices to save the capital from
the Nationalist army, solidarity was not universal 'and there were many workers who
could be described as individualistic'. Emphasizing the role of the trade unions (in
particular the CNT – National Confederation of Labour, and the UGT – General
Workers' Union), and notably those acquisitive individuals within the unions,
Seidman demonstrates how inflated price rises, thefts and deception took place to such
an extent as to alter the traditional emphasis on collective militancy during the
Spanish Civil War. Thorough and scholarly, the author concludes that future research
on this subject might not only explore the struggle of class and gender but also analyse
the conflict between the individual and society.

**Madrid 1931: mujeres entre la permanencia y el cambio.** (Madrid 1931:
women amidst tradition and change.)
*See* item no. 170.

**Las elecciones municipales de 1931 en Madrid.** (The municipal elections
of 1931 in Madrid.)
*See* item no. 205.

**Ideology and political patronage: workers and working-class movements
in republican Madrid, 1931-4.**
*See* item no. 241.

**La Escuela de Madrid: un ensayo de filosofía.** (The Madrid School: a study
of philosophy.)
*See* item no. 296.

**The fell of dark.**
*See* item no. 334.

**Trilogía de Madrid: memorias.** (Madrid trilogy: memoirs.)
*See* item no. 346.

# Post-Civil War

136 **El Madrid de Juan Carlos I.** (The Madrid of Juan Carlos I.)
Margerita Jiménez. Madrid: EFCA, 1995. 332p. bibliog.
Massive both in size and scope, this beautifully produced and illustrated volume has been published in a limited edition, but is available from all major bookshops in Madrid. Various chapters consider Madrid's history generally; the Plaza Mayor; Madrid in the year 2000; urban planning and society; the role of the King and his relationship with Madrid and its people; and another section contains extracts from literary and historical writings on Madrid. Jiménez also wrote several other books on Madrid, including two on the city's squares, parks and gardens (qq.v.).

137 **El Madrid de la postguerra, 1940-1960.** (Post-war Madrid, 1940-60.)
Eugenio Salas Morales, Juan Antonio Palacios Antón, José Jiménez Díaz. Madrid: The Authors, 1995. 158p.
This is one of the few books which covers Madrid under the Franco régime. During this twenty-year period Madrid underwent much development and many changes, and witnessed important events such as: the opening of the first electric railway between Madrid and El Escorial (1944); urban development plans; the creation of the Instituto de Estudios Madrileños (Institute of Madrid Studies) (1951); the withdrawal of Civil War ration cards (1952); military agreements between Spain and the United States (1953); the first transmissions from TVE (Spanish television) (1956); the opening, by Franco, of the *Valle de los Caídos* monument (Valley of the Fallen) (1959); and the visit to Madrid of President Eisenhower (1959).

**Solo se vive una vez: esplendor y ruina de la movida madrileña.** (You only live once: the rise and fall of the Madrid movement.)
*See* item no. 162.

**Trilogía de Madrid: memorias.** (Madrid trilogy: memoirs.)
*See* item no. 346.

# Population

## Demography

138 **La población de la villa de Madrid: desde finales del siglo XVI hasta mediadas del siglo XIX.** (The population of the town of Madrid: from the end of the 16th century to the middle of the 19th.)
María F. Carbajo Isla. Madrid: Siglo XXI, 1987. 401p. bibliog.

This has become a standard work on the demographic history of Madrid and is particularly useful for its detail, scholarship and documentation. Two other important studies of Madrid's population during the 19th and early part of the 20th century have been written by one of Spain's most noted sociologists, Amando de Miguel: *La población de Madrid a lo largo del último siglo* (The population of Madrid during the last century) (Madrid: Asamblea de Madrid, 1991. 223p.) which gathers together information relating to demographic movement in Madrid and the area now covered by the Autonomous Community; and *La población de Madrid en los primeros años del siglo* (The population of Madrid at the beginning of the century) (Madrid: Instituto de Estudios Madrileños, 1984. 32p.), a short but interesting survey. Readers might also refer to Javier Ruiz Almansa's much older article, 'La población de Madrid, su evolución y crecimiento durante el presente siglo (1900-1945)' (The population of Madrid, its evolution and growth during the present century [1900-45]) in the *Revista Internacional de Sociología*, vol. 4 (1946), p. 389-411. He also wrote an article on Madrid's population since 1800 in the same journal (vol. 3 [1945], p. 245-67, 389-420), and was author of the booklet, *El censo español y el censo de Madrid* (The Spanish census and the census of Madrid) (Madrid: Consejo Superior de Investigaciones Científicas, 1984. 50p.).

139 **Urban dynamics and life cycle of Madrid's population.**
Aurora García Ballesteros. *Geographia Polonica*, vol. 61 (1993),
p. 121-32.
This article analyses the relationship between Madrid's urban expansion and demographic trends. In particular the author considers age-groups and the changes that recent urban renewal has made on the traditional pattern of an old urban city centre versus a new young periphery. Various sections look at Madrid's growth stages, life cycle and household structure, and urban dynamics and age structure in Madrid's districts. Although certain parts of the article will be of interest to the general reader, it is aimed in particular at specialists in human geography. The author also collaborated with Dolores Brandis and Isabel de Río Lafuente on the article, 'Los movimientos migratorios de la población de Madrid' (The migratory movements of Madrid's population) (*Revista Internacional de Sociología*, vol. 22 [1977], p. 193-224).

140 **La población de Madrid.** (The population of Madrid.)
Madrid: Comunidad Autónoma, Servicio de Documentación y
Publicaciones, 1994. 264p.
Covering the region of Madrid, this up-to-date study analyses the spatial distribution of the population, the demographic characteristics and trends during the period 1981-91. Other useful general works and statistical surveys of the city's population include: *Movimiento natural de la población español, 1992: Madrid* (Spanish population movement, 1992: Madrid) (Madrid: Instituto Nacional de Estadística, 1995. 134p.), an annual publication; and *La población de Madrid en 1991* (The population of Madrid in 1991) (Madrid: Ayuntamiento de Madrid, Departamento de Estadística, 1991. 334p.).

141 **Demografía y sociedad en el Madrid decimonómico (1787-1857).**
(Population and society in 19th-century Madrid [1787-1857].)
Federico José Ponte Chamorro. Madrid: Ayuntamiento; Turner,
1991. 223p. bibliog.
This prize-winning book presents a detailed, comprehensive survey of Madrid's population growth and changing society over a seventy-year period. During that time the city's population grew dramatically from around 160,000 in 1787 to over 300,000 by the mid-19th century. The book includes numerous graphs and statistics as well as illustrations, plans and indexes.

142 **Madrid culpable: sobre el espacio y la población en las ciencias
sociales.** (Madrid to blame: on space and population in the social
sciences.)
Juan Salcedo. Madrid: Tecnos, 1977. 199p. (Colección de Ciencias
Sociales; Serie de Sociología).
This is one of the best studies of Madrid's population and one of the most informative generally on the social geography and problems of space in the city, including issues such as overcrowding, traffic, transport and housing.

**Madrid en la sociedad del siglo XIX.** (Madrid in 19th-century society.)
*See* item no. 120.

**The social ecology of Madrid: stratification in comparative perspective.**
*See* item no. 155.

**Estadísticas del movimiento natural de la población de la Comunidad de Madrid: 1992.** (Statistics on native population movements for the Community of Madrid: 1992.)
*See* item no. 250.

# Minority groups

143  **Madrid y sus judíos.** (Madrid and its Jews.)
Juan Antonio Cabezas.    Madrid: El Avapiés, 1987. 206p. bibliog.

Little has been written on the history of the Jews of Madrid, and certainly during the 19th century the subject was virtually taboo. This is all the more surprising when one considers that the area around the Plaza de Lavapiés and the Calle la Fe was the centre of Madrid's mediaeval Jewish community (and the location of a synagogue) until the expulsion of the Jews from Spain by Queen Isabella in 1492. Cabezas provides an extensive historical survey of the Jews in Madrid from their earliest presence there, through the years of persecution from 1391 until their expulsion. He then proceeds to consider the consequences of the expulsion edict, with the creation in Madrid of the new social class of *conversos* (Jews who converted to Catholicism in order to remain in Spain). Subsequent chapters study the *conversos* in the newly-established capital during the 16th century, and their persecution under the Inquisition until the end of the 18th century. Finally, Cabezas considers Jews returning to Spain during the 20th century, in relation to Primo de Rivera's decree of 1924 (allowing Sephardic Jews the right to a Spanish passport); Nazi persecution and the 'final solution'; and the present-day situation with the growth of Jewish communities in Spain generally and the opening of new synagogues in Madrid and Toledo. The only other historical study of the Jews of Madrid of any note is *Madrid: judíos, herejes y brujas: el Tribunal de Corte (1650-1820)* by Juan Blázquez Miguel (q.v.).

144  **Inmigrantes extranjeros en Madrid.** (Foreign immigrants in Madrid.)
Coordinated by C. Giménez Romero.    Madrid: Comunidad, Secretaría General Técnica, 1993. 2 vols.

Surprisingly, perhaps, there are very few up-to-date surveys published on this subject, and this work, which considers the region of Madrid, represents the only in-depth analysis available. Volume one provides a general overview and social profile as well as giving a full history of the development of foreign immigration into Madrid. It also contains an analysis of the principal problems and a series of recommendations for overcoming them. Volume two reports on specific groups of immigrants (Latin Americans, Moroccans, Portuguese, Africans and Filipinos). Both volumes include a wealth of statistical data. Another interesting study, although somewhat dated, is the article, 'Valor de la inmigración madrileña' (The value of immigration to Madrid), by A. Alonso Cabo in *Estudios Geográficos*, vol. 22 (1961), p. 353-74.

145   **La comunidad mudéjar de Madrid: un modelo de análisis de aljamas mudéjares castellanas.** (The *mudéjar* community of Madrid: a model for analysing Castilian *mudéjar* communities.)
Juan Carlos de Miguel Rodríguez, prologue by Cristina Segura Graíño.
Madrid: Asociación Cultural Al-Mudayna, 1989. 139p. 2 maps.
bibliog. (Colección Laya Madrid, no. 4).

This is an important study on the minority *mudéjar* community of Madrid who had a presence in the city from the end of the 11th century right up until the beginning of the 17th century. The recapture of Toledo from the Moors (1085) marked the turning point in the Christian reconquest of Spain, and the process of *convivencia* or 'living together' was introduced to allow the Moslems to live in Spain under Christian rule. A person who elected to stay was known as a *mudéjar*, a word derived from the Arabic *al-mudajjar* meaning 'persons allowed to remain'. Among historians of today the word *mudéjar* is widely used (both as an adjective and a noun) to label the culture and architecture of the Moslems who chose to remain in mediaeval Spain – just as the term *mozarab* is used to denote Christians who lived under Moslem rule. The author of the present work painstakingly analyses the origins and development of the *mudéjar* community in Madrid, its religious and institutional organizations, its economic and social history, and its cultural assimilation and forced conversion. Miguel Rodríguez is a respected historian of mediaeval Madrid and also edited *El Madrid medieval: sus tierras y sus hombres* (Mediaeval Madrid: its land and its people) (Madrid: Asociación Cultural Al-Mudayna, 1990. 255p.), a useful work which gathers together information from a wide range of sources.

146   **La minoría gitana en la Comunidad de Madrid.** (The gypsy minority in the Community of Madrid.)
Juan Manuel Montoya.   Madrid: Instituto Regional de Estudios, 1987. 105p.

One of the standard sources of information, this work covers the wider region of Madrid and contains statistical and other useful data. Another book, *Gitanos al encuentro de la ciudad* (Gypsy encounter with the city) by Equipo Giens (Madrid: Cuadernos para el Diálogo, 1977. 202p.), considers how the gypsies of Madrid deal with life in the capital.

147   **Foreign minorities from developing countries in Madrid.**
V. Rodríguez, M. J. Aguilera, M. P. González-Yanci.   *GeoJournal*, vol. 30, no. 3 (July 1993), p. 293-300.

In this survey the authors selected the six nationalities which provide the highest numbers of immigrants from the developing world in Madrid (metropolitan area). Racial and cultural contrasts are considered, together with regularization processes, the reactions of the Madrid population towards immigrants, and detailed profiles of the minorities (location, mobility and segregation). Despite the occasional misspelling or mistranslation, the article is clear, concise and packed with a wealth of useful statistical data. Currently there are over 100,000 officially registered immigrants in Madrid, with another 50,000 or more in the city who are there illegally. Most arrived in the 1980s, when Madrid's thriving economy began to attract an increasing flow of people from the Third World and Eastern Europe. As this article emphasizes, most immigrants can only find poorly-paid work in the service industries, and Latin American and Filipino women work particularly in cleaning jobs and as private maids.

Many North Africans work at the cheaper end of the construction industry and on road-building.

148 **Kinship, marriage, law and leadership in two urban gypsy settlements in Spain.**
Teresa San Román Espinosa. In: *Gypsies, tinkers and other travellers*. Edited by Farnham Rehfisch. London; New York: Academic Press, 1975, p. 169-99. bibliog.

Based on material included in the author's MPhil thesis, 'A comparative study of three gypsy urban settlements in Spain' (University of London, 1974), this interesting chapter provides a background history to the gypsies' presence in Spain, their lineage organization, their views of the family and marriage, their code of law and morality, and concepts of honour and prestige. Her study is based upon research undertaken in La Alegría settlement in Madrid (which at the time of writing had a population of about 500 gypsies) and San Roque in Barcelona. San Román Espinosa also wrote *Gitanos de Madrid y Barcelona: ensayos sobre aculturación y etnicidad* (Gypsies of Madrid and Barcelona: essays on acculturation and ethnicity) (Barcelona, Spain: Universidad Autónoma, 1984. 132p.). The gypsies of Madrid were also the focus of a fascinating newspaper article by Justin Webster, entitled 'Gypsies for Jesus' in *The Independent Magazine* (Feb. 11th 1995, p. 30-34). Webster noted that over the years drink, drugs and flamenco were the common means of escape for the Madrid gypsies. However, he describes how an evangelical creed called the Church of Philadelphia, or simply 'the cult', bearing the hallmarks of charismatic Christianity, transformed their outlook and way of life.

# Language

149  **El habla de la ciudad de Madrid: materiales para su estudio.**
(The spoken language of Madrid: study material.)
M. Esgueva, M. Cantarero.   Madrid: Consejo Superior de
Investigaciones Científicas, Instituto Miguel de Cervantes, 1981. 449p.
(La Norma Lingüística Culta de la Lengua Española Hablada en
Madrid, no. 1).

The work constitutes a small anthology of interviews which were conducted in order to study the learned linguistic norm of Spanish as spoken in Madrid. It comprises a variety of transcripted talks with inhabitants of the city (all educated men and women) from different backgrounds, and illustrates the variations in speech and use of language by people born and bred in Madrid. Three other volumes in this series of studies were subsequently published: *Encuestas léxicas del habla culta en Madrid* (Lexical surveys of educated speech in Madrid) by José C. Torres Martínez (Madrid: CSIC, Instituto Miguel de Cervantes, 1981. 737p.); *La concordancia gramatical en la lengua española hablada en Madrid* (Grammatical agreement in the Spanish spoken in Madrid) by Antonio Quilis (Madrid: CSIC, Instituto Miguel de Cervantes, 1983. 126p.); and *El pronombre personal sujeto en la lengua española hablada en Madrid* (The personal subject pronoun in the Spanish spoken in Madrid) by Emilia V. Enríquez (Madrid: CSIC, Instituto Miguel de Cervantes, 1984. 393p.).

**Catálogo de manuscritos de la Real Academia Española.** (Catalogue of the manuscripts of the Spanish Royal Academy.)
*See* item no. 534.

# Religion

150 **Guía diocesana de Madrid y los pueblos de su provincia.** (Diocesan guide to Madrid and its provincial towns.)
Luis Béjar. Madrid: Imp. del Asilo de Huérfanos del S. C. de Jesús, 1913. 527p.

Old and difficult to obtain, this is nonetheless a fascinating guidebook to the history of the religious organization of Madrid. Other interesting studies relevant to the study of the city's religious history are: *Hermandades y cofradías establecidas en Madrid* (Brotherhoods and guilds established in Madrid) by Joaquín Tello Jiménez (Madrid: Camarasa, 1942. 266p.); *La semana santa de Madrid en el siglo XVII* (Holy Week in 17th-century Madrid) by Miguel Herrero García (Madrid: Gráfica Universal, 1935. 64p.); *La iglesia secular en Madrid en el siglo XVIII* (The lay church in 18th-century Madrid) by Gloria Angeles Franco Rubio (Madrid: Universidad Complutense, 1986. 2 vols.); *La Almudena y su significación en la vida y en la cultura madrileñas* (The Almudena and its meaning in the life and culture of Madrid) (Madrid: Concejalía de Cultura, 1990. 13p.); and *Madrid y su santo patrono* (Madrid and her patron saint) by José del Corral (Madrid: Ayuntamiento, Centro de Orientación Pedagógica y Extensión Cultural, 1956. 35p.).

151 **Madrid: judíos, herejes y brujas: el Tribunal de Corte (1650-1820).**
(Madrid: Jews, heretics and witches: the Court Tribunal, 1650-1820.)
Juan Blázquez Miguel. Toledo, Spain: Arcano, 1990. 218p. maps. bibliog. (Inquisitio; no. 2).

This detailed study recounts and analyses the work of the Inquisition's Tribunal Court, from its creation in 1650 until its demise in 1820. During this period of 170 years the Tribunal exercised a direct and total control over the inhabitants of the capital. The permanent Tribunal of Madrid was technically known as *Corte* (Law Court) and its jurisdiction was strictly limited to the city, while the surrounding country remained under the control of Toledo. The present work covers the history of the *Corte*, the Inquisition in Madrid and all aspects of the Tribunal's procedures and trials in the city. A wide range of statistical information is included, together with an extensive bibliography and numerous illustrations and maps.

152 **Response to urbanization: Madrid and Barcelona, 1850-1930.**
William James Callahan. *Hispania Sacra*, vol. 42, no. 86 (1990),
p. 445-51.

Callahan's short paper was originally presented at the International Congress on Comparative Ecclesiastical History on the subject of churches in the city in modern times. Callahan is a prolific writer on the subject and in this short article he compares the negative effect of urbanization on religious practice and belief in Madrid and Barcelona. He demonstrates, in a general way, that religious indifference among the working classes was a major problem for the Spanish Church at the time of Spain's 19th-century industrial revolution. Measures were taken by some of the clergy to try to remedy the situation, but it was not until after the Spanish Civil War (1936-39) that parochial reform programmes were successfully introduced. Callahan also wrote *La Santa y Real Hermandad del Refugio y Piedad de Madrid, 1618-1832* (The Holy and Royal Brotherhood for Sanctuary and Compassion of Madrid, 1618-1832) (Madrid: Consejo Superior de Investigaciones Científicas, Instituto de Estudios Madrileños, 1980. 186p.), a definitive history of the religious fraternity.

153 **The English College at Madrid, 1611-1767.**
Edited by Canon Edwin Henson. London: Catholic Record Society,
1929. 383p. (Publications of the Catholic Record Society, vol. 29).

Edwin Henson was rector of the English College in Valladolid when he compiled this detailed historical and documentary record of the English College of St George at Madrid. The Jesuit College was founded and endowed by an Italian, Caesar Bogacio, although its foundation was strenuously opposed by both Spanish Jesuits and Benedictines. In 1767 the Jesuits were expelled from Spain, and all their property and the property under their care (including the colleges for the education of priests in Madrid, Seville and Valladolid) were taken possession of by Charles III. The documents included in this volume are primarily made up of texts by one of the rectors of St George's, Fray Juan de Cabrera (1658-1730), who provides a summary of its foundation and of its work over subsequent years. The original Spanish texts are followed by corresponding English translations. Also included are account books, miscellaneous documents and letters and several appendices, all of which shed light on the Jesuits and the training of priests in Madrid over a period of 150 years.

154 **Una ciudad ante el hecho religioso: Madrid en la Edad Media.**
(Religion in the city: Madrid in the Middle Ages.)
Angela Muñoz Fernández. PhD thesis, Universidad Complutense,
Madrid, 1993. 1 vol.

There are plans to publish this thesis, as it presents an excellent survey of religiosity in mediaeval Madrid.

**Kinship, marriage, law and leadership in two urban gypsy settlements in Spain.**
*See* item no. 148.

**Iglesias de Madrid.** (Churches of Madrid.)
*See* item no. 292.

**Aproximación a la escultura religiosa contemporánea en Madrid.**
(Introduction to contemporary religious sculpture in Madrid.)
*See* item no. 391.

**From Madrid to purgatory: the art and craft of dying in sixteenth-century Spain.**
*See* item no. 425.

# Society

## Social conditions

155  **The social ecology of Madrid: stratification in comparative perspective.**
Mark Abrahamson, Paul Johnson. *Demography*, vol. 11, no. 3 (Aug. 1974), p. 521-32.
This article examines the characteristics of residential zones in Madrid. At the time it was written the primary difference between zones lay in 'a new bourgeoisie life-style dimension'. Working women were found to be the best indicator of this factor, and fertility and socio-economic status were also identified as interrelated features. Although over twenty years old, the authors' discussions and conclusions are still relevant when considering the historical development of the population and social stratification of Madrid. Maps, tables and references are also included. The original version of this study was published under the same title in the Maxwell Graduate School of Citizenship and Public Affairs Metropolitan Studies Program as Occasional Paper no. 12 (Syracuse, New York: Syracuse University, 1974). Readers may also wish to refer to *Una estrategía de futuro para la sociedad madrileña* (A future strategy for Madrid society) by Jesús Leal Maldonado (Madrid: ProMadrid, 1989. 63p.).

156  **La cohabitación en España: un estudio en Madrid y Barcelona, marzo 1988.** (Cohabitation in Spain: a study in Madrid and Barcelona, March 1988.)
Edited by Ana Alabert.   Madrid: Centro de Investigaciones Sociológicos, 1988. 157p. bibliog. (Estudios y Encuestas; no. 8).
The results of a comparative study of cohabitation trends and figures in Spain's two principal cities are presented in this work.

157 **Mujeres del Madrid barroco: voces testimoniales.** (Women in baroque Madrid: testifying voices.)
Isabel Barbeito Carneiro. Madrid: Dirección General de la Mujer; Horas y Horas, 1992. 223p. bibliog. (Mujeres en Madrid).

This is a fascinating survey of what life was like for women in 17th-century Madrid. Through a series of biographical portraits and personal testimonies, it demonstrates how they were unable to control their own destinies in a male-dominated society. The testimonies themselves make compelling reading, encompassing as they do the accounts of women from different class and social backgrounds. The book presents an excellent, illustrated, social history of the period. The author also wrote a shorter study on women during the same period, entitled *Mujeres del siglo XVII entre Europa y Madrid* (17th-century women in Europe and Madrid) (Madrid: Instituto de Estudios Madrileños, 1990. 25p.). An extensive and scholarly survey of the subject is Pilar Tenorio Gómez's *Realidad social y situación femenina en el Madrid del siglo XVII* (Social reality and the position of women in 17th-century Madrid) (Madrid: Universidad Complutense, 1992. 740p.)

158 **Madrid vivo: estudio sociológico de la ciudad.** (Living Madrid: a sociological study of the city.)
José Manuel Caballero Bonald et al. Madrid: Horizonte, 1964. 120p. bibliog.

Though dated, this still remains an interesting analysis of the population of Madrid. The author also wrote *Festivals and rituals of Spain* (New York: Abrams, 1994. 276p.). For more up-to-date social studies of Madrid, readers could usefully refer to: *Estudio social sobre Madrid* (A social study of Madrid) (Madrid: Servicio de Mutualismo Laboral, 1976. 5 vols.); and *El Madrid tremebundo* (Savage Madrid) by Francisco Hernández Castanedo (Madrid: El Avapiés, 1993. 215p.).

159 **The making of an urban social movement: the citizen movement in Madrid towards the end of the Franquist era.**
Manuel Castells. In: *The city and the grassroots: a cross-cultural theory of urban social movements.* The Author. London: Edward Arnold, 1983, p. 213-88. maps. bibliog.

The social mobilization around urban issues that occurred in the neighbourhoods of most Spanish cities in the 1970s was regarded by most experts as the largest and most significant urban movement in Europe since 1945. In particular, the most important aspect of the Spanish neighbourhood movement was its performance as an agent of social change. Through systematic fieldwork in the late 1960s and 1970s, Castells thoroughly analyses the 'Madrid Citizen Movement' and its role in mobilizing citizens to demand more say in planning policy and building programmes in order to alleviate the urban crisis.

160 **Jóvenes en Comunidad: plan de juventud de la Comunidad de Madrid.** (Young people in the Community: youth plan for the Community of Madrid.)
Comisión Interdepartamental de Juventud.    Madrid: Comunidad Autónoma, 1992. 92p. bibliog.

Containing useful information on the youth of Madrid, this report highlights the various aspects of the Community's youth action plan. Works of related interest are: *La juventud de Madrid* (The youth of Madrid) (Madrid: Ayuntamiento, 1985. 162p. bibliog.); and *La juventud en la Comunidad de Madrid: conocer para actuar* (Young people in the Community of Madrid: understanding for action) (Madrid: Comunidad, Dirección General de la Juventud, 1991. 3 vols. bibliog.).

161 **Mujeres de Madrid.** (Women of Madrid.)
Paloma Fernández Quintanilla.    Madrid: El Avapiés, 1986. 174p. bibliog.

The author has dedicated her professional life to the study of women in Spain generally and in Madrid in particular. This book has become the standard work on the subject and looks at how women have influenced the character of the city. Surveying the last three centuries, she concentrates on providing the reader with an evocative history in an account which does not simply rely on lists of dates and statistical data. She recreates important moments in the history of women in Madrid and links their backgrounds, customs and ideas to the events of the time. Some fascinating black-and-white illustrations are also included. Another general and more wide-ranging study is *La mujer en la Comunidad de Madrid* (Women in the Community of Madrid) (Madrid: Consejería de Presidencia, Dirección General de la Mujer, 1989. 102p.) which also considers women in the workforce and their right to equality of opportunity. This topic is examined in more detail in the *Segundo plan para la igualdad de oportunidades de las mujeres de la Comunidad de Madrid* (Second plan for equal opportunities for women in the Community of Madrid) (Madrid: Dirección General de la Mujer, 1993. 23p.) which contains the objectives and action proposed to improve the situation of women during the period 1993-95.

162 **Sólo se vive una vez: esplendor y ruina de la movida madrileña.**
(You only live once: the rise and fall of the Madrid movement.)
José Luis Gallero.    Madrid: Ediciones Ardora, 1991. 416p. bibliog.

After Franco's death in 1975, Madrid's inhabitants awoke from imposed hibernation and set about making up for lost time by demonstrating their love of life and living. A cultural renaissance took place, and during the 1980s the city witnessed an explosion of art, counter-culture, nightlife and creativity. Certain characters are often associated with this *movida*, including the film director, Pedro Almodóvar, and Madrid's much-loved Socialist mayor, Enrique Tierno Galván. Gallero's fascinating and entertaining book concentrates on the liberalism and creativity that were synonymous with the movement, but also chronicles its decline towards the end of the decade.

163 **Madrid adolescents express an interest in gender roles and work possibilities.**
Judith L. Gibbons, Rachel Bradford, Deborah A. Stiles. *Journal of Early Adolescence*, vol. 9, nos. 1-2 (May 1989), p. 125-41.
This fascinating study details the results of a survey of over 300 Madrid adolescents, in which they were asked to rate ten qualities of the ideal man or woman. Their responses not only reflected young Spaniards' concerns, including an interest in gender roles and a commitment to work, but also demonstrated responses related to Madrid. A number of illustrations, graphs and statistical tables accompany the text.

164 **Madrid bajo el punto de vista médico-social.** (Madrid from a medico-social point of view.)
Philip M. Hauser. Madrid: Editora Nacional, 1979. 1 vol.
Originally published in 1902 (Madrid: Suc. de Rivadeneyra. 2 vols.), this work remains a standard source of information relating to the social condition of the city at the turn of the century.

165 **Estudio de la diferenciación residencial en la ciudad de Madrid.**
(A study of the residential differences in the city of Madrid.)
Beatriz Cristina Jiménez Blasco. Madrid: Universidad Complutense, 1988. 691p. bibliog.
This massive work is the result of extensive research and represents a comprehensive survey of social and housing factors in Madrid. The author also wrote: *Almagro, estudio geográfico de un barrio de Madrid* (Almagro, a geographical survey of a district of Madrid) (Madrid: Universidad Complutense, 1981. 178p.); and *Análisis geográfico y representación del mosaico social de Madrid* (A geographical analysis and representation of the social fabric of Madrid) (Madrid: Instituto Geográfico Nacional, 1987. 229p.).

166 **Spain's Institute for Women.**
Anny Brooksbank Jones. *European Journal of Women's Studies*, vol. 2, no. 2 (May 1995), p. 261-69. bibliog.
Created in 1988, this Madrid-based government organization is a branch of the Ministry of Social Affairs, and coordinates and promotes the activities of its various member bodies, including the Dirección General de la Mujer de la Comunidad de Madrid (State Office for Women in the Community of Madrid), which publishes numerous books on women in the city. The Institute's aim is to promote equality between the sexes as well as the greater involvement of Spanish women in social, economic, political and cultural life. This article briefly assesses the strengths and weaknesses of this sometimes controversial force in Spanish women's issues.

167 **The labor force participation and fertility of Spanish women, Madrid, 1980.**
Teresa Ann Keenan. PhD thesis, Cornell University, New York, 1993. 197p. bibliog.
This thesis examines the balance between the competing demands of work and family life for women in Madrid. Keenan investigates the nature of the relationship between work and fertility through her sample of 1,584 married women in the city during 1980.

168   **Boys, girls and the discourse of identity: growing up in Madrid.**
Virginia Maquieira, translated by D. E. Hanson.   In: *Teenage
*lifestyles and criminality in Spain, France and Holland.*   Virginia
Maquieira, Jean Charles Lagrée.   Florence, Italy: European University
Institute, 1987, p. 1-14. (EUI Working Paper; no. 87/299).

This paper refines and elaborates the results of an investigation carried out by a
research team, between 1981 and 1983, into the urban youth of Madrid. It generally
addresses the question of changes in values and morality and the reasons behind these
changes. In particular, the author shows how young people of Madrid see themselves
on the one hand as 'bearers . . . of attitudes and styles which are different from those
of the adult world; but, on the other, they believe that this will be a short-lived
identity, a passing phase'.

169   **La masonería en Madrid.** (Freemasonry in Madrid.)
F. Márquez et al.   Madrid: El Avapiés, 1987. 238p. bibliog.

Pioneering and comprehensive, this illustrated survey has become a standard history
of the freemason movement in Madrid. After an introduction which includes an
analysis of freemasonry and its place in Spanish history, the author considers its
ideology, finance, members and role in the city's society. Much of the book's contents
are based upon (and offer a critique of) documents held by several freemason lodges
in Madrid. Consideration is also given to the influence of the masons on social,
political, cultural and religious matters from the end of the 19th century up until the
early years of the 20th.

170   **Madrid 1931: mujeres entre la permanencia y el cambio.** (Madrid
1931: women amidst tradition and change.)
María Gloria Núñez Pérez.   Madrid: Dirección General de la Mujer,
1993. 199p. bibliog. (Mujeres en Madrid).

What did the coming of the Second Republic in 1931 mean to the women of Madrid?
This excellent analysis considers what the repercussions were for women in politics,
work and society generally. Other works in the same series (all published in Madrid
by the same publisher) include: *Las madrileñas del mil seiscientos: imagen y realidad*
(The women of Madrid in the 1600s: image and reality) by Pilar Tenorio Gómez
(1993); *Hispanoamericanas en Madrid (1800-1936)* (Latin American women in
Madrid, 1800-1936) by Juana Martínez Gómez and Almudena Mejías Alonso (1994);
*Acciones e intenciones de mujeres en la vida religiosa de los siglos XV y XVI* (The
actions and intentions of women in religious life in the 15th and 16th centuries) by
Angela Muñoz Fernández (1995); *Mujer y sociedad en el siglo XVII a través de los
avisos de Barrionuevo* (Woman and society in the 17th century through the
admonishments of Barrionuevo) by Pilar Ríos Izquierdo (1994); and *Carmen de
Burgos 'Colombine'* by Paloma Castañeda (1994), the story of the first female war
correspondent in Spain (1867-1932), nicknamed Colombine, who published over 150
literary texts.

171   **Citizen action and participation in Madrid.**
Janice E. Perlman.   *Planning and Administration*, vol. 8, no. 2
(autumn 1981), p. 77-97.

This interesting article looks at the role of citizen participation and action in public
decision-making and service provision in Madrid. The author notes how effective the
neighbourhood associations are and how, at the time of writing, urban planning was
'neighbourhood-oriented, citizen-based and openly participatory'. Her study provides
a detailed analysis of the PAI – Programa de Acciones Inmediatas (Programme for
Immediate Action) – a participatory planning process for the entire Madrid metropolitan area. Three case studies follow, focusing on three distinct areas of the city, and
the article is completed with conclusions and references.

**The vulgar sort: common people in 'siglo de oro' Madrid.**
*See* item no. 102.

**Tradition and change in the Madrid bourgeoisie, 1900-1914.**
*See* item no. 108.

**La sociedad madrileña durante la Restauración 1876-1931.** (Madrid society
during the Restoration 1876-1931.)
*See* item no. 109.

**Gentlemen, bourgeois, and revolutionaries: Madrid and the formation of
the Spanish bourgeoisie, 1750-1850.**
*See* item no. 112.

**Madrid en la sociedad del siglo XIX.** (Madrid in 19th-century society.)
*See* item no. 120.

**Economic crisis, social conflict and the Popular Front: Madrid 1931-6.**
*See* item no. 130.

**Demografía y sociedad en el Madrid decimonómico (1787-1857).** (Population and society in 19th-century Madrid, 1787-1857.)
*See* item no. 141.

**Response to urbanization: Madrid and Barcelona, 1850-1930.**
*See* item no. 152.

**Local economic policies and social citizenship in Spanish cities.**
*See* item no. 211.

**Ciudad, democracia y socialismo: la experiencia de las asociaciones de
vecinos en Madrid.** (City, democracy and socialism: the experience of the
residents' associations in Madrid.)
*See* item no. 242.

**Trabajo y participación económica: la actividad de las mujeres madri-
leñas.** (Work and economic participation: the occupations of Madrid's
women.)
*See* item no. 244.

**Foreign women in domestic service in Spain.**
*See* item no. 246.

**Labour market and gender in the Autonomous Community of Madrid.**
*See* item no. 247.

**Information for equality: the Documentation Center of the Women's Institute in Madrid.**
*See* item no. 452.

# Social problems

172 **Mujer y delincuencia en la Comunidad de Madrid.** (Women and criminality in the Community of Madrid.)
Andrés Canteras Murillo.   Madrid: Consejería de Presidencia, Dirección General de la Mujer, 1992. 141p. bibliog.

In an attempt to outline a theory on female criminality, this study analyses the results of a survey and the statistical sources of the Ministries of Justice and the Interior. The nature of the delinquent woman and the incidence and evolution of criminal behaviour are all covered in this valuable sociological work.

173 **La prostitución femenina en Madrid.** (Female prostitution in Madrid.)
Amparo Comas.   Madrid: Consejería de la Presidencia, Dirección General de la Mujer, 1991. 108p. bibliog.

Based upon a survey of prostitutes in the city-centre area of Madrid (undertaken between 1984 and 1990), this interesting report highlights the women's personal histories, their place in social networks and their ambitions. *Caídas, miserables, degeneradas: estudio sobre la prostitución en el siglo XIX* (Fallen women, wretches, degenerates: a study of 19th-century prostitution) by Aurora Rivière Gómez (Madrid: Dirección General de la Mujer, 1994. 214p. bibliog.) presents a detailed survey of prostitution in 19th-century Madrid, looking at its political control and social marginalization, and at the social status and life of the city's prostitutes. Various appendices include personal histories and other helpful documentation.

174 **Consumo de drogas en el municipio de Madrid.** (Drug-taking in Madrid.)
Madrid: Ayuntamiento, Area de Servicios Sociales, 1989. 334p. bibliog.

This report, published by Madrid's Social Services Department, paints a detailed and worrying picture of drug abuse in the city. To combat the problem, several plans have been developed by Social Services, including the *Plan municipal contra las drogas* (Municipal plan against drugs) (Madrid: Ayuntamiento, Area de Servicios Sociales, 1991).

175 **Pobreza y desigualdad en la Comunidad de Madrid: necesidades, recursos y balance social.** (Poverty and inequality in the Community of Madrid: needs, resources and social evaluation.)
Equipo de Investigación Sociológica, Cáritas. Madrid: Editorial Popular, 1989. 381p. maps. (Trabajo Social, Política Social; no. 3).

Prepared by a team of professional researchers and a respected charity association in Madrid, this report provides a full and detailed survey of the social situation in the Autonomous Community of Madrid. All aspects of social deprivation and inequality are examined and analysed, linked to specific areas of population. The first part of the work considers the social problems including poverty, illiteracy, work and unemployment, health, alcoholism, drug addiction, child abuse and battered women. Part two looks at the resources available to deal with these problems, including social services and charitable organizations in Madrid, and concludes that these are inadequate and often poorly placed to have any real impact. The majority of the text deals specifically with the different districts of the city, and numerous maps and statistical tables are also included. Readers might also usefully refer to the following: *La mendicidad infantil: menores en situación de marginación* (Child beggars: the young outcasts) (Madrid: Concejalía de Servicios Sociales, 1986. 90p.) by Alvaro Rodríguez Díaz; and *La mendicidad en Madrid: sus causas y sus remedios* (Begging in Madrid: its causes and remedies) (Madrid: R. Velasco, 1916. 40p.) by Francisco García Molinas, which provides an interesting study of the problem at the beginning of the century.

176 **The impact of drug-related deaths on mortality among young adults in Madrid.**
Luis de la Fuente et al. *American Journal of Public Health*, vol. 85, no. 1 (Jan. 1995), p. 102-05.

The authors studied the trend of drug-related deaths (defined as the sum of deaths from acute drug reactions and AIDS in drug-users) among the population of fifteen- to thirty-nine-year-olds in Madrid, and compared these figures with mortality rates from all causes during the period 1983-90. Through detailed analysis and statistical comparisons, the authors demonstrate that drug-related deaths represented 60 per cent of the increase in the rate in males, and 170 per cent of the increase in females. Their worrying, although understated, conclusion was that 'increases in drug-related mortality are likely to continue in the future'. The authors are all members of the government's delegation for the *Plan nacional sobre drogas* (National plan on drugs) based in the Ministry of Health and Consumer Affairs in Madrid.

177 **Tobacco smoking, alcohol consumption, and laryngeal cancer in Madrid.**
Gonzalo López-Abente et al. *Cancer Detection and Prevention*, vol. 16, nos. 5-6 (1992), p. 265-72.

This short, scholarly article examines the associations between cigarette smoking, alcohol consumption and laryngeal cancer in a case-control study carried out between 1982 and 1985 in Madrid. Statistical tables and references are included.

178 **Embarazo, aborto y maternidad entre las adolescentes de la Comunidad de Madrid.** (Pregnancy, abortion and motherhood amongst adolescent girls in the Community of Madrid.)
Clemente Martín Barroso.   Madrid: Dirección General de la Mujer, 1992. 103p. bibliog.
Focusing on the views and feelings of both family-planning practitioners and the young girls themselves, this qualitative survey analyses the incidences and repercussions of youth pregnancy, abortion and motherhood. Needless to say, the views of both parties conflict in many areas, although there is some common ground.

179 **A cross-cultural comparison of social reform: the growing pains of the battered women's movements in Washington, D.C., and Madrid, Spain.**
Susan L. Miller, Rosemary Barberet.   *Law and Social Enquiry*, vol. 19, no. 4 (1994), p. 923-66.
In this detailed study the authors compare responses to domestic violence in the two designated cities, using a range of interview data provided by representatives of social services, criminal justice and policy-making agencies in both capitals. The article clearly demonstrates the various differences that exist in the history, funding, development and participants of the battered women's movements. In Madrid, for example, the government determined the appropriate response to domestic violence from the outset, whereas in Washington the power to respond to the issue related to a large extent to the more insidious process of state co-optation. The authors conclude that the battered women's movements, in both Spain and the United States, have gained legitimacy in terms of official acknowledgement and enforcement of some policy changes. However, they qualify their positive comments with the view that until women's subordination in the family and elsewhere is recognized as political, the criminalizing of battering women 'will not significantly alter unequal gender relations or create lasting changes in society'. A large number of references are also included in this interesting study.

180 **Paro y empleo juvenil en la periferia urbana madrileña.** (Youth unemployment and work in Madrid's urban outskirts.)
Madrid: Consorcio Rector del Plan de Prevención de la Delincuencia y la Marginación Social, 1988. 231p. bibliog.
This volume presents a thorough and detailed analysis of the problem of youth unemployment in Madrid and the various types of work undertaken by the city's young people.

181 **La cultura del alcohol entre los jóvenes de la Comunidad de Madrid.** (The alcohol culture amongst the young people of the Community of Madrid.)
Anselmo Peinado, Francisco Pereña, Paloma Portero.   Madrid: Consejería de la Salud, 1993. 55p. bibliog.
Despite its size, this work offers a thorough and detailed analysis of the place of alcohol in youth society and the problems that arise when it is misused. Another useful report on the subject is *Estudio sobre conocimiento y actitud hacia el*

*alcoholismo en la juventud de la Comunidad Autónoma de Madrid* (A study of understanding and attitudes towards alcoholism amongst the youth of the Autonomous Community of Madrid) (Madrid: Consejería de Integración Social, 1989. 81p.).

182 **Problemática de la drogodependencia en Madrid.** (The problem of drug addiction in Madrid.)
Madrid: Consejería de Salud, Secretaría General Técnica, 1988. 224p. bibliog.

The report contains the views of lawyers, health workers and psychiatrists which were expressed at a round-table meeting in Madrid in 1987. All the medical and legal aspects of drug addiction in the capital were discussed and possible solutions put forward in the hope of alleviating the problem.

183 **Adolescent drug use in Madrid and in the United States of America.**
Juan-Luis Recio Adrados, Lana Harrison. *Contemporary Drug Problems,* vol. 20, no. 1 (spring 1993), p. 93-131.

This article focuses on the comparison of adolescent drug use patterns in Madrid and the United States which emerged from surveys undertaken amongst youths in high school and the general population between 1988 and 1989. The authors explain their methodology and look at the use of the whole range of drugs from alcohol and tobacco to 'hard' drugs. The differences and similarities in the patterns of use are illustrated with data from the surveys which demonstrate how more Madrid youths used cannabis, analgesics, tranquillizers and sedatives, and regularly used tobacco and alcohol, while more American youths used the 'harder' drugs. Attitudes towards the use of drugs, age and drug availability are also considered. Recio Adrados has subsequently published an article which considers the socializing impact of the family amongst Madrid's youth. 'The influence of family, school and peers on adolescent drug misuse' (*International Journal of the Addictions*, vol. 30, no. 11 [1995], p. 1,407-23) presents a scholarly report based on an analysis of drug abuse amongst the school population of the city.

184 **Delincuencia y seguridad en el Madrid de Carlos II.** (Criminality and security in Charles II's Madrid.)
Rosa Isabel Sánchez Gómez. Madrid: Ministerio del Interior, Secretaría General Técnica, 1994. 273p. bibliog.

Madrid declined dramatically under Charles II (1665-1700), the last of the Spanish Habsburg monarchs. His ill-health, coupled with the effect of wars, social decay and population decline, meant that the economy and administration of the country suffered. Subsequently, crime increased and the severe fall in Madrid's population (from around 170,000 in 1665 to 100,000 in 1700) was inextricably linked to widespread poverty and disillusion. This interesting study considers the legal and social factors involved in criminal behaviour and personal safety in Madrid during this period.

185   **La segregación social en Madrid.** (Social segregation in Madrid.)
Madrid: Ayuntamiento, 1990. 160p. bibliog.

Produced by the city council, this report looks at the various issues surrounding the
subject of social segregation in Madrid, including housing, begging and unemployment. Other studies of related interest are: *Segregación social en Madrid* by Miguel
Roiz (Madrid: Castellote, 1973. 131p.); and *Estudio sobre la problemática social y
humana de Madrid* (An investigation of social and human problems in Madrid) by
Carmen Sánchez Moro (Madrid: Cáritas Diocesana, 1980. 283p.).

186   **Poverty in eighteenth-century Spain: the women and children of
the Inclusa.**
Joan Sherwood.   Toronto: University of Toronto Press, 1988. 239p.
bibliog.

The foundling hospital of the Inclusa of Madrid during the 18th century forms the
focus of this thorough study of poverty in Spain. A detailed analysis is made of the
unbroken records of the hospital from its founding in 1572 to the present day. The
lives and deaths of the poor were meticulously documented and these records shed a
great deal of light on the experiences of both women and children in Madrid at this
time. Part one of the book discusses the institution itself, while part two covers the
wet-nurses and part three deals with the children of the Inclusa. A large number of
statistical tables and figures are included. Another useful general study of Madrid
during the 18th century is *Conflicto y reforma en el Madrid del siglo XVIII* (Conflict
and reform in 18th-century Madrid) by Carmen de la Guardia (Madrid: Caja de
Madrid, 1993. 291p.) which considers the social and political problems of the period.

**La Farola.** (Street Light.)
*See* item no. 506.

# Health and welfare

187   **Los hospitales de Madrid de ayer y de hoy.** (The hospitals of Madrid
of today and yesteryear.)
José Alvarez Sierra.   Madrid: Ayuntamiento, 1952. 202p. bibliog.

There are very few studies of Madrid's hospitals and this has become the standard
history of the subject. Alvarez Sierra also wrote *Historia de la medicina madrileña* (A
history of medicine in Madrid) (Madrid: Editorial Universitaria Europea, 1968.
181p.). Another relevant and more up-to-date work is Domingo Melón Ovalle's
*Sistema hospitalario: situación y función de la organización sanitaria de la
Comunidad Autónoma de Madrid* (The hospital system: the position and operation of
health organization in the Autonomous Community of Madrid) (Madrid: Universidad
Complutense, 1990. 301p.).

188 **Corporate charity in Spain: the Hermandad del Refugio of Madrid 1618-1814.**
William J. Callahan. *Histoire Sociale – Social History*, vol. 9, no. 17 (1976), p. 159-86.

In 17th- and 18th-century Spain the presence of mendicants, vagabonds and the idle poor in virtually every city and town presented a major problem for government authorities. After 1750 the Spanish crown attempted to develop a system of poor-relief designed to limit the distribution of alms to the deserving poor and to impose severe restrictions upon beggars, with the establishment of institutions of confinement. Nevertheless, during the 17th century a number of charitable organizations emerged which were prepared to fight poverty and aid the needy. Callahan's interesting article focuses on the work of the most important charitable corporation of Madrid, the 'Santa y Real Hermandad del Refugio y Piedad' (Holy and Royal Brotherhood for Sanctuary and Compassion), which assisted nearly a million persons between 1618 (when it was founded) and 1800. By 1630 membership of this body 'had become a social necessity for the capital's nobility'. All aspects of the Brotherhood's organization and operation are examined, together with the question of how effective it was in the relief of Madrid's poor. Eventually (over several decades in the early 19th century) the traditional charitable orders declined as a result of liberal legislation, taxation and forced loans. Callahan concludes that the lack of a traditional structure of assistance to respond to the needs of the poor contributed to the social and political unrest which characterized Spanish political history between 1808 and 1873. Unfortunately, contemporary Madrid (particularly in the centre) still has a large number of homeless people begging on its streets.

189 **Historia del cuerpo de bomberos de la Comunidad de Madrid.** (A history of the Community of Madrid's fire brigade.)
José Luis Calle García et al. Madrid: Comunidad, Dirección General de Protección Ciudadana, 1991. 149p. bibliog.

Emphasizing the importance of Madrid's fire brigade, this comprehensive history includes an analysis of the brigade's fire prevention and development programmes, as well as a survey of its human and technical resources. Those interested in the early history of Madrid's firefighters should refer to Antonio Mendoza de Lozoya's *Proyecto de organización de una compañía de bomberos, al socorro de incendios de Madrid* (Plan for the organization of a company of firemen to combat Madrid's fires) (Madrid: Imp. Tomás Núñez, 1863. 16p.), an old but fascinating pamphlet which describes the embryonic stages of Madrid's fire service.

190 **Policía municipal de Madrid: siete siglos de historia, 1202-1987.**
(Madrid's local police force: seven centuries of history, 1202-1987.)
Joaquín Carrascosa. Madrid: Ayuntamiento, Area de Seguridad, Circulación y Transportes, 1987. 160p. bibliog.

Nowadays, like many other European countries, Spain has several police forces – local, national and civil guard. The present work provides a wide-ranging historical survey of Madrid's municipal police force. Other works of related interest include: *Policía de barrio* (District police forces) by Francisco J. Lobo García et al. (Madrid: Federación Española de Municipios y Provincias, 1987. 75p.); and *Los policías locales: su imagen en la Comunidad de Madrid* (Local police forces: their image in the Community of Madrid) (Madrid: Comunidad, Servicio de Documentación y

Publicaciones, 1991. 233p.). For a general English-language examination of Spain's police forces readers should refer to 'The police system in Spain' by Iain R. Macdonald in *Police and public order in Europe*, edited by John Roach and Jürgen Thomaneck (London: Croom Helm, 1985, p. 215-54. bibliog.). As a matter of interest, Carrascosa also wrote *Historia de los escudos de la villa de Madrid* (A history of the coats of arms of Madrid) (Madrid: Giner Méndez, 1981. 29p.).

191  **La Cruz Roja en España: fundación en Madrid de la primera junta de la Cruz Roja en España.** (The Red Cross in Spain: the foundation in Madrid of the first Red Cross committee in Spain.)
Josep Carles Clemente.  Madrid: Cruz Roja, 1989. 166p. bibliog.
Founded as an international relief agency by the Geneva Convention in 1864, the Red Cross has had a long and worthy history in Spain. Clemente's book considers the setting up of the first Spanish Red Cross committee in Madrid and the development of the agency in the country as a whole.

192  **Changing mental health services in Madrid: international issues.**
David A. Dowell, José María Poveda de Augustín, Alan Lowenthal.
*Hospital and Community Psychiatry*, vol. 38, no. 1 (Jan. 1987), p. 68-72.
This short, but detailed, article focuses on the shift away from institutional and custodial care in Spain's mental health services towards community-based services. The authors show how, in Madrid, mental health service priorities include preventing psychiatric hospitalization, developing a range of residential facilities, reducing the population of chronic patients in hospitals and improving the quality of hospital care. At the time of writing, a network of twenty health promotion centres was being developed to serve new patients, whilst long-stay hospital patients who could be discharged were being transferred to the care of social services. Nevertheless, the authors emphasize that the most difficult aspect of change is in dealing with the problems encountered while actually implementing system reforms.

193  **Identifying management training needs for social service workers in Madrid, Spain.**
John P. Flynn, Ana A. Díaz.  *International Social Work*, vol. 31 (April 1988), p. 145-56.
Presents a report on a project which assessed the training needs of social service workers in Madrid, in the areas of policy, planning and administration. The project developed a training plan in twelve key areas: this was based on survey respondents' replies to questionnaires and their ratings for over a hundred tasks involved in their jobs related to frequency of performance and perceived importance. Interesting as it is, readers should note that the article is specifically written for trainers and professional social workers.

194  **Madrid, ciudad saludable.** (Madrid, healthy city.)
Ricardo Iglesias García.  Madrid: Ayuntamiento, Area de Sanidad y Consumo, 1991. 95p. bibliog.
This short study details all the factors that make Madrid a healthy city in which to live, including its good social health and welfare services. Other useful works on the

city's health and welfare system include: *Estudios de calidad de servicios sanitarios públicos en Madrid* (A survey of the quality of public health services in Madrid) by María Luisa Nadal Ortega et al. (Madrid: Comunidad Autónoma, Servicio de Documentación y Publicaciones, 1994. 268p.); *Servicios sociales municipales* (Local social services) (Madrid: Ayuntamiento de Madrid, Area de Servicios Sociales y Comunitarios, 1993); *Aproximación a los servicios sociales* (An introduction to the social services) by Patricia Restrepo Ramírez (Madrid: Consejería de Integración Social, 1990. 140p.); and *Equipamiento de servicios sociales en el municipio de Madrid* (The resourcing of social services in Madrid) (Madrid: Ayuntamiento, 1980. 213p.).

195 **Normas para el abastecimiento de agua.** (Water-supply standards.)
Madrid: Canal de Isabel II, 1991. 163p.

In 1858 the *Canal de Isabel II* (Canal of Isabella II), bringing water from the Guadarrama mountains, was completed. For years Madrid's water supply had been poor and wholly inadequate to the needs of the population. The canal removed one of the major obstacles to the city's growth, and this study details the standards set for its construction and the actual supply of water. Works of related interest are: *El abastecimiento de aguas a Madrid* (The supply of water to Madrid) by Jesús Muñoz Muñoz (Madrid: Universidad Complutense, 1983. 2 vols.); and *El agua en la higiene del Madrid de los Austrias* (Water in the hygiene of Habsburg Madrid) by Jacinta Landa Goñi (Madrid: Canal de Isabel II, 1986. 258p.), a historical analysis of the health factors involved in the use of water in 16th-century Madrid.

196 **Feeding practices and growth of children under 20 months of age in Madrid.**
Suzanna A. M. van den Boom. PhD thesis, University of Surrey, England, 1994. 163p. bibliog.

This study analyses the feeding habits of 344 children under twenty months of age. The data were obtained from mothers using the dietary history method, together with responses to questions on milk-feeding and weaning. Meal contents and patterns were evaluated and the children weighed and measured to establish energy and nutrient intake and growth rates. Several appendices are included.

197 **Las cárceles de Madrid en el siglo XVII.** (The prisons of Madrid in the 17th century.)
María Dolores Vázquez González. Madrid: Universidad Complutense, 1992. 694p. bibliog.

This illustrated history of Madrid's prisons is thorough and fascinating. Ironically, one of the prisons described – *Cárcel de Corte* (Court Prison) – which was built between 1629 and 1643, is now home of the Ministry for Foreign Affairs. Other books of related interest include *Las viejas cárceles madrileñas: (siglos XV al XIX)* (Madrid's old prisons: 15th-19th centuries) by Julio de Ramón Laca (Madrid: Ayuntamiento, Instituto de Estudios Madrileños, 1973. 59p.); and *Las cárceles de la villa* (The prisons of Madrid) by Pablo de Fuenmayor Gordón (Madrid: Ayuntamiento, Instituto de Estudios Madrileños, 1958. 34p.).

# Politics, Local Government and Administration

198 **El ayuntamiento de Madrid y su organización.** (Madrid's city council and its organization.)
Madrid: Alcaldía, 1989. 32p.

Produced by local government officers, this short guide introduces the responsibilities and workings of Madrid's local administration. Readers may also be interested in *Historia del ayuntamiento de Madrid* (A history of Madrid's city council) by Carlos Bonet y Galea (Madrid: Ayuntamiento, 1936. 244p.), which provides a reliable history of the evolution of Madrid's town hall and local government. The *Guía del ayuntamiento de Madrid* (Guide to Madrid's city council) (Madrid: Ayuntamiento, Dirección de Servicios de Organización e Informática, 1992. 632p.) is an internal directory of addresses and telephone numbers, covering local government offices, officers and areas of service, and includes a comprehensive index.

199 **Madrid and the ethnic homelands: is consociational democracy possible in post-Franco Spain.**
Robert P. Clark. In: *Politics and change in Spain.* Edited by Thomas D. Lancaster, Gary Prevost. New York: Praeger, 1985, p. 64-93. map. bibliog.

Now primarily of interest from a historical viewpoint, this chapter nevertheless provides an important consideration of the crucial question of regional policy in Spain, whilst viewing the participants in a coalition process (central, regional and local government), from a territorial and ethnic perspective. Surveying the regional divisions and autonomous communities like Madrid, Clark relates them to the terms 'regionalism' and 'nationalism' in the context of Spanish political culture. He also discusses the importance of the 1978 Constitution with regard to Madrid and the other sixteen autonomous communities, and in particular those articles of the Constitution which have a direct bearing on the mechanics of autonomy.

200 **Aproximación a las instituciones de la Comunidad de Madrid.** (An introduction to the institutions of the Community of Madrid.)
Blanca Esther Fernández Nieto, Antonio García Sanjuán. Madrid: Comunidad de Madrid, Consejería de Educación y Cultura, 1995. 137p. maps. bibliog.

Without claiming to be an exhaustive study, this book offers a panoramic view of local administration in the Autonomous Community of Madrid, and also contains useful information relating to the city of Madrid. Five principal sections describe: the Spanish State and the Autonomous Communities; the Community of Madrid; its institutions (including the Asamblea de Madrid [Madrid Assembly], the Consejo de Gobierno [Council of Government] and the Tribunal Superior de Justicia de Madrid [Upper/Higher Court of Justice of Madrid]); the relationship between regional government and the city council of Madrid (Ayuntamiento); and the Autonomous Community in relation to other institutional bodies. This clearly written study also includes numerous illustrations, diagrams and extracts from the *Estatuto de Autonomía de la Comunidad de Madrid* (Statute of Autonomy of the Community of Madrid) (Madrid: Ministerio de la Presidencia, 1994).

201 **El Fuero de Madrid.** (The municipal charter of Madrid.)
Translated and introduced by Agustín Gómez Iglesias. Madrid: Ayuntamiento, 1994. 154p.

Madrid's *Fuero* represents the city's mediaeval law code and charter. Written in 1202, the original text was a mixture of Latin and Romance language. Originally published by Madrid's city council (Ayuntamiento) in 1932, it has subsequently appeared in several editions. The current edition contains a preliminary discussion of the *Fuero* and the *derechos locales castellanos* (local Castilian laws), a transcript of the *Fuero* (with Spanish translation), a glossary and the full, beautifully illustrated, original manuscript.

202 **Alcaldes de Madrid.** (Mayors of Madrid.)
Germán Lopezarias. Madrid: El Avapiés, 1994. 210p. bibliog. (El Oso y El Madroño).

The most important mayors of Madrid, including Enrique Tierno Galván (1979-86), are covered in this interesting, illustrated biographical survey. It contains biographies for mayors from the 15th century to the present, and also provides a full chronology of mayors by century. Readers may also be interested in a much shorter, selective survey of the same title by Juan A. Marreno and Santiago Ferrer (Madrid: Cronos, 1979. 20p.).

203 **Madrid: legislación de las Comunidades Autónomas, 1994.**
(Madrid: legislation of the Autonomous Communities.)
Madrid: Editorial Aranzadi, 1995. 784p.

This annual publication (first published in 1983) details the current legislation of the Autonomous Community of Madrid, much of which directly affects the city. Similarly, *Repertorio de legislación de la Comunidad* (Catalogue of legislation for the Community of Madrid) (Madrid: Civitas; Comunidad de Madrid, 1995. 1,903p.) is a massive compendium of laws, decrees and orders which have come into force from the inauguration of the Community (1983) up to 1995.

204 **Regionalismo: Madrid, capital y región.** (Regionalism: Madrid, capital and region.)
Nicolás Piñeiro. Madrid: The Author, 1991. 260p. bibliog.

This is an interesting study of the various tiers of authority and government that exist in Madrid. Not only is the city the capital of Spain and home of the national government, but it also houses the offices of the Autonomous Community of Madrid and has its own city council and provincial (regional) government. Other works of related interest include: *Madrid, fronteras y territorio* (Madrid, frontiers and territory) by Antonio García Martín, Carmen Gavira and Jorge Ruiz Varela (Madrid: Ayuntamiento, 1992. 215p.); and *Funcionamiento administrativo de la ciudad* (The administrative workings of the city) by Fidel Revilla González (Madrid: Ayuntamiento, Servicio de Educación, 1990. 14p.).

205 **Las elecciones municipales de 1931 en Madrid.** (The municipal elections of 1931 in Madrid.)
Pablo Villalaín. Madrid: El Avapiés, 1987. 152p. bibliog.

Madrid's election history is a varied and interesting topic, and one which sheds a great deal of light on its society generally. In this detailed study different chapters analyse distinct aspects of the local elections (held during the year in which the Second Republic was proclaimed) including: the social structure of Madrid; the crisis of the monarchy; electoral legislation; the political parties and candidates; election campaigns; and the results. Several appendices complete the work. Two other relevant volumes that examine Madrid's political and electoral history and which were both written by one of Spain's most prominent political historians, Javier Tusell Gómez, are: *Sociología electoral de Madrid 1903-1931* (Electoral sociology of Madrid 1903-31) (Madrid: Cuadernos para el Diálogo, 1969. 219p.); and *La Segunda República en Madrid: elecciones y partidos políticos* (The Second Republic in Madrid: elections and political parties) (Madrid: Tecnos, 1970. 220p.).

**Madrid: audiencia, provincia, intendencia, vicaría, partido y villa.** (Madrid: court, province, government, vicariate, district and town.)
*See* item no. 117.

**Citizen action and participation in Madrid.**
*See* item no. 171.

**Local economic policies and social citizenship in Spanish cities.**
*See* item no. 211.

**Tribuna.** (Tribune.)
*See* item no. 493.

**Boletín Oficial del Estado.** (Official Gazette.)
*See* item no. 504.

# Economy

206 **Impacto del mercado interior europeo sobre la economía de Madrid.** (Impact of the Single Market on the economy of Madrid.)
M. Ahijado et al. Madrid: Comunidad, Dirección General de Cooperación con el Estado y Asuntos Europeos; Instituto Madrileño de Desarrollo, 1991. 5 vols. bibliog.

This extensive survey of the effect of the Single Market on Madrid's economy covers the whole of the Autonomous Community of Madrid. However, it concentrates on the city itself in the three volumes which examine effects upon industry, financial services and foreign investment. The other two volumes provide a theoretical framework for evaluation and a synthesis of views on the overall effect.

207 **La reestructuración de la economía madrileña.** (The restructuring of Madrid's economy.)
José María Alvarez Perla. Madrid: Ayuntamiento, 1989. 106p.

This useful study of Madrid looks at various aspects of the economic and industrial structure of the city. A similar historical work covering the wider region of Madrid is *La economía madrileña en sus sectores* (Madrid's economy by sector) (Madrid: Comunidad, Dirección General de Economía y Planificación, 1988. 130p.).

208 **Anuario Económico y Financiero.** (Economic and Financial Yearbook.)
Madrid: Ayuntamiento, 1985- . annual.

Each annual volume contains around 250 pages and examines all the principal areas of the city's economy and financial structure.

209 **La Cámara de Comercio e Industria de Madrid, 1887-1987.**
(The Madrid Chamber of Commerce and Industry, 1887-1987.)
Angel Bahamonde Magro, Jesús A. Martínez Martín, Fernando del
Rey Reguillo. Madrid: CCIM, 1988. 391p. bibliog.

Published to celebrate the centenary of the Madrid Chamber of Commerce and
Industry, this historical survey also represents an excellent economic and social
history of the city. The Chamber of Commerce, although oriented towards local
business, also provides a wide range of information and legal services for foreign
investors, particularly if they are exporting from Spain. The book includes a wealth of
economic and business detail as well as statistical data.

210 **Madrid, presente y futuro.** (Madrid, present and future.)
Edited by José Estébanez Alvarez. Madrid: Akal, 1990. 264p.
bibliog. (Akal Geografía).

Provides an excellent summary of the economic development of Madrid, and the city
and region's potential for industrial and economic growth in the future. The book
contains a wealth of statistical data. Three other works of related interest are:
*Situación Económica y Social de la Comunidad de Madrid* (The Economic and Social
Position of the Community of Madrid) (Madrid: Consejo Económico y Social, 1985- .
annual) which analyses population structure, income and expenditure, social services,
the economy, labour, industry and unemployment; *Madrid futuro: plan estratégico de
Madrid* (Future Madrid: strategic plan for Madrid), produced by the Ayuntamiento
(Madrid: ProMadrid, 1993. 167p. bibliog.) which again looks at the economic and
social aspects of Madrid's development as expounded in the council's strategic plan for
the city; and *Plan estratégico: IMADE, 1992-1995* (Strategic plan: IMADE, 1992-95)
(Madrid: IMADE, 1992. 112p.), produced by the Instituto Madrileño de Desarrollo
(Madrid Development Institute), which contains the text of the Institute's economic
and social development plan.

211 **Local economic policies and social citizenship in Spanish cities.**
Soledad García. *Antipode*, vol. 25, no. 3 (July 1993), p. 191-205.

This article examines the restructuring of the local economy in Spain's principal cities
(particularly Barcelona, but also Madrid and Seville) in relation to the main changes
that have taken place in the urban environment since local democracy was re-
established after the 1979 elections. Local council intervention in the economy and the
extension of the social dimension of citizenship are analysed. This idea of social
citizenship, embodied in the social rights accorded by the government to citizens in
areas such as social security, health care, education and pensions, was developed in
the 1980s. Since the granting of regional autonomy some of these rights have come
under local (as opposed to national) jurisdiction. García shows that, despite relatively
small resources, local administrations have attempted to create a more dynamic
approach of leading economic and social reconstruction. Despite this fact, conflicting
interests and priorities with the state government have caused problems for local
government, and the control which the regional governments seek to exercise over
cities has only served to exacerbate these problems. Madrid is fortunate in that, as
capital city, it has been able to develop a strong sense of locality based on economic
and cultural initiatives and social policies. Clear and concise, the article contains a
number of statistical tables and references.

212 **Madrid in the 1990s: a European investment region.**
Edward Pincheson. London: Economist Intelligence Unit, 1992. 90p.
maps. (EIU European Investment Regions Series; Special Report,
no. M608).

The author is a respected authority on Spanish business and finance, and has written
numerous reports on the economies of Spain and Turkey. In this detailed study he
considers the region of Madrid in the context of economic growth and its
attractiveness for foreign investors. Most of the work refers primarily to the city of
Madrid, and areas covered include: the regional economy; Madrid's economic
structure; industrial sectors (including the automobile, pharmaceutical, food,
telecommunications and construction industries); services sector (including banking,
retail, communications and the property market); foreign investment; regional
resources; and economic forecasts for the region. Clearly laid out and well presented,
the report is also enhanced by maps, figures, statistical tables and a list of useful
addresses for the city of Madrid.

213 **Madrid and the Spanish economy, 1560-1850.**
David R. Ringrose. Berkeley, California: University of California
Press, 1983. 405p. 18 maps. bibliog.

Historians have long been fascinated by Madrid's rise and dominance as capital city of
Spain. Ringrose's seminal study is staggering in its detail and painstaking in its
analysis. He was the first scholar to undertake such an exhaustive study into the nature
and consequence of Madrid's dominance, and the result is a classic, totally original
work. Its pioneering nature can be glimpsed in the amount of primary and secondary
source material consulted in the extensive bibliography. Having been nominated
capital of Spain in 1561, the city had grown to a large metropolis by 1630. By the
middle of the 17th century the city dominated the interior, and other urban centres had
declined in importance. 'The uneven distribution of urban income directed demand
toward agricultural staples from the interior and quality merchandise from the ports,
discouraging diversification in the regional economy'. Ringrose's study, amongst
other things, helps to explain Spain's slow industrialization, and how Madrid assisted
in the creation of an inflexible economy and a political class that tried to insulate the
economy from modernization. For a concise study of related aspects of the subject,
readers should refer to Ringrose's article, 'Madrid and the Castilian economy', in the
*Journal of European Economic History*, vol. 10, no. 2 (Fall 1981), p. 481-90. He is
also author of the article, 'The impact of a new capital city: Madrid, Toledo and New
Castile 1560-1660' (q.v.), in the *Journal of Economic History*, vol. 33, no. 4 (Dec.
1973), p. 761-91.

**The impact of a new capital city: Madrid, Toledo, and New Castile,
1560-1660.**
*See* item no. 106.

**Revolutionary wars and public finances: the Madrid treasury, 1784-
1807.**
*See* item no. 110.

**Cinco Días.** (Five Days.)
*See* item no. 470.

**Expansión.** (Expansion.)
*See* item no. 472.

**Actualidad Económica.** (Economic News.)
*See* item no. 479.

# Finance

214 **El sector financiero en la Comunidad de Madrid.** (The financial
sector in the Community of Madrid.)
Susana Feito Crespo. Madrid: Comunidad, Dirección General de
Economía y Planificación, 1988. 216p.

This volume offers a good, general survey of the most important aspects of, and
developments in, the region's financial sector. Special attention is paid to the city of
Madrid.

215 **The foundation of the Bank of Spain.**
Earl J. Hamilton. *Journal of Political Economy*, vol. 53, no. 2
(June 1945), p. 97-114.

The Bank of Spain in Madrid is the country's central bank. Owing its origin to the
18th-century banks (the Banco Nacional de San Carlos [San Carlos National Bank]
and the Banco de San Fernando [San Fernando Bank]), it was given the name Banco
de España [Bank of Spain] in 1856 and remained nominally in private hands until it
was nationalized in 1962. Its present-day role is very much the same as that of central
banks in other countries. Hamilton (a prolific writer on Spain's economic history)
provides a very detailed history of the Bank's early origins in the 1780s. He also wrote
other relevant articles in the same journal on the Bank of Spain specifically, and
banking in Spain generally: 'Spanish banking schemes before 1700' (vol. 57 [April
1949], p. 134-56); 'Plans for a national bank in Spain, 1701-83' (vol. 57 [Aug. 1949],
p. 315-36); and 'The first twenty years of the Bank of Spain (Parts I-II)' (vol. 54 [Feb.
1946], p. 17-37 [part I], and vol. 54 [April 1946], p. 116-40 [part II]).

216 **Investing in Madrid.**
Madrid: Chamber of Commerce and Industry, 1994. 26p. maps.

Available in Spanish, English and French, this small guide (prepared by the Research
Service of the Madrid Chamber of Commerce and Industry) is packed with useful
information, including a wealth of up-to-date statistics. Updated on an irregular basis
(every few years), it offers an overview of Madrid's commercial and industrial

sectors. Information and statistics are provided under a number of headings, proving useful for any prospective investor or company looking to locate in Madrid. Headings include Madrid's industrial and commercial sector; the market for office space; trade; foreign investment; tourism; conferences, congresses and trade fairs (including a trade fair calendar); business incentives and assistance; foreign banks; new business areas (map included); and a list of relevant addresses. Those requiring more information on doing business in Madrid should contact the Chamber of Commerce directly (see the address section at the front of this book). The Chamber also publishes a number of works on Madrid's population, economy and industry (including a number of statistical yearbooks), a catalogue of which can also be provided.

217  **Investigating the behavior and characteristics of the Madrid Stock Exchange.**
M. Ratner.  *Journal of Banking and Finance*, vol. 20, no. 1 (1996), p. 135-49. bibliog.

This study examines the efficiency and characteristics of the nine major indexes of the Madrid Stock Exchange (Bolsa de Madrid) from 1941 up to 1992. The Exchange was founded in 1831 and it accounts for eighty-five per cent of the trading in Spain's four stock markets. In 1884 Enrique María Repullés y Vargas won a competition to design the building which has housed the Bolsa ever since. It was inaugurated by Queen María Cristina in 1893, whence trading began. The building (situated in the Plaza de la Lealtad next to the Ritz Hotel) consists of two areas: one where the trading is conducted, and the second (open to the public) housing an exhibition on the Exchange's history. Readers should also consult the comprehensive *Historia de la Bolsa de Madrid* (History of the Madrid Stock Exchange) by José Antonio Torrente Fortuño (Madrid: Colegio de Agentes de Cambio y Bolsa, 1974-88. 4 vols.).

**El Mundo Financiero.** (Financial World.)
*See* item no. 488.

# Business and Trade

218 **Tiendas de Madrid.** (Shops of Madrid.)
Luis Agromayor.   Madrid: Susaeta, 1995. 155p.

Beautifully produced and containing excellent colour illustrations, this coffee-table book presents a history of Madrid's commercial establishments. All types of shops are considered for food, wine and other products. Of related interest are: *Once siglos de mercado madrileño* (Eleven centuries of trade in Madrid) (Madrid: MercaMadrid, 1988; originally published Madrid: Ayuntamiento, 1985); *Los sectores mercantiles en Madrid en el primer tercio del siglo XX: tiendas, comerciantes y dependientes de comercio* (Commercial sectors in Madrid during the first third of the 20th century: shops, traders and shop assistants) by Gloria Nielfa Cristóbal (Madrid: Ministerio de Trabajo y Seguridad Social, 1985. 334p.); and *El mercado en Madrid en la baja edad media: estructura y sistemas de abastecimiento de un concejo medieval castellano (s. XV)* (The market-place in Madrid during the late Middle Ages: structure and systems for supplying a mediaeval Castilian town council [15th century]) by Tomás Puñal Fernández (Madrid: Caja de Madrid, 1992. 280p.), which is an excellent history of commerce during the period and includes information relating to commercial laws, food products and traders.

219 **Comercio Exterior de la Comunidad de Madrid.** (Overseas Trade of the Community of Madrid.)
Madrid: Consejería de Economía, Departamento de Estadística, 1994-annual.

A complete package of statistical information is provided in this useful publication. Trade data are given both by country and product.

220 **Madrid as a business centre: Financial Times survey.**
*Financial Times* (14th Nov. 1988), p. 41-44.

Although a little dated, this brief survey still provides some helpful information relating to the city, the way in which the Spanish conduct business, and developments within the business and financial sectors in Madrid. Readers should also refer to the

Spanish periodical, *Madrid – Centro de Negocios* (Madrid – Business Centre) (Madrid: s.n., 1995- . monthly), which contains information for foreign investors and has a circulation of around 140,000.

**Vip Madrid: guide for the business visitor.**
*See* item no. 52.

**La Cámara de Comercio e Industria de Madrid, 1887-1987.** (The Madrid Chamber of Commerce and Industry, 1887-1987.)
*See* item no. 209.

**Madrid in the 1990s: a European investment region.**
*See* item no. 212.

**Investing in Madrid.**
*See* item no. 216.

**Guía del Comercio y de la Industria de Madrid.** (Guide to Commerce and Industry in Madrid.)
*See* item no. 223.

**Cinco Días.** (Five Days.)
*See* item no. 470.

**Expansión.** (Expansion.)
*See* item no. 472.

**La Gaceta de los Negocios.** (Business Gazette.)
*See* item no. 473.

**Actualidad Económica.** (Economic News.)
*See* item no. 479.

**Mercado.** (Market Place.)
*See* item no. 487.

**Tribuna.** (Tribune.)
*See* item no. 493.

**En Directo.** (Live.)
*See* item no. 505.

**Reseña bibliográfica y documental en las áreas de trabajo, industria y comercio en la Comunidad de Madrid.** (A bibliographical and documentary report on the subjects of work, industry and trade in the Community of Madrid.)
*See* item no. 528.

# Industry

221 **Atlas de la industria en la Comunidad de Madrid.** (Atlas of industry in the Community of Madrid.)
Madrid: Comunidad, Consejería de Economía, 1994. 210p.

Using a historical approach, this work charts the growth of industry in the region and provides detailed economic analysis of the characteristics of the different manufacturing industries. The same publisher (the Community's Council for the Economy) produces a range of useful publications, including a number of statistical and analytical studies of Madrid's industrial sector, such as: *Estructura industrial de la Comunidad de Madrid* (The industrial structure of the Community of Madrid) by Fernando del Castillo Cuervo-Arango, Antonio Gil Huerres and Juan Leyva Salmerón (Madrid: Consejería de Economía, Departamento de Estadística, 1994. 215p.); *La industria madrileña a través de sus cuentas: 1986-1987* (Madrid's industry as seen through its accounts: 1986-87) by Fernando del Castillo Cuervo-Arango and Luis González Calbet (Madrid: Consejería de Economía, Departamento de Estadística, 1990. 68p.); and *El sector de servicios a empresas en la Comunidad de Madrid* (The business service sector in the Community of Madrid) (Madrid: Consejería de Economía, Departamento de Estadística, 1992. 2 vols.).

222 **Industrial subcontracting and the informal sector: the politics of restructuring in the Madrid electronics industry.**
Lauren A. Benton. In: *The informal economy: studies in advanced and less developed countries.* Edited by Alejandro Portes, Manuel Castells, Lauren A. Benton. Baltimore, Maryland; London: Johns Hopkins University Press, 1989, p. 228-44. bibliog.

Benton examines the role of the informal (as opposed to the regulated) economy and industrial subcontracting in the process of industrial restructuring in the Madrid electronics industry. This high-tech industry was specifically chosen as the case study because of its importance in the Spanish economy and because over seventy per cent of all electronics production is concentrated in Madrid. A number of statistical tables are included, although these have now become rather dated. Benton also wrote the ground-breaking study, *Invisible factories: the informal economy and industrial development in Spain* (Albany, New York: State University of New York Press, 1990. 231p.).

92

223 **Guía del Comercio y de la Industria de Madrid.** (Guide to
Commerce and Industry in Madrid.)
Madrid: Cámara de Comercio e Industria de Madrid, 1971- . annual.

Compiled and published by Madrid's Chamber of Commerce, the 1995 edition
constituted ten volumes providing information on all aspects of the region's industrial
sector. It includes the food, chemical, leather, wood, paper and textile industries as
well as the building and iron and steel sectors. Over 4,000 products and 7,000
manufacturing companies are classified and indexed in the guide. The Chamber of
Commerce published a number of other useful studies on Madrid's trade and industry
including: *Guía de exportadores de la Comunidad de Madrid* (Guide to exporters in
the Autonomous Community of Madrid) (1995) which gives information relating to
over 3,000 exporting companies in the region, many of which are based in and around
the city; and *Informe de Coyuntura de la Industria/Comercio de Madrid* (Report on
Industry/Business Trends in Madrid) (1971- . two-monthly) which comprises two
pamphlets (one dealing with industry, one with commerce) surveying the latest
developments and analysing individual sectors. For a full and detailed centenary
history of the Madrid Chamber of Commerce, readers should refer to *La Cámara de
Comercio e Industria de Madrid, 1887-1987* (q.v.).

224 **INI: 50 años de industrialización en España.** (INI: 50 years of
industrialization in Spain.)
Pablo Martín Aceña, Francisco Comín. Madrid: Espasa Calpe, 1991.
648p. (Biblioteca de Economía: Serie Perfiles).

Written by prolific and respected authors on the subjects of Spain's economy and
industry, this is a thoroughly detailed study of the history and development of Spain's
National Institute for Industry (INI) since its foundation in 1941. Based in Madrid, it
is a particularly significant organization as regards the wide range of industrial activity
in and around the city. Packed with valuable statistical data, the work is also
noteworthy for its extensive bibliography. The authors also wrote *Historia de la
empresa pública en España* (History of the public sector company in Spain) (Madrid:
Espasa Calpe, 1991. 408p.), another authoritative work which includes references to
public sector companies in Madrid.

225 **La industria de Madrid.** (The industry of Madrid.)
Ricardo Méndez Gutiérrez del Valle. Madrid: Universidad
Complutense, Facultad de Geografía e Historia, 1981. 2 vols. bibliog.

This academic study of Madrid's industries looks at the historical and geographical
development of different industries and sectors. Two standard historical works on this
subject are: *Historia de la industria en Madrid* (A history of industry in Madrid) by
Antonio Sánchez Trasancos (Madrid: The Author, 1972. 394p.); and *La industria en
Madrid: ensayo histórico-crítico de la fabricación y artesanía madrileña* (Industry in
Madrid: a historical-critical essay on Madrid's manufacturing and craftsmanship) by
Miguel Capella Martínez (Madrid: Cámara Oficial de la Industria, 1962-63. 2 vols.).
For a helpful overview of Spain's industrialization in the post-war period (including
the factors involved in its development and the economic crisis of the 1980s), readers
should refer to the chapter by Antonio Vázquez-Barquero, entitled 'Transformation of
the industrial system in Spain' in *Industrialization in developing and peripheral
regions*, edited by I. F. E. Hamilton (London: Croom Helm, 1986, p. 114-35).

226 **Spanish guns and pistols: including 'An historical account of the gunmakers of Madrid from their origin until the present day' by Isidro Soler, gunmaker to our Lord the King, Madrid MDCCXCV.**
William Keith Neal. London: G. Bell & Sons, 1955. 102p. bibliog.
This was the first study of Spanish firearms to appear in English and is particularly noteworthy for its inclusion *in toto* of a translation of the book written by the Madrid royal gunmaker, Isidro Soler, in 1795. Soler goes into the methods of barrel forging, as well as giving an interesting general history of gunmaking in Madrid, and the names and dates of the principal gunsmiths. The first part of Neal's work provides a general description of gunsmithing in Spain from the 16th century. Numerous black-and-white photographs are included, together with a list of Spanish gunmakers and their marks. Those interested in this subject should also refer to James Duncan Lavin's *A history of Spanish firearms* (London: Jenkins; New York: Arco, 1965), which is a superbly illustrated history of the firearms industry from the introduction of gunpowder into Spain in the 14th century to the death of Soler in 1825.

227 **Nuevas tecnologías en la industria madrileña.** (New technology in Madrid's industry.)
Compiled by Luis Sanz Menéndez. Madrid: Comunidad, Consejería de Trabajo, Industria y Comercio, 1987. 121p. bibliog.
Various aspects of the effects of new technology on industrial processes and development are examined in this interesting study. Another work of related interest is *Patrones del cambio tecnológico y política industrial: un estudio de las empresas innovadores madrileñas* (Patrons of technological change and industrial policy: a survey of Madrid's innovative companies) by Mikel Buesa and José Molero (Madrid: Civitas; Instituto Madrileño de Desarrollo, 1992. 171p.).

**Economic crisis, social conflict and the Popular Front: Madrid 1931-6.**
*See* item no. 130.

**La Cámara de Comercio e Industria de Madrid, 1887-1987.** (The Madrid Chamber of Commerce and Industry, 1887-1987.)
*See* item no. 209.

**Madrid, presente y futuro.** (Madrid, present and future.)
*See* item no. 210.

**Madrid in the 1990s: a European investment region.**
*See* item no. 212.

**Labour market and gender in the Autonomous Community of Madrid.**
*See* item no. 247.

**Reseña bibliográfica y documental en las áreas de trabajo, industria y comercio en la Comunidad de Madrid.** (A bibliographical and documentary report on the subjects of work, industry and trade in the Community of Madrid.)
*See* item no. 528.

# Transport and Communications

228   **Madrid: 101 años de tranvías.** (Madrid: 101 years of trams.)
Agustín Burgaleta Simón.   Madrid: Proyecto Brainstorm, 1988. 360p.
maps.

The author has spent most of his professional life working in Madrid's tram and bus systems. The trams transformed the way people travelled around the city, operating from 1871 when the first horse-drawn trams appeared until 1972 when the last electric tram made its final journey. This fascinating book describes all aspects of the tram's operation and includes chapters on: horse-drawn, steam and electric trams; tram-operating companies; types of tram; and routes. Clearly written, the work is particularly noteworthy for its magnificent illustrations which include numerous colour plates of the different trams, together with photographs of the trams in operation and examples of posters, tickets and routes of the period. Readers could also usefully refer to Carlos López Bustos' *Tranvías de Madrid* (Trams of Madrid) (Madrid: Aldaba, 1992. 2nd ed. 287p.), a study which is comprehensive and rich in detail; and his shorter survey, *Historia de los tranvías de Madrid* (History of the trams of Madrid) (Madrid: Ayuntamiento; Instituto de Estudios Madrileños, 1984. 39p.).

229   **El aeropuerto de Madrid Barajas: estudio geográfico.** (Madrid's
Barajas airport: a geographical study.)
J. A. Córdoba Ordóñez.   Madrid: Universidad Complutense, Facultad
de Geografía e Historia, 1980. 3 vols. maps. bibliog.

Very little has been written on Madrid's Barajas airport, and this academic study represents the only detailed survey. For an interesting article on the airport's history, readers should refer to 'El aeropuerto de Madrid – Barajas' by M. Dastis Quecedo, in *Estudios Geográficos*, vol. 34 (1973), p. 303-58.

230 **The growth of metro systems in Madrid, Rome and Athens.**
Frank J. Costa, Allen G. Noble. *Cities*, vol. 7, no. 3 (August 1990),
p. 224-29.

The Madrid Metro system was inaugurated in 1919 and the basic network of three main lines, intersecting beneath the Puerta del Sol in the centre of Madrid, was completed by the end of the 1920s. The system is held in high regard by passengers for its comprehensiveness, efficiency and low ticket prices. It is also safe and clean, and provides the simplest way of getting around the city. The ten lines are identified by a number and colour on maps and station platforms. At the time of writing, the network was still being extended, with completion of the stretch of line between Laguna and Ciudad Universitaria creating a continuous circular route. The authors of this article compare and contrast the metro systems of the three capital cities and demonstrate how the Madrid system provides the city with one of the most extensive networks in Europe. Both authors are respected Professors of Geography in the United States, and their article is supplemented with a number of useful figures and statistical tables.

231 **The postal markings of Madrid, 1900-31.**
Anthony C. Crew. Hove, England: Ronald G. Shelley, 1984. 32p.
map. (Bookclub; no. 13).

The author has collected postmarks of Madrid for a number of years, and this book is devoted to those covering the period from 1900 up to the beginning of the Second Republic (1931). Aimed primarily at postmark collectors and students, it was printed in limited numbers and may prove difficult to obtain. Of related interest is the old, but fascinating, article by C. Alcázar Molina, 'Historia de los carteros de Madrid en el siglo XVIII' (A history of Madrid's 18th-century postmen) in *Revista de Archivos, Bibliotecas y Museos*, vol. 20 (1951), p. 57-74.

232 **Coverage of rail transport networks (metro and commuter railway) in the city of Madrid, using a geographic information system.**
Carlos Cristóbal Pinto, Antonio García Pastor. *PTRC Publications P*, no. I385 (1994), p. 61-69. map.

The four different networks which make up Madrid's public transport system, namely the Metro network, the commuter rail network, the urban bus network and the city's metropolitan bus network, are discussed in this short, scholarly article. Focusing on the rail transport networks, the authors provide a detailed, and sometimes technical, analysis of the system, including the population served and the location of stations.

233 **Transporte, espacio y capital.** (Transport, space and capital.)
Ramón Fernández Durán. Madrid: Nuestra Cultura, 1980. 405p.

This extensive study considers the interlinked factors concerning Madrid's role as capital city, its space and planning problems, and the history and development of the city's transport system. Other short works of related interest include: *Estrategía de transportes en la región metropolitana de Madrid* (Transport strategy for the metropolitan area of Madrid) (Madrid: Consejería de Política Territorial, 1988. 32p.); *Estudio del sistema de transportes en el área metropolitana de Madrid* (A survey of the transport system in the metropolitan area of Madrid) by Juan Javier Pérez Sanz and Guillermo Vázquez (Madrid: Diputación, Area de Urbanismo y Ordenación Territorial, 1982. 91p.); *Plano de los transportes de Madrid* (Transport plan of Madrid) (Madrid: Consorcio Regional de Transportes de Madrid, 1994. 24p.); and *Plano de los transportes del centro de Madrid* (Transport plan for Madrid city centre) (Madrid: Consorcio de Transportes de Madrid, 1994. 3rd ed. 18p.). Both the 'Consejería de Transportes' (Transport Council) and the 'Consorcio Regional de Transportes' (Regional Transport Consortium) for Madrid publish useful annual reports on all aspects of the city's transport system.

234 **Los accesos ferroviarios a Madrid: su impacto en la geografía urbana de la ciudad.** (Rail access to Madrid: its impact on the urban geography of the city.)
María Pilar González Yanci.   Madrid: Instituto de Estudios Madrileños, 1977. 520p. maps. bibliog. (Biblioteca de Estudios Madrileños, no. 21).

Based on her doctoral thesis at Madrid's Complutense University's Faculty of Geography and History, this pioneering work presents a minutely detailed analysis of the railway as the agent of change which, from the beginnings of the industrial revolution, put an end to Madrid's isolation at the centre of the peninsula. Providing a vital communication route, it linked the city with the periphery and set in motion its rapid development as a major industrial centre. The railways also ensured that major changes occurred in the urban planning of Madrid to accommodate the new railway stations and tracks. Chapters cover: the birth of the Spanish rail network (1851-81); its competition with other forms of transport (1929-41); the evolution of rail transport in Madrid (1941-61); the commercial function of the city's railway stations; and an analysis of the railway's influence on Madrid. Thoroughly researched and supported by numerous maps and appendices, this volume has become the standard work on the history and importance of Madrid's rail network. The author also wrote *Los inicios del ferrocarril en Madrid* (The beginnings of the railway in Madrid) (Madrid: Ayuntamiento de Madrid, 1994. 40p.), a short historical survey of rail transport in Madrid. Of related interest is *El ferrocarril metropolitano de Madrid, 1917-1953* (Madrid's metropolitan railway, 1917-53) by Miguel Otamendi (Madrid: Compañía Metropolitano, 1953. 27p.), whose author wrote widely on the history of the city's railways.

235 **Guía de la comunicación de la Comunidad de Madrid.** (Guide to communications in the Community of Madrid.)
Madrid: Comunidad, Oficina del Portavoz del Consejo de Gobierno, 1995. 300p.

This annual publication forms a directory of public institutions and other communications media for professionals and specialists in this field.

236 **Los transportes urbanos de Madrid.** (Urban transport in Madrid.)
Antonio López Gómez.   Madrid: Instituto Juan Sebastián Elcano; Consejo Superior de Investigaciones Científicas, 1983. 314p. maps. bibliog.

The author has written widely on the subject of Madrid and its transport system. In this standard work he considers the history and development of all areas of public transport in the city, opening with the era of the tram (1871-1919) and concluding with a general survey of transport circulation in the city, and the problems relating to public and private forms of transport, parking and city-centre congestion. In between, there are some interesting chapters on the Metro system, the bus (and trolleybus), taxis, general transport development, the population of Madrid and transport routes in the city. Readers might also find useful some of the author's other articles on this and related subjects, including: 'Los transportes urbanos en Madrid: el ferrocarril metropolitano (metro)' (Urban transport in Madrid: the metropolitan railway [metro]) in *Estudios Geográficos*, vol. 30, no. 144 (1969), p. 5-105; and 'Los transportes urbanos en Madrid: el trolebús' (Urban transport in Madrid: the trolleybus) in the same journal (vol. 37, no. 143 [1976], p. 129-42): although somewhat dated, these remain useful for their historical detail and views.

237  **Assessment of congestion costs in Madrid (Spain).**
Andrés Monzón de Cáceres, Javier Villanueva Gredilla.  *PTRC Publications P*, no. I376 (1994), p. 197-208. 2 maps. bibliog.

High levels of traffic congestion in Madrid frequently exhaust the capacity of the road infrastructure and also have serious economic and social costs. In this paper the authors provide a systematic and technical assessment of the economic effects of traffic congestion in the city. Since the mid-1980s much work has been done to reduce pollution levels and provide an integrated urban transport system. The Regional Government of Madrid, in conjunction with the Transport Consortium (Consorcio de Transportes), has recently carried out a regional transport survey which identified the scale and nature of the main transport problems of Madrid. The survey established medium- and long-term objectives with the year 2001 highlighted as the year of full implementation of the strategy and packages of measures. Madrid's public transport system relies on the cooperation of the three administrative levels (national, regional and local), with the role of successfully coordinating policy between these three having fallen to the Transport Consortium, created in 1986. Further details relating to Madrid's local and regional transport strategies can be obtained from the Consejería de Transportes at the address listed at the front of this book. Of related interest is the Transport Council's strategic road plan for the city and region: *Plan de carreteras: 1994-2001; memoria resumen* (Road plan: 1994-2001; summary report) (Madrid: Consejería de Transportes, 1994. 124p.).

238  **Metro de Madrid, 1919-1989: setenta años de historia.** (Madrid metro, 1919-89: seventy years of history.)
Aurora Moya Rodríguez.  Madrid: Metro de Madrid, 1990. 339p. maps.

Exhaustive and full of detail and illustrations, this is the most up-to-date, comprehensive study of Madrid's Metro system. Another standard Spanish book on the history of the Madrid Metro is *El metro de Madrid: medio siglo al servicio de la ciudad, 1919-1969* (The Madrid Metro: half a century of serving the city, 1919-69) by Marino Gómez Santos (Madrid: Escelicer, 1969. 141p.) which celebrates in words and pictures the fiftieth anniversary of the opening of the system.

239 **Riding the AVE: Madrid to Seville to Madrid in a day.**
Robert J. Sladky. *Passenger Train Journal*, vol. 26, no. 8
(Aug. 1995), p. 30-35.
This short, illustrated article provides an overview of the value and performance of the
AVE (Alta Velocidad – High Speed), Spain's high-speed train. One of the most
controversial and expensive projects undertaken around Seville's Expo '92, opinions
still vary about whether it was worth it or not. Madrid's Atocha railway station was
lavishly refurbished to provide a suitable home for the twelve trains which depart each
day for Seville. For a more detailed survey of the AVE, readers should refer to the
chapter by Mitchell P. Strohl, 'Iberia and the Spanish tren de alta velocidad' in
*Europe's high speed trains: a study*, edited by the author (Westport, Connecticut:
Praeger, 1993, p. 223-50. bibliog.).

240 **Las telecomunicaciones de la región de Madrid, 1990-2000.**
(Telecommunications in the Madrid region, 1990-2000.)
Mario Tanco, Cristóbal Guzmán.   Madrid: IMADE, 1992. 255p.
Little has been published on Madrid's telecommunications systems and networks.
This useful report covers the Madrid region and examines the current situation, recent
developments and the prospects for the year 2000.

**Caminos y caminantes por las tierras del Madrid medieval.** (Tracks and
travellers through the lands of mediaeval Madrid.)
*See* item no. 99.

**Late nineteenth-century Spanish progressivism: Arturo Soria's linear
city.**
*See* item no. 275.

**Grand terminus: Atocha railway station, Madrid.**
*See* item no. 291.

# Labour

241 **Ideology and political patronage: workers and working-class movements in republican Madrid, 1931-4.**
Aviva Aviv, Isaac Aviv. *European Studies Review*, vol. 11, no. 4 (Oct. 1981), p. 487-515.

The authors are respected writers on the history of European working-class movements. In this article they consider how, with the establishment of the Second Republic in April 1931, the Madrid working class became a key element in influencing the destiny of the new régime. They analyse various aspects of this group – their numbers, economic and social conditions, political affiliations and unemployment levels – and relate them to the political and economic events of the time. A number of statistical tables and references are also included. The two authors also collaborated to produce a follow-up article, entitled 'The Madrid working-class, the Spanish Socialist Party and the collapse of the Second Republic (1934-1936)' in the *Journal of Contemporary History*, vol. 16, no. 2 (April 1981), p. 229-50. The study focuses on the Madrid working-class socialist federations and trade unions and concludes that, despite the radicalization of the Socialist Party (PSOE) after 1933, the Madrid working class was certainly not more revolutionary in 1936 than in 1931 or 1934, and that it is impossible to claim that war was inevitable or that there was no other solution to the country's problems but revolution and counter-revolution. Another interesting historical analysis is *La condición obrera hace un siglo: los trabajadores madrileños y la Comisión de Reformas Sociales* (Working conditions a century ago: Madrid's workers and the Commision for Social Reform) by María Angeles Montoya Tamaño et al. (Madrid: Universidad Autónoma, 1991. 150p.).

242 **Ciudad, democracia y socialismo: la experiencia de las asociaciones de vecinos en Madrid.** (City, democracy and socialism: the experience of the residents' associations in Madrid.)
Manuel Castells. Madrid: Siglo Veintiuno de España, 1977. 249p. bibliog.

Castells is the author of a number of sociological studies. In this detailed and scholarly work he analyses the foundation, development and experiences of the working-class residents' associations of the capital.

243 **Divergent paths: labor politics in Barcelona and Madrid.**
Robert M. Fishman. In: *Politics, society, and democracy: the case of Spain.* Edited by Richard Gunther. Boulder, Colorado; Oxford: Westview Press, 1993, p. 196-213. bibliog. (Essays in Honor of Juan J. Linz).

In many respects this chapter updates the study of the labour movements in Madrid and Barcelona which appear in an earlier chapter in this book by Edward E. Malefakis: 'A comparative analysis of workers' movements in Spain and Italy' (p. 57-69). Both studies examine, and attempt to explain, the political behaviour of workers in Spain's two major cities. Malefakis explores workers' movements in the late 19th and early 20th centuries, whilst Fishman focuses on the contemporary situation through an inter-regional approach. Of related interest is Alejandro Tiana's *Maestros, misioneros y militantes: la educación de la clase obrera madrileña, 1898-1917* (Masters, missionaries and militants: the education of the Madrid working class, 1898-1917) (Madrid: CIDE, 1992) which provides an excellent source of information for working-class conditions at the turn of the century, using the disastrous year of the Spanish-American War and that of the national General Strike as boundaries.

244 **Trabajo y participación económica: la actividad de las mujeres madrileñas.** (Work and economic participation: the occupations of Madrid's women.)
Cristina García Sainz. Madrid: Dirección General de la Mujer, 1995. 250p. bibliog.

The author analyses the different types of activity or employment of women in the Community of Madrid, and includes a great deal of useful statistical data. Readers interested in this subject should also refer to another study by the same author: *Mujer y empleo en la Comunidad de Madrid* (Women and employment in the Community of Madrid) (Madrid: Dirección General de la Mujer, 1992. 95p.).

245 **Mercado de trabajo, política de empleo y desarrollo local: territorio, economías locales y formas flexibles de regulación.**
(Labour market, employment policy and local development: territory, local economies and flexible methods of regulation.)
Juan Mayoral Lobato. Madrid: Iniciativas Regionales Madrileñas; Fundación Universidad-Empresa, 1992. 360p. bibliog.

This comprehensive study of Madrid's labour market considers the different factors which influence employment policies, economic and industrial development and the movement of labour. A similarly rigorous study was carried out in relation to unemployment by I. Ezquiaga, entitled *Determinantes poblacionales, productivos y espaciales del paro en un mercado local de trabajo: el caso de Madrid* (The population, profit and spatial factors of unemployment in a local labour market: the case of Madrid) (Madrid: Universidad Autónoma, 1984. 1 vol.). Other works of related interest are: *Conciencia social, sindical y política de los trabajadores industriales en el área metropolitana de Madrid* (The social, trade-union and political conscience of industrial workers in the metropolitan area of Madrid) (Madrid: Centro de Investigaciones Sociológicas, 1980. 1 vol.); *Empleo y paro en la Comunidad de Madrid* (Employment and unemployment in the Community of Madrid) (Madrid: Comunidad, Consejo Económico y Social, 1994. 64p.), which presents a detailed analysis of Madrid's labour market and unemployment levels; and *Informe Anual sobre Formación y Mercado de Trabajo en la Comunidad de Madrid* (Annual Report on Training and the Labour Market in the Community of Madrid) (Madrid: Instituto para la Formación de la Comunidad, 1993- . annual. c.100p.).

246  **Foreign women in domestic service in Spain.**
Miguel de Prada, Walter Actis, Carlos Pereda.  Geneva: ILO World Employment Programme, 1991. 58p. (International Migration for Employment Working Paper, no. 51).

Examines the employment situation and living conditions of foreign domestic workers in Spain, which upon investigation prove to be somewhat precarious. The paper focuses on the city of Madrid, to which women are attracted principally from, in order of importance, the Philippines, Morocco, Dominica, Cape Verde, Chile, Colombia and Peru. Copies of this study may prove difficult to obtain, but a copy is held in microfiche format by the British Library.

247  **Labour market and gender in the Autonomous Community of Madrid.**
Juana María Rodríguez Moya, María Angeles Díaz Muñoz.  *Iberian Studies*, vol. 20, nos. 1-2 (1991), p. 113-34.

The Autonomous Community of Madrid is one of the most important industrial and commercial areas in Spain. The authors discuss the economic reorganization of the Community, and whilst studying the area as a whole emphasize the importance of the growth of the tertiary sector in the central districts of the city of Madrid. They proceed to note the decline in industry and the social differences in the Community between those districts housing the professional élites and those where the unskilled live. They argue that economic reorganization has allowed more and more women to enter the labour market, but that this has all too often meant poorly-paid and insecure manual work in small factories. A number of maps, statistical tables and graphs illustrate the study, and it also contains a number of useful references including their earlier article on the subject, 'Spatial variations of the female and male labour force participation in the Madrid metropolitan area', in *Espace, Populations, Sociétés* (vol. 1 [1989], p. 43-52). An article of related interest directly follows the main item from *Iberian Studies*: written by Ana Sabaté Martínez et al., it is entitled 'Economic restructuring and the gender division of labour: the clothing industry in the rural areas of the Autonomous Community of Madrid' (p. 135-54).

**Economic crisis, social conflict and the Popular Front: Madrid 1931-6.**
*See* item no. 130.

**Individualisms in Madrid during the Spanish Civil War.**
*See* item no. 135.

**The labor force participation and fertility of Spanish women, Madrid, 1980.**
*See* item no. 167.

**Oficios tradicionales en Madrid.** (Traditional crafts of Madrid.)
*See* item no. 431.

**Reseña bibliográfica y documental en las áreas de trabajo, industria y comercio en la Comunidad de Madrid.** (A bibliographical and documentary report on the subjects of work, industry and trade in the Community of Madrid.)
*See* item no. 528.

# Statistics

248  **Anuario Estadístico de la Comunidad de Madrid.** (Statistical
Yearbook for the Community of Madrid.)
Madrid: Comunidad de Madrid, Consejería de Economía,
Departamento de Estadística, 1984- . 2 vols. maps. annual.

This publication is the most authoritative compilation of statistical data on the
Autonomous Community of Madrid, and is produced by the Community's Department
of Statistics. Volume one covers the Community as a whole and provides data on
topics such as: geography; climate; environment; population; the labour market;
industry; agriculture; housing; transport and communications; tourism; health and
social services; education; sport; the legal system; the economy and finance (including
the Madrid Stock Exchange); public administration; and elections. Numerous maps
and diagrams illustrate the numeric information. Volume two ranges across similar
subject areas, but this time provides data relating to the municipalities which make up
the Autonomous Community, and as such it is particularly relevant for data on the city
of Madrid. Detailed colour maps are again included. Both volumes are clearly
presented and excellently produced. A small booklet accompanies the two-volume set
and provides an extremely helpful, alphabetical, thematic index to the work as a
whole. In 1995 volume two became available on computer software as part of the
'Matriz' program produced by the Department of Statistics, allowing easier access to
the data on PCs and more flexibility in the tailoring of information for specific
geographical areas such as Madrid.

249  **Boletín Estadístico Municipal: Datos y Análisis.** (Municipal
Statistical Bulletin: Data and Analysis.)
Madrid: Ayuntamiento, 1986- . irregular.

Although its irregularity of publication is a negative feature, the bulletin contains a
wide range of useful statistical data on the city of Madrid, on subjects including
population, economy, employment, health, and society. Of related interest for economic and financial statistical data is the publication, *Estadísticas Presupuestarias
Municipales* (Municipal Budgetary Statistics) (Madrid: Comunidad de Madrid, 1985- .
annual).

250 **Estadísticas del movimiento natural de la población de la Comunidad de Madrid: 1992.** (Statistics on native population movements for the Community of Madrid: 1992.)
Madrid: Comunidad, Consejería de Economía, Departamento de Estadística, 1994-95. 3 vols.

Each volume in this huge statistical work contains around 500 pages and represents a comprehensive survey of the Community's population trends. Volume one provides data on births; volume two covers marriages; and volume three details deaths. In conjunction with these volumes, the Community also published the massive ten-volume set providing data on its 1991 census, entitled *Censos de población y vivienda de 1991 de la Comunidad de Madrid* (Population and housing censuses of 1991 for the Community of Madrid) (Madrid: Comunidad, Consejería de Economía, Departamento de Estadística, 1993-95. 10 vols.).

251 **Historia del Instituto Nacional de Estadística, 1945-1981: resumen de su actividad.** (History of the National Institute for Statistics, 1945-81: summary of its activity.)
Manuel García Alvarez. Madrid: Ministerio de Economía y Comercio, Instituto Nacional de Estadística, 1981. 208p.

This is a standard work on Spain's National Institute for Statistics (INE), based in Madrid. It relates the history and development of the Institute from its creation in 1945 until the beginning of the 1980s. From 1989 it became an autonomous organization, although it remains assigned to the Ministry of Economy and Trade. For a more up-to-date summary of its history and role, together with a wide-ranging survey of statistical information on Spain, readers could usefully refer to a whole journal issue devoted to this topic: 'La estadística en España hoy' (Statistics in Spain today) in *Situación*, nos. 3/4 (1992). 192p.

252 **Madrid data guide.**
Madrid: Consejería de Economía, Departamento de Estadística, 1993. 1 vol. map.

This fold-out leaflet is generally available from tourist offices and certain bookshops in Madrid, and is produced in English, French and Spanish editions. It contains a map of the region of Madrid and statistical data covering the region's population, industry, towns and cities, employment and socio-economic indicators. Another fold-out publication (updated annually) is *Madrid in figures* (Madrid: Cámara de Comercio e Industria de Madrid) which provides similar information as well as statistics on education, the Madrid Stock Exchange and the consumer prices index. It is available in English, French or Spanish directly from the Madrid Chamber of Commerce (see addresses section at the front of this book).

**La población de Madrid.** (The population of Madrid.)
*See* item no. 140.

**Comercio Exterior de la Comunidad de Madrid.** (Overseas Trade of the Community of Madrid.)
*See* item no. 219.

# Environment and Urban Planning

## General

253 **Madrid a la búsqueda de su naturaleza.** (Madrid in search of its natural environment.)
Miguel A. Acero. Madrid: Acción Divulgativa, 1995. 266p. maps. bibliog. (Colección El Buho Viajero: Serie Aire Libre, no. 92).

This is an up-to-date detailed study of the region's environment and wildlife. The clearly-written text is enhanced by many illustrations (mostly in colour) and includes descriptions of protected areas and itineraries for those interested in exploring places of natural beauty. Detailed maps assist the reader, and appendices explain legislation relating to the environment and provide catalogues of threatened species and natural beauty spots. Other standard Spanish-language works on this topic are: *Madrid verde* (Green Madrid) by J. Izco (Madrid: Comunidad, Ministerio de Agricultura, Pesca y Alimentación, 1985); *La naturaleza en Madrid* (Nature in Madrid) by Antonio López Lillo (Madrid: Incafo, 1992. 2nd ed. 191p.); *Madrid y su medio ambiente* (Madrid and its environment) by F. Cadarso González and F. Parra Supervía (Madrid: Comunidad, Agencia de Medio Ambiente, 1991. 140p.); and *Desarrollo y medio ambiente en Madrid: un equilibrio necesario* (Development and the environment in Madrid: a necessary balance) (Madrid: Cámara de Comercio e Industria, 1990. 62p.).

254 **Landscape planning in Spain.**
Miguel Aguiló, Santiago González Alonso, Angel Ramos. *Built Environment*, vol. 16, no. 2 (1990), p. 98-110.

The main purpose of landscape planning is to help reconcile the needs of competing land uses and to incorporate them into a landscape within which people can prosper without destroying the natural and cultural resources: in a nutshell, it is creative conservation. The main focus of this article is to demonstrate how Spain has made considerable progress in introducing landscape values into the planning process, particularly during the late 1980s. The authors use the region of Madrid as a case study of this progress and consider areas such as legislation and ecological and agricultural factors. Nevertheless, they conclude that further progress is severely restricted by the total lack of schools or faculties in Spanish universities to teach this subject. A number of tables and illustrations accompany the text.

255 **Residential satisfaction in council housing.**
María Amérigo, Juan Ignacio Aragonés. *Journal of Environmental Psychology*, vol. 10 (Dec. 1990), p. 313-25.
In this study, which was based on primary research in an area of council housing in Madrid, the principal aim is to analyse the physical and social factors which influence council-housing residents' satisfaction. A sample of 447 housewives responded to a questionnaire which demonstrated that the physical environment (house and neighbourhood) and social aspects (neighbours) were the most important factors in variations in residential satisfaction. Tables, illustrations and a list of references are also included with the text.

256 **Air quality in the greater Madrid area: monitoring campaign in November 1990.**
C. Cerutti, A. Noriega, S. Sandroni. Luxembourg: Commission of the European Communities, Directorate-General Telecommunications, Information Industries and Innovation, 1992. 72p. maps. bibliog. (Environment and Quality of Life, EUR, no. 13999).
Growing concern about the air quality in the greater Madrid area during the 1980s, when extensive urban development was taking place, led the authorities to commission a series of investigations. Supplementing a long-term monitoring campaign, a survey on pollutants and emissions took place in November 1990 when the meteorological conditions were expected to be favourable to an accumulation of pollutants released by fumes from traffic and from domestic heating. Measurements made by specially equipped mobile units in different parts of the city enabled the investigators to obtain a detailed view of pollutant distribution in Madrid. Most of the volume is taken up with detailed maps, graphs and figures illustrating different levels of air pollution. Weather forecasts on Madrid's local television channel, 'TeleMadrid', also provide viewers with facts and figures relating to daily pollution levels and air quality in the vicinity.

257 **Madrid.**
Adriana dal Cin, Javier de Mesones, Jonás Figueroa. *Cities*, vol. 11, no. 5 (Oct. 1994), p. 283-91.
This clear, primarily descriptive article provides a concise profile of the city, charting its historical evolution from a small Moslem settlement in the 9th century to its present-day situation as capital of Spain, seat of the national government and central administration, and headquarters of large national and multinational companies. The authors describe how the growth of the city has always been strongly linked to immigration, internal as much as external, which has influenced facilities, services and housing policies. They also consider the current (1994) planning process (which at the time was under revision) and note how the planners are aiming to make good what the city lacks in order to be fully integrated into European development axes. Several plans, maps and diagrams illustrate the evolution and growth of the city over the centuries.

258 **Characterization of the air pollution in the urban area of Madrid.**
Aurelio Climent-Font, Erik Swietlicki, Antonio Revuelta. *Nuclear Instruments and Methods in Physics Research, Section B*, vol. 85, no. 1/4 (1994), p. 830-35.

The authors attempt to characterize the urban pollution of Madrid using the combination of conventional gas measurements and an ion-beam analytical technique for aerosol monitoring. This represents a preliminary study, the results of which (the authors hoped) would supply the trends and strategies for a more thorough investigation. Detailed and highly technical, it will be of interest only to specialists in the field.

259 **High-rise food waste separation in Madrid.**
Patricia Conway. *Biocycle*, vol. 32, no. 6 (June 1991), p. 36-38.

This short but interesting article describes the development of a pilot programme to test the feasibility of separating domestic solid wastes in Madrid and treating them in order to recover recyclable products. The author is co-director of Equipo Verdegaia in Madrid, the company which initiated the proposal (directed to the Office for the Environment in the city) to develop such a programme. At the time of writing the article, the success of the project led Conway to predict that it would be expanded.

260 **Waste management in Madrid: back to the future?**
J. Cooper. *Wastes Management* (March 1995), p. 20-21.

Although very brief, this is an interesting and more up-to-date article than that by Patricia Conway (q.v.), which looks at the problems of waste disposal and recycling in Madrid. The city generates over 3,600 tonnes of municipal waste per day. In 1995 the final phase of an elaborate materials recycling, energy recovery and composting system, handling 1,200 tonnes of this waste per day, was completed.

261 **Evolving planning systems in Madrid, Rome, and Athens.**
Frank J. Costa, Allen G. Noble, Glenna Pendleton. *GeoJournal*, vol. 24, no. 3 (July 1991), p. 293-303.

Provides an overview and comparison of the planning institutions and activities of three southern European capitals – Madrid, Rome and Athens. Each city experienced rapid growth during the 19th century, which was particularly due to their status and function as capital cities. As the authors demonstrate, over the decades there have been strong growth pressures and many city planning policies were subverted by private sector interests. In fact, it is only in the latter part of the 20th century that planning measures have really become effective in controlling and managing urban growth. This short, clearly-written article also contains a number of illustrations (maps and plans) and a list of references.

262 **Water and landscape in Madrid: possibilities and limitations.**
Fernando González Bernáldez. *Landscape and Urban Planning*, vol. 16, nos. 1-2 (Oct. 1988), p. 69-79.

This short, scholarly study considers the landscape diversity in the Madrid area related to water. The biological, microclimatic, aesthetic and agricultural interests are all considered, and the author concludes that conservation and protection policies need to reflect the requirements not only of surface and underground water quality, but also of the landscape characteristics and their associated ecosystems. Illustrated, it also contains a number of references. The same author collaborated with J. P. Ruiz on the article, 'Landscape perception by its traditional users: the ideal landscape of Madrid livestock raisers', in *Landscape Planning*, vol. 9 (1982), p. 279-97; and with F. Parra Supervía and M. A. García Quintas on 'Landscape preferences in outdoor recreation areas in Madrid' in *Journal of Environmental Management*, vol. 13, no. 1 (July 1981), p. 13-22. A further article relating to Madrid's landscape and water (although very technical in nature) is 'Quantitative study of fluvial landscapes: case study in Madrid, Spain' by V. Castillo, A. Díaz Segovia and S. González Alonso in *Landscape and Urban Planning*, vol. 16, nos. 1-2 (Oct. 1988), p. 201-17.

263 **Madrid.**
E. A. Gutkind. In: *Urban development in southern Europe: Spain and Portugal.* The Author. New York: Free Press; London: Collier-Macmillan, 1967, p. 396-409. maps. bibliog. (International History of City Development, vol. 3).

The book as a whole represents a massive survey of the origin and growth of urban civilization in Iberia, and remains a standard work on the subject. The section on Madrid describes its history, growth and topography in relation to geographic, economic and historic factors, and captures the essential features (non-architectural) of the city's development over the centuries. The clear text is complemented by detailed illustrations and maps, and this particular chapter provides the reader with an excellent and concise starting-point for understanding the growth of Madrid.

264 **Urban growth under an authoritarian regime: Spain 1939-1975: the case of Madrid.**
John Naylon. *Iberian Studies*, vol. 15, nos. 1-2 (spring-autumn 1986), p. 3-16.

This article is the first of six in a theme issue of the journal devoted to urban growth in Spain during the Franco era, with particular reference to Madrid. Versions of the papers were originally presented at the conference on 'Economic Development and Urbanization in the Periphery and Semi-Periphery' held at the Universidad Complutense de Madrid (27-30 August 1986). This introductory article emphasizes the political climate in which urban growth took place. The five case studies which follow are: 'Government policy in the production and development of Madrid's peripheral urban space: El Gran San Blas' by Fermina Rojo Pérez (p. 17-23); 'Urbanization in the western area of Madrid during the period of economic development' by Mercedes Arranz Lozano (p. 23-30); 'Accelerated urbanization and economic change in the metropolitan area of Madrid: Alcobendas – San Sebastián de los Reyes' by Enrique Pozo Rivera (p. 30-39); 'The urban transformation of Fuenlabrada: a consequence of the metropolitanization of Madrid' by José Miguel Santos Preciado (p. 39-49); and 'The dynamics of land prices and spatial development in Madrid 1940-1980' by Joaquín Bosque Maurel et al. (p. 49-59). All the articles present detailed analyses and contain maps, graphs, illustrations and bibliographies, and each of the authors are highly respected experts in the field of human geography.

265 **Analysis of the 1985 General Plan for Madrid.**
Angela Rose O'Hagan.   MSc thesis, University of Strathclyde,
Scotland, 1988. 1 vol.

This concise study presents a survey of the evolution of urban planning from the time
of Franco up to, and including, the changes experienced with the transition to a
democratic state. Part one considers the Socialist government's revision of the existing
1963 General Plan and includes coverage of the reasons behind this plan and the
effects of financial administration on it. Part two analyses the Plan of 1985 in detail.
Land policy and regulations are considered together with the housing market and
housing policy. Appendices offer insight into activities in Madrid in the late 1980s,
showing the trends in the housing market and effects of the Plan on the people of the
city. Of related interest are two Spanish-language publications: *Madrid: cuarenta años
de desarrollo urbano (1940-1980)* (Madrid: forty years of urban development [1940-
80]) (Madrid: Ayuntamiento, 1981. 239p.) which contains an interesting collection of
articles; and Sofía Diéguez Patao's *Un nuevo orden urbano: 'El gran Madrid' (1939-
1951)* (A new urban order: greater Madrid [1939-51]) (Madrid: Ministerio de
Administración Pública, 1991) that describes the plan of the first Republican
government for a 'Greater Madrid' which, rather than being based on concentric
circles spreading from the old centre, was based on transport axes centred on Cibeles
fountain.

266 **Los primeros cien años del Canal de Isabel II.** (The first hundred
years of the Canal of Isabella II.)
Madrid: Ministerio de Obras Públicas, 1954. 505p. bibliog.

In 1858 the Canal de Isabel II, bringing water from the Guadarrama mountains, was
opened, ferrying an almost unlimited supply of fresh water to Madrid. Its success as
an engineering achievement and its beneficial effects upon the lives of the population
are detailed in this interesting book, commemorating its centenary. It includes over
seventy pages of illustrations. Other works of related interest include: *El Canal de
Isabel II* by Emilio Zurano (Madrid: Pueyo, 1925. 16p.); and *Antecedentes del Canal
de Isabel II* (Forerunners of the Canal of Isabella II) by Bernardo López-Camacho y
Camacho, María Bascones Alvira and Irene de Bustamente Gutiérrez (Madrid: Canal
de Isabel II, 1986. 199p.).

267 **Planning heritage cities: comparing Madrid, Quebec City, Fez, and
Tripoli.**
Amer Shehubi Rghei.   PhD thesis, University of Waterloo, Canada,
1992. 404p. maps. bibliog.

Rghei's thesis opens with a survey of the argument that has continued over the years
as to whether heritage conservation and planning strategies should be promoted in
historic cities for economic, educational and aesthetic purposes. The importance of
preservation is emphasized and the study strongly supports the view that heritage
resources in cities like Madrid should be enhanced and promoted so that people will
be encouraged to visit, work and live in these areas. The four case studies provide in-
depth analysis of each city, and the work as a whole contains a large number of
illustrations and appendices to supplement the text.

268   **The remodelling of housing districts in Madrid.**
Fermina Rojo Pérez.   *Iberian Studies*, vol. 18, no. 1 (1989), p. 50-69.
maps. bibliog.

At the beginning of the 1970s the deterioration of Madrid's official housing schemes led to a rising tide of protest among the residents. The author describes the historical origins of the crisis in the 1950s, when industrialization led to huge migration into the capital. Housing schemes sacrificed quality for cheapness, so that twenty years later the official working-class housing estates were under threat both from physical deterioration and the efforts of land developers to move them out in the hope of profiting from rising land values. Taking advantage of Spain's democratic transition in the mid-1970s, pressure was brought to bear by residents upon central and city governments to create a housing renovation programme which embraced thirty administrative districts, almost 39,000 dwellings and over 147,000 people. A number of tables, figures, plans and photographs are included in this article.

269   **El Manzanares: río de Madrid.** (The Manzanares: river of Madrid.)
José María Sanz García.   Madrid: La Librería, 1990. 171p.
(Biblioteca Básica de Madrid).

Few geographical features of the city have so consistently failed to impress as Madrid's Manzanares river. Often ridiculed by visitors and natives alike ('a ditch learning how to be a river'), an expensive clean-up operation in the early 1980s has made a walk along its bank quite a pleasant experience. This attractive little book recounts its history (from the times it was used by washerwomen), its role in traditions and society, and the plans for the river over the centuries. Other relevant studies include: *Madrid en torno al río Manzanares* (Madrid and the Manzanares river) by Miguel Angel Torremocha (Madrid: Ayuntamiento, Servicio de Educación, 1989. 21p.); *El pequeño gran Manzanares* (The small great Manzanares) by Lucas Pellicer (Madrid: Consejería de Gobernación, 1986. 80p.); and *El río Manzanares* (The Manzanares river) (Madrid: Comunidad, Dirección General de Educación, 1986. 206p.).

270   **Ildefonso Cerdá's general theory of 'urbanización'.**
Arturo Soria y Puig.   *Town Planning Review*, vol. 66, no. 1 (Jan. 1995), p. 15-39.

This article highlights the distinctive contributions of the Spanish engineer, Ildefonso Cerdá (1815-76), to the theory and practice of modern town planning. It first examines the development of Cerdá's thought from the mid-1840s, and his definition of the term, *urbanización*, for the new scientific and integrative study and activity he proposed. Soria y Puig draws upon examples from his proposals for the 'reform' and expansion of Barcelona (1859, 1863 and 1867) and Madrid (1861), and considers in detail Cerdá's analysis and ideas for housing, the functions of streets and the vital role of *intervías* (street-blocks) in urban design. Illustrations and a bibliography are also included. Readers of Spanish who wish to investigate Cerdá's life and work more fully could usefully refer to *Teoría de la viabilidad urbana; Cerdá y Madrid* (Theory of urban viability: Cerdá and Madrid) (Madrid: Instituto Nacional de Administración Pública, 1991. 362p.), which also contains an extensive bibliography. Other studies of related interest include: *La urbanización de la Gran Vía* (The urbanization of the Gran Vía) by Eulalia Ruiz Palomeque (Madrid: Ayuntamiento; Instituto de Estudios Madrileños, 1985. 40p.), a well illustrated work by a writer who has written several books on Madrid's urban history; and *Urbanismo en Madrid durante la II República (1931-1939): política y ciudad 1931-1939* (Urban development in Madrid during the

Second Republic [1931-39]: politics and the city 1931-39) by Aurora Fernández Polanco (Madrid: Ministerio para las Administraciones Públicas, 1990. 302p. maps).

271　**New planning experiences in democratic Spain: the metropolitan planning of Madrid and the implementation of citizens' participation.**
Fernando de Terán. *International Journal of Urban and Regional Research*, vol. 5, no. 1 (1981), p. 96-105.

Urban planning had little practical success under the Franco régime. During the 1970s a massive growth in urban social movements was particularly important on the political level, most notably in the years immediately preceding and following Franco's death. This study describes the development of a programme of democratic planning in Madrid during the late 1970s. The article should be read in conjunction with Castell's article on the citizens' movement in Madrid (q.v.). The author also wrote an in-depth Spanish-language study, entitled *Madrid* (Madrid: Mapfre, 1992. 358p.), which presents a detailed survey of the planning experience in Madrid.

272　**Planeamiento urbano en la España contemporánea (1900-1980).**
(Urban planning in contemporary Spain, 1900-80.)
Fernando de Terán.　Madrid: Alianza, 1982. 631p. maps. bibliog.
(Alianza Universidad Textos, no. 39).

This remains one of the most detailed and authoritative studies of urban planning in Spain. Emphasizing the continuity and persistence of virtually unaltered principles in Spanish urban planning, the book surveys all the major plans for the development of Madrid including the *Plan General de Extensión* (State Expansion Plan) (1931) and Arturo Soria's plan for the *Ciudad lineal* (q.v.). The post-war years saw plans for the reconstruction of the city with the *Plan General de Ordenación y Extensión de Madrid* (State Organization and Expansion Plan for Madrid) (1939) and the particularly important *Plan General de Urbanización de Madrid* (State Urban Development Plan for Madrid) (1941 and 1946 law). Subsequent planning concentrated on trying to control the frightening speed of growth of the city, through the *Plan de Urgencia Social de Madrid* (Social Emergency Plan for Madrid) (1957) and the *Plan de Descongestión de Madrid* (Plan to ease congestion in Madrid) (1959). The 1941 *Plan General* (State Plan) was revised in 1963 and approved in 1964 to become the *Plan General de Ordenación Urbana del Area Metropolitana de Madrid* (State Urban Organization Plan for the Madrid Area), and witnessed the first use of the term, 'metropolitan area', in official documents. Continually revised since that time, Madrid's *Plan General* now reflects planning proposals and developments to take the city into the 21st century.

273　**Economic and social restructuring in the metropolitan area of Madrid (1970-85).**
Constanza Tobío Soler.　*International Journal of Urban and Regional Research*, vol. 13, no. 2 (June 1989), p. 324-38.

Although covering a wider area than Madrid city itself, this article presents an important study of the effects of industrial crisis and an expanding service sector on the social structure of the area. Based upon the author's Master's thesis of the same title (Madrid: Universidad Complutense, 1988. 2 vols.), it demonstrates how the immediate effect of the industrial crisis was unemployment and the way in which urban space was also affected indirectly by economic restructuring. New suburbs for professional people appeared, and a growing 'ghettoization' of the traditional residential areas of industrial workers was apparent at the time. The article includes a number of bibliographical references.

274 **Urban policies and gentrification trends in Madrid's inner city.**
Carmen Vázquez. *Netherlands Journal of Housing and the Built Environment*, vol. 7, no. 4 (1992), p. 357-76.

This interesting article was written as part of a wider research project on Madrid's social geography supported by the Spanish Ministry of Education and Science. Although based on 1986 census data (the 1991 census results had not been published at the time), the points raised and conclusions drawn by Vázquez are still relevant in the fields of housing policy and the property market in Madrid. Different sections consider a variety of topics including planning in Madrid, inner-city demography, housing rehabilitation policy, and the pilot project of the Conde-Duque area. Maps, statistical tables and references are included.

275 **Late nineteenth-century Spanish progressivism: Arturo Soria's linear city.**
Diana Vélez. *Journal of Urban History*, vol. 9, no. 2 (Feb. 1983), p. 131-64.

Arturo Soria y Mata (1844-1920) was a pioneering city planner. He was the first modern linear planner and actually constructed a pilot linear city (Ciudad Lineal) on the north-eastern outskirts of Madrid (Chamartín de la Rosa and Pueblo Nuevo districts) – the only such plan carried out until the Russian linear communities of the 1930s. Soria was a great advocate of technological innovation at a time when Spanish cities were undergoing tremendous transformations. He applied (unsuccessfully) for a permit to install Madrid's first telephone system and founded one of the early tram lines in the city. Indeed it was Soria who originated the loop tramway system which became common in many Spanish cities. For him, transportation was the key factor in planning a modern city. Thus the 'Ciudad Lineal' represented the embodiment of his planning ideas and political ideology. Conceived during the 1880s, it was not until 1894 that actual implementation of the project finally began. Political and social instability over a five-year period from 1918 to 1923, and Soria's death in 1920, eventually brought the operation to a halt. Nevertheless, the appeal of the linear city with its use of tracks as the focal point of urban organization (facilitating the quick and efficient circulation of goods and people) became the object of considerable interest outside Spain. Soria's concept of modern urban living was neatly summarized in his statement, 'For each family a house; for each house a garden'. Vélez's article provides a very good analysis of Soria's philosophy and genius in an interesting style. A number of references are included together with some fascinating plans and diagrams. For those wishing to read more on Soria's linear city there is not (as yet) any English-language treatment in book form, but the volume edited by George R. Collins and Carlos Flores, entitled *Arturo Soria y la Ciudad Lineal* (Arturo Soria and the Linear City) (Madrid: Ediciones de la Revista de Occidente, 1968. 410p.), presents a helpful anthology of articles, speeches and excerpts from books by, and about, Soria. It also contains a short biography, a useful introduction describing the development of the linear city, articles from Soria's own planning journal (the first of its kind), *La Ciudad Lineal*, and an excellent bibliography of Spanish and other linear planning. Collins also wrote two very useful articles in English describing and appraising

Soria's contribution to linear planning: 'The Ciudad Lineal of Madrid' in the *Journal of the Society of Architectural Historians*, vol. 18, no. 2 (May 1959), p. 38-53; and 'Linear planning throughout the world' in the same journal (vol. 18, no. 3 [Oct. 1959], p. 74-93).

276   **La vivienda en Madrid.** (Housing in Madrid.)
      Madrid: Comunidad, C. P. T., 1995. 193p. bibliog.

This up-to-date study contains a spatial analysis of all aspects of district housing in the Community of Madrid and includes some useful statistics on the city, including population figures by area.

277   **Conserving Madrid.**
      Martin Wynn.   *Town & Country Planning*, vol. 49 (Feb. 1980), p. 53-54.

Although short and somewhat dated, this article remains an interesting study (and the first in English) of conservation in Madrid. Wynn, an authority on town planning and conservation, concentrates on the problems of Madrid's historic centre and the steps being taken to protect it. Illustrations are included as well as a short list of references. For a more extensive study of housing policy in Spain during the same period, readers could usefully refer to Wynn's chapter, 'Spain', in *Housing in Europe* (edited by Wynn) (London: Croom Helm; New York: St. Martin's Press, 1984, p. 124-54). Focusing on the cities of Madrid and Barcelona, he discusses the early State Housing Acts, loan systems for house buyers and housing policy generally.

278   **Many plans for Madrid.**
      Martin Wynn.   *Geographical Magazine*, vol. 57, no. 4 (April 1985),
      p. 193-97.

This is an interesting, well illustrated review of the growth of Madrid. Wynn concentrates on its modern development and looks at the structural changes envisioned in the 1984 city plan. Although now primarily of interest for its historical overview, the article is still relevant when one considers the pertinent comments relating to the city's legacy of more than a century of haphazard and ill-planned growth. It includes a useful map which illustrates the expansion of the city since its earliest settlement.

**Madrid: city of the Enlightenment.**
*See* item no. 119.

**The making of an urban social movement: the citizen movement in Madrid towards the end of the Franquist era.**
*See* item no. 159.

**Citizen action and participation in Madrid.**
*See* item no. 171.

**Assessment of congestion costs in Madrid (Spain).**
*See* item no. 237.

**Golf: a conflicting recreational activity in the Madrid autonomous area (Spain).**
*See* item no. 440.

**Alfoz: Madrid, Territorio, Economía y Sociedad.** (Alfoz: Madrid, Land, Economy and Society.)
*See* item no. 502.

# Parks and gardens

279 **Parques y jardines de Madrid.** (Parks and gardens of Madrid.)
Edited by Carmen Añón Feluí.    Madrid: El Avapiés, 1994. 9 vols.
maps. bibliog.

Each volume extends to around 100 pages, describing the most famous and attractive parks or gardens of the city. Beautifully illustrated, the aim of the set is to emphasize the history and beauty of Madrid's environment. Places covered are: El Prado; Casa de Campo; Buen Retiro; Jardines de Palacio; Fuente del Berro; Parque del Oeste; Real Jardín Botánico; El Capricho de la Alameda de Osuna; and the Parque de Juan Carlos I. Readers could also refer to: *Los jardines del Buen Retiro de Madrid* (The gardens of the Buen Retiro of Madrid) by Carmen Ariza Muñoz (Madrid: Ayuntamiento, 1990. 2 vols.); and *Los jardines de Madrid en el siglo XIX* (The gardens of Madrid in the 19th century) (Madrid: El Avapiés, 1988. 307p.).

280 **El Retiro: sus orígenes y todo lo demás (1460-1988).** (The Retiro: its origins and other matters [1460-1988].)
María del Rosario Mariblanca Caneyro.    Madrid: Ayuntamiento, 1989. 317p. bibliog.

Covering nearly 300 acres, the gardens of Madrid's Retiro Park date from the 1630s when they were laid out as part of the Buen Retiro palace of Philip IV. The park itself dates back to the 15th century and in this interesting book its history and development are juxtaposed with other fascinating facts and anecdotes. Of related interest are the following works: *El Retiro, parque de Madrid* (The Retiro, park of Madrid) by María del Carmen Simón Palmer (Madrid: La Librería, 1991. 142p.), an illustrated history of the park and its attractions by a respected historian, bibliographer and member of the Institute of Madrid Studies; and *El Parque del Retiro* (The Retiro Park) by Miguel Angel Torremocha (Madrid: Ayuntamiento, Servicio de Educación, 1989. 24p.).

281 **Jardines históricos de Madrid.** (Historic gardens of Madrid.)
María Carmen Martínez, illustrated by Esther Montero.    Madrid: La Librería, 1993. 128p. maps. bibliog.

This guide proposes seven different walks through some of Madrid's historic gardens, in order to discover their historical significance, their flora and fauna and their function within the city. It is beautifully illustrated with plans of the layout of each garden and magnificent sketches of the flora and fauna to be found in each park. The same author and illustrator also collaborated on a similar work, entitled *Parques de Madrid* (Parks of Madrid) (Madrid: La Librería, 1993. 128p.). Readers may also find *Jardines madrileños* (Madrid's gardens) by Pedro Navascués Palacio of interest (Madrid: El Avapiés, 1994).

282 **The Garden of Three Cultures in Madrid.**
Francesca Mazzini. *Spazio e Societa – Space and Society*, vol. 16,
no. 62 (April-June 1993), p. 90-97.

The creation of the Juan Carlos I Park, between the airport and the Feria de Madrid
trade-fair centre, is part of the city's continuing effort to make the inner city less
congested by guiding development outwards and reducing the intensive use of the
Retiro Park in the city centre. A state-of-the-art park, it is very large and includes an
artificial river and other water features. Unfortunately, at the time of writing, it v. as
little used, principally because of the difficulty in getting there by public transport.
Many people also feel that it needs more shade. Within the park the grounds are laid
out within a ring of olive trees, flanked by cycle and jogging tracks. Inside the circle is
a series of six gardens, one of which is called the Garden of Three Cultures. This
draws on Spain's historical and cultural legacy, made up of the Arabic, Jewish and
Christian elements. Mazzini's interesting article (with parallel English/Italian text)
describes the design and highlights of the garden, and includes a number of
photographs and plans.

283 **The Alameda of the Duchess of Osuna: a garden of ideas.**
Juan F. Remón Menéndez. *Journal of Garden History*, vol. 13, no. 4
(Oct.-Dec. 1993), p. 224-40.

In 1787 the Duchess of Osuna hired the French gardener, Jean Baptiste Mulot (who
had worked on the gardens at Versailles), to create a landscape garden in the pre-
Romantic style. Cool and peaceful, the gardens are something of a romantic fantasy,
and include an artificial lake with islands in the middle. Work on restoration of the
gardens began in 1974. This illustrated article discusses different cultural aspects and
meanings of the garden, which is located close to Madrid's Barajas airport. The author
argues that the Alameda (or Capricho, as it is more formally known) was a 'Garden of
Ideas' and that its purpose 'was to be an instrument of social and moral reform within
Spanish culture'. He also challenges the belief that in Spain there were no significant
English landscape gardens. Those interested in reading more about the garden's
history and features should refer to Alice Jane McVan's 'The Alameda of the Osunas'
(*Notes Hispanic*, vol. 4 [1944], p. 113-32) and Tony Venison's 'A caprice well
named' (*Country Life* [Dec. 20th 1990], p. 46-49). Remón Menéndez is also author of
*El Parque del Oeste* (Western Park) (Madrid: El Avapiés, 1994. 120p.) in the series,
'Parques y Jardines de Madrid'.

**Guía de la Casa de Campo.** (Guide to the Casa de Campo.)
*See* item no. 59.

**Madrid en sus plazas, parques y jardines.** (Madrid's squares, parks and
gardens.)
*See* item no. 65.

# Flora and fauna

284  **Atlas provisional lepidópteros de Madrid.** (Provisional atlas of the butterflies and moths of Madrid.)
C. Gómez de Aizpurua.   Madrid: Comunidad, Agencia de Medio Ambiente, 1987. 101p. 153 maps.
Using the European map of lepidoptera as a base, the author has produced an atlas and catalogue of Madrid's lepidoptera, classifying species and incidences of sightings. Of related interest is the descriptive work, *Los anfibios y reptiles de Madrid* (The amphibia and reptiles of Madrid), by Mario García-París et al. (Madrid: Ministerio de Agricultura, Pesca y Alimentación, 1989).

285  **El Parque Zoológico de Madrid 1774-1994.** (The Zoological Park of Madrid 1774-1994.)
Miguel Jiménez de Cisneros y Baudín.   Madrid: Incipub, 1994. 126p.
Situated in the huge Casa de Campo Park (covering nearly 4,500 acres), Madrid's attractive zoo houses over 2,000 animals with over 150 species of mammals and 100 species of birds, including 29 which are endangered. Highlights include a giant panda, a parrot show and the dolphinarium. This book examines the history and development of the zoo, from its inauguration in 1774 when the people of Madrid saw exotic animals in the city for the first time. The clear, chronological survey includes detailed plans and colour illustrations of the animals. It could also be read in conjunction with the following: *El zoo de la Casa de Campo* (The zoo of the Casa de Campo) by Nieves Martín, Miguel Muñoz and Paloma Ramírez-Montesinos (Madrid: Ayuntamiento, 1987. 56p.); and Ramírez-Montesinos' *Guía didáctica del zoo de la Casa de Campo* (Educational guide to the Casa de Campo zoo) (Madrid: The Author, 1986. 91p.), which is a fully-illustrated, instructional guide to the animals in the zoo.

286  **Aves en los parques de Madrid.** (Birds in the parks of Madrid.)
Miguel Lomas, Angel Jaramillo.   Madrid: Ayuntamiento, Area de Urbanismo e Infraestructuras, 1985. 105p. (Colección Cuadernos).
Beautifully illustrated, this book is aimed at the dedicated ornithologist, but will also be useful for anyone with a general interest in the subject. It describes all the different types of birds to be seen, feeding methods, and plans of the parks. Detailed indexes are included for species and parks.

287  **Los árboles de Madrid.** (The trees of Madrid.)
Antonio López Lillo.   Madrid: Comunidad, Consejería de Agricultura y Ganadería, 1995. 212p. maps.
First published in 1948, this standard work covers the Madrid region. Beautifully produced with stunning colour photographs, it describes the range of species, their habitat and identifying features. López Lillo also wrote *Arboles singulares de Madrid* (Outstanding trees of Madrid) (Madrid: Comunidad, Consejería de Presidencia, 1994). Interested readers should also refer to Luis Martín Martín's *Arboles del Retiro* (Trees of the Retiro) (Madrid: Ayuntamiento, 1990. 245p. bibliog.), which contains a full botanical survey of species and includes numerous illustrations, indexes and plans.

288 **Guía de la flora mayor de Madrid.** (Guide to the principal flora of Madrid.)
Juan Ruiz de la Torre et al.   Madrid: Consejería de Agricultura y Ganadería, 1983. 1 vol.

This book represents a standard guide to the varied flora of Madrid. A historical study of the same subject is Carmen Añón Feluí's *Flora y paisaje del Madrid medieval* (The flora and landscape of mediaeval Madrid) (Madrid: Instituto de Estudios Madrileños, 1986. 64p.).

**Madrid a la búsqueda de su naturaleza.** (Madrid in search of its natural environment.)
*See* item no. 253.

# Architecture

289 **La Ciudad Universitaria de Madrid.** (The University City of Madrid.)
Madrid: Colegio Oficial de Arquitectos de Madrid; Universidad Complutense, 1988. 2 vols. maps. bibliog.

The University (Complutense) City was one of the largest building projects in Madrid this century, and was opened in 1928 by King Alfonso XIII. The initial project was still unfinished when it became a major battlefield during the Civil War and was severely damaged. Rebuilt by Franco, it expanded into the sprawling, monotonous compound that stands today. By far the largest campus in Madrid, it caters for around 130,000 students. The present work details the architectural plans and development of the building project and includes numerous illustrations and diagrams. For analysis of other remarkable architectural achievements in the city readers should refer to: *La Castellana, escenario de poder: del Palacio de Linares a la torre Picasso* (La Castellana, an imposing setting: from the Palace of Linares to the Picasso tower) by Francisco Azorín García and María Isabel Gea Ortigas (Madrid: La Librería, 1990. 222p.), which describes the architectural developments along Madrid's great arterial thoroughfare from 1860 (when its route was laid by Carlos María de Castro, the developer of the city's *ensanche* – 'expansion') to the present day and its high-rise, glass-tower architecture; and *Madrid no construido* (Unbuilt Madrid) by Alberto Humanes Bustamente et al. (Madrid: Colegio Oficial de Arquitectos de Madrid, 1986. 324p.), a fascinating and often surprising book which describes a series of architectural projects for the city which never left the drawing-board.

290 **Spanish design and architecture.**
Emma Dent Coad.   London: Studio Vista, 1990. 208p. bibliog.

Over the past fifteen years Spanish design, fashion and architecture have projected themselves to the forefront of the international scene. This book attempts to capture the essence of these arts in contemporary Spain, and includes a number of examples and numerous references for Madrid. Beautifully illustrated and presented, it focuses on major names (individuals, groups and companies), providing an essential analysis in a historical context. Separate chapters deal with architecture, interior design, fashion, graphic design, furniture and product design. The book also contains a chronology of 20th-century Spanish design and more than 200 colour photographs. Coad also wrote *Javier Mariscal: designing the new Spain* (London: Fourth Estate, 1991. 112p.), which considers one of Spain's most prodigious designers of the new era. Readers will also find the following useful for their references to a variety of aspects of design and fashion in Madrid: *New Spanish design* by Guy Julier (London: Thames & Hudson, 1991. 191p.); and *Spanish style* by Suzanne Slesin, Stafford Cliff and Daniel Rozensztroch, with photographs by Gilles de Chabaneix (London: Thames & Hudson, 1991. 297p.).

291 **Grand terminus: Atocha railway station, Madrid.**
Colin Davies. *Architecture*, vol. 83, no. 1 (Jan. 1994), p. 62-69.

Atocha railway station has become famous for its exciting architectural styles and use of interior space. Housing four transport centres in one (Metro, commuter station, long-distance and high-speed trains), its most prominent feature, a late 19th-century arched train shed, now contains an indoor tropical garden and food court. The new commuter terminus, designed by José Rafael Moneo, has expanded the station on to a number of different levels, all of them sunken below the surrounding roads. Davies' article clearly describes the station's architectural highlights and contains a number of photographs and plans. Of related interest is *Las estaciones ferroviarias de Madrid: su arquitectura e incidencia en el desarrollo de la ciudad* (The railway stations of Madrid: their architecture and importance in the development of the city) (Madrid: Colegio Oficial de Arquitectos de Madrid, 1980. 250p.).

292 **Iglesias de Madrid.** (Churches of Madrid.)
Pedro Francisco García Gutiérrez. Madrid: El Avapiés, 1993. 567p. bibliog. (Colección Avapiés, no. 40).

Art, religion and tradition come together in this comprehensive study of Madrid's churches. It principally details their architecture, but also examines their history and the anecdotes surrounding them. Well illustrated, the book includes an appendix listing the addresses of all the churches mentioned in the text. Readers should also refer to *Iglesias antiguas madrileñas* (Madrid's old churches) by Ramón Hidalgo Monteagudo (Madrid: La Librería, 1993. 176p.).

293 **Guía de Madrid: nueva arquitectura.** (Guide to Madrid: new architecture.)
Ramón Guerra de la Vega. Madrid: Guías de Arquitectura en la Comunidad de Madrid, 1992. 4 vols. (Guías de Arquitectura de Madrid).

This series of illustrated guides looks at Madrid's contemporary architecture and new buildings and provides a brief history and description of each. The author is the most prolific writer on the city's architecture and has written a number of standard historical and contemporary studies including: *Historia de la arquitectura en el Madrid de los Austrias, 1516-1700* (A history of architecture in Madrid under the Habsburgs, 1516-1700) (Madrid: The Author, 1984. 220p.); *Madrid, guía de arquitectura 1700-1800: del Palacio Real al Museo del Prado* (Madrid, an architectural guide 1700-1800: from the Royal Palace to the Prado Museum) (Madrid:

The Author, 1980. 85p.); *Guía de Madrid: siglo XIX* (Guide to Madrid: 19th century) (Madrid: The Author, 1993. 2 vols.); *Madrid, guía de arquitectura, 1800-1919* (Madrid, an architectural guide, 1800-1919) (Madrid: The Author, 1980. 96p.); *Madrid, guía de arquitectura, 1900-1920* (Madrid, an architectural guide, 1900-20) (Madrid: The Author, 1990. 127p.); *Madrid, 1920-1980: guía de arquitectura contemporánea* (Madrid, 1920-80: a guide to contemporary architecture) (Madrid: The Author, 1981. 141p.); and *Madrid, nueva arquitectura, 1980-1985* (Madrid, new architecture, 1980-85) (Madrid: The Author, 1985. 94p.).

294 **Guía de arquitectura y urbanismo de Madrid.** (Guide to the architecture and urban development of Madrid.)
Madrid: Colegio Oficial de Arquitectos de Madrid, 1987. 4th ed. 2 vols. maps. bibliog.

Produced by a team of architects and art historians, under the auspices of the Official College of Madrid Architects, this excellent two-volume work provides a distinct architectural guide to the city, relating the buildings to successive plans, reforms and urban renewal in Madrid. Volume one covers the old central part of Madrid up to the middle of the 19th century, whilst volume two considers the *ensanche* (expansion), the periphery of the city, the growth northwards and growth since the 1940s. The winner of a local government prize in 1984, the guide is very well produced with detailed illustrations and descriptions of buildings. It includes comprehensive indexes by building, street and name, as well as an extensive bibliography and cartography. Readers interested in this subject should also refer to another useful publication produced by the College, entitled *Guía de arquitectura de Madrid* (Guide to the architecture of Madrid) (Madrid: Colegio Oficial de Arquitectos de Madrid, 1992. 369p.), which considers the architecture of the 300 most important buildings in the city and is profusely illustrated.

295 **Arquitectura y arquitectos madrileños del siglo XIX.**
(Nineteenth-century architecture and architects of Madrid.)
Pedro Navascués Palacio. Madrid: Instituto de Estudios Madrileños, 1973. 391p.

This is one of the best works on the subject of Madrid's 19th-century architectural growth and includes forty pages of illustrations. Of related interest are: *Arquitectura madrileña del siglo XVII: datos para su estudio* (Seventeenth-century architecture of Madrid: study data) by Virginia Tovar Martín (Madrid: Instituto de Estudios Madrileños, 1983. 904p.), an expert in this field and one of the most prolific writers on the city's architectural history; *Arquitectura y clases sociales en el Madrid del siglo XIX* (Architecture and social classes in 19th-century Madrid) by Clementina Díez de Baldeón (Madrid: Siglo XX, 1986. 608p.), another excellent study; and *Juan Gómez de Mora (1586-1648): arquitecto y trazador del rey y maestro mayor de obras de la villa de Madrid* (Juan Gómez de Mora, 1586-1648: royal architect and planner and master craftsman of the town of Madrid) (Madrid: Ayuntamiento, Concejalía de Cultura, 1986. 417p.), a superb, illustrated biography of Philip III's chief architect and the man who was responsible for buildings such as the Plaza Mayor (completed in 1619), the Casa de la Villa (Town Hall) and the Real Monasterio de la Encarnación (Royal Monastery of the Incarnation).

**El Observatorio Astronómico de Madrid: Juan de Villanueva, arquitecto.**
(The Astronomical Observatory of Madrid: Juan de Villanueva, architect.)
*See* item no. 62.

**El ayer de Madrid, el Madrid de hoy.** (The Madrid of yesteryear, Madrid today.)
*See* item no. 91.

**The new Plaza Mayor of 1620 and its reflections in the literature of the time.**
*See* item no. 105.

**Royal palaces of Spain: a historical and descriptive account of the seven principal palaces of the Spanish kings with 164 illustrations.**
*See* item no. 384.

**Enciclopedia de Madrid.** (Encyclopaedia of Madrid.)
*See* item no. 509.

**Bibliografía básica de arquitectura en Madrid: siglos XIX y XX.** (A basic bibliography of architecture in Madrid: 19th and 20th centuries.)
*See* item no. 530.

# Education

296 **La Escuela de Madrid: un ensayo de filosofía.** (The Madrid School: a study of philosophy.)
José Luis Abellán, Tomás Mallo. Madrid: Asamblea de Madrid, 1991. 200p. bibliog.

The Madrid School was the name given by Julián Marías Aguilera to characterize the philosophy of a group of 20th-century thinkers, including Miguel de Unamuno, Ortega y Gasset and Marías himself. This interesting study recounts the influence of their philosophy on the process of renewal and innovation in the city's education system during the period of the Second Republic (1931-36).

297 **Alcalá before reform: the decadence of a Spanish university.**
George M. Addy. *Hispanic American Historical Review*, vol. 48 (Nov. 1968), p. 561-85.

The University of Alcalá de Henares was founded in 1508 by Cardinal Jiménez de Cisneros, and soon rivalled Salamanca as one of the great Spanish seats of learning. The old university town (19 miles/31 km from Madrid) is also famous as the birthplace of Miguel de Cervantes (1547) and as the place of publication of the first polyglot Bible (1514-17), with simultaneous translations into Greek, Latin and Hebrew. The University was moved to Madrid in 1836 and Alcalá's importance as a centre of learning consequently diminished (in 1977 a new university was opened in what is now a fairly industrial city of 50,000 inhabitants). Addy explores the university's history, focusing on the aspiration of its founder for it to 'give Spain a great center of learning that would marry humanism and theology'. However, through a detailed study of its administration and educational standards, he argues that the University suffered from a 'stifling institutional decadence, which was doing grave damage to both teaching and learning'. Eventually, in the 1760s and 1770s, changes were brought to bear through the work of reformers and ministers in Alcalá and Madrid, although Addy concludes that 'Spanish universities of the nineteenth century continued to bear marks of the earlier decadence'. For an interesting and colourful history of Madrid's universities readers should refer to *La universidad en Madrid:*

*presencias y aportes en los siglos XIX y XX* (The university in Madrid: its presence and contribution during the 19th and 20th centuries) (Madrid: Consejo de Universidades, Secretaría General Madrid, 1992. 394p.), which represents a catalogue of an exhibition held in Madrid's Cultural Centre in 1992. The corresponding texts and commentaries describe the university's place in Madrid's cultural life and provide a detailed, historical analysis of university development in the city.

298 **Oxford y Cambridge en Madrid: la residencia de estudiantes, 1910-1936, y su entorno cultural.** (Oxford and Cambridge in Madrid: the student hall of residence, 1910-36, and its cultural environment.) John Crispin.   Santander, Spain: Sur, 1981. 171p. bibliog. (La Isla de los Ratones: Narración y Ensayo, no. 23).

Born in Belgium in 1934, the author emigrated to the United States in 1954, and has written extensively on the subject of Spanish literature, where his principal interest is the Generation of 1927 poets. The present work recounts the history of the student residence in Madrid (subsequently home to researchers of the CSIC – Higher Council for Scientific Research). The building is particularly important as many of its residents were prominent writers, artists and thinkers of the 1920s, including García Lorca, Emilio Prados, Salvador Dalí and Luis Buñuel. Future Nobel Prize-winners began their careers researching in its laboratories and H. G. Wells, Marie Curie and Paul Valéry were amongst its long list of notable speakers at conferences which were held there. Crispin's chronicle of the Residence's history is aimed at the general reader, and the second part of the book reproduces texts and documents of the time relating to the Residence generally, music and its science laboratories. Several photographs and illustrations are also included.

299 **Evaluation and decision making in the Complutense University of Madrid.** Juan Fernández.   *Higher Education Management*, vol. 4, no. 3 (Nov. 1992), p. 336-45.

Founded in 1508, the Complutense University of Madrid is one of the largest universities in the world, with over 5,000 teaching staff and around 130,000 students. In 1983 the Rectorate of the University selected a group of researchers to prepare a questionnaire with which to carry out the evaluation of the teaching quality. This article analyses the evaluation and decision-making processes, emphasizing the importance of students and faculty members within them. Examples of the questionnaire are included, together with a number of references. The University publishes two periodicals which contain a wealth of data and statistics relating to its courses and teaching: *Gaceta de la Complutense* (Complutense Gazette); and *Memoria de la UCM* (Annual Report of the UCM).

300 **Professional expectations and career motivations among engineering students: a case study of the students of the Telecommunications School of the 'Universidad Politécnica de Madrid', Spain.**
Santiago Lorente. *Frontiers in Education Conference* (1994), p. 245-49.

This short paper summarizes a survey which was carried out in February 1994, and focuses on the relationships between career motivations and the professional expectations of the students. Of related interest is the paper presented at the previous year's conference by S. Lorente, G. L. Araujo and R. Meza, entitled 'Academic failure in the first school year of the Telecommunications School of the "Universidad Politécnica de Madrid"' in *Frontiers in Education Conference*, vol. 38, no. 9 (1993), p. 326-31.

301 **Case study analyses of the origin and evolution of two American university study-abroad programs in Madrid, Spain.**
Maureen McCabe. EdD thesis, George Peabody College for Teachers of Vanderbilt University, Tennessee, 1991. 169p. bibliog.

McCabe's research outlines two study-abroad programmes that offer American students a dual opportunity of cultural integration and foreign-language acquisition. In particular, she highlights and analyses student impressions of their stay in Madrid.

302 **La enseñanza en Madrid: análisis de una función urbana.**
(Education in Madrid: analysis of its function.)
Ana Olivera Poll. Madrid: Instituto de Estudios Madrileños, 1978. 420p. maps. bibliog. (Biblioteca de Estudios Madrileños; no. 23).

Thorough and highly detailed, this study was the first to fully survey and analyse the education system and its functioning in Madrid. Four principal aspects are considered: firstly, facts, data and statistics are presented relating to all aspects of education provision in the city; secondly, the theory and practice of the services offered to, and demanded by, the citizens of Madrid are discussed; thirdly, every facet of university education is examined, including demographic and social factors; and finally, a concluding chapter looks at the impact of education in the city, including student mobility and student transport services. An outcome of the author's doctoral thesis, this work is aimed at specialists in education, urban geography and sociology. Despite its age, its value is retained through its wealth of statistical data, detailed city maps and plans, and the continuing validity of many of the author's arguments and conclusions. Unfortunately, the lack of an index presents a problem for the reader wishing to study a particular topic comprehensively.

303 **La educación de la mujer en el Madrid de Isabel II.** (The education of women in Madrid during the reign of Isabella II.)
Aurora Rivière Gómez. Madrid: Dirección General de la Mujer, 1993. 199p. bibliog. (Mujeres en Madrid).

With the development of the industrial society it became clear to governments that there was a need to extend education to the population as a whole. In Spain, during the reign of Isabella II (1833-68), a national system of education was established, but as the division of labour by sex persisted, it led to a somewhat different system for women. The present book considers the arguments which were made for this split, and examines education laws and the practicalities and possibilities for women wishing to educate themselves at this time.

304 **La enseñanza privada seglar de grado medio en Madrid (1820-1868).** (Private lay education at college level in Madrid [1820-68].)
María del Carmen Simón Palmer.   Madrid: Instituto de Estudios Madrileños, 1972. 438p. bibliog. (Biblioteca de Estudios Madrileños, no. XV).

By a prolific writer on Madrid, this detailed study examines private education in Madrid from its introduction in 1820 until 1868 when a revolution overthrew the monarchy of Isabella II. Various chapters discuss distinct aspects of Madrid's private education system including its aims, the people involved, its administration, the education of women, the colleges of Madrid (including women's colleges) and the subjects taught. Numerous appendices, an extensive bibliography and indexes complete the work. For a very brief survey of the British Council's private school in Madrid, readers should refer to Catherine Ormell's article, 'Far too good to be unique' in the *Times Educational Supplement*, no. 4,053 (4 March 1994), p. A3. Noting that it is the only British Council School in the world (known locally as 'El Británico'), she describes how it has grown rapidly since it was opened in 1940. Offering a bilingual and bicultural education, it charges high fees but still has nearly 2,000 students.

305 **El movimiento estudiantil en la crisis del franquismo: la Universidad Complutense (1973-1976).** (The student movement during the crisis of the Franco years: the Complutense University [1973-76].)
Gregorio Valdelvira González.   Madrid: Universidad Complutense, 1992. 1,080p. bibliog.

This massive study of the student movement during the critical periods of Franco's rule and the transition to democracy presents a comprehensive analysis of the subject. The historical perspective, political and educational factors, and the many problems involved are all considered and given due attention and space. Other works of related interest include: *Los movimientos estudiantiles (1900-1936)* (Student movements [1900-36]) by José Cepeda Adán (Madrid: Ayuntamiento; Instituto de Estudios Madrileños, 1985. 54p.); *El movimiento estudiantil en Madrid* (The student movement in Madrid) by A. Camarero González (Madrid: Universidad Complutense, Facultad de Ciencias Políticas y Sociología, 1979. 1 vol.); and *Los estudiantes de Madrid en el siglo de oro* (The students of Madrid during the Golden Age) by José Simón Díaz (Madrid: Ayuntamiento; Instituto de Estudios Madrileños, 1966. 48p.).

306 **The Free School of Madrid: a limited discussion.**
D. A. K. Whitlock.   MA thesis, University of Sussex, England, 1970. 73p. bibliog.

The Free School of Madrid (Institución Libre de Enseñanza) opened its doors to students on 29 October 1876. Its founder was Spain's great educational reformer, Francisco Giner de los Ríos (1839-1915), whose aim was to create a new educational environment equally free of Church and State control. He saw reform in the education of Spain's youth as the only sure path towards permanent reform elsewhere, and dedicated his life to the education of a 'generation more cultured, more serious, more worthy, more honourable'. Labelled the Spanish Socrates by Unamuno, Giner was appointed Rector of the School in 1880, and in his inaugural address officially declared that henceforth the School would be mainly a junior-secondary institution. The School closed in the spring of 1937 when the siege of Madrid and the Civil War generally made teaching impossible: identified with the Republican Left, it could never be reopened under the Franco régime. Whitlock's dissertation provides a clearly-written outline history and evaluation of the School. The *Boletín de la Institución Libre de Enseñanza* (Bulletin of the Free School of Madrid), which first appeared in 1877, was revived in 1987 (Madrid: Fundación Francisco Giner de los Ríos, 1987- . quarterly), and carries articles relating to education, philosophy and culture. The standard work for the history of the School is *La Institución Libre de Enseñanza y su ambiente: período parauniversitario* (The Free School of Madrid and its milieu: the para-university period) by Antonio Jiménez-Landi Martínez (Madrid: Taurus, 1973-87. 3 vols.).

**La Ciudad Universitaria de Madrid.** (The University City of Madrid.)
*See* item no. 289.

**Information science in the Universidad Autónoma de Madrid: developments with the times.**
*See* item no. 450.

**Revista de la Universidad Complutense.** (Journal of the Complutense University.)
*See* item no. 507.

# Science and Technology

307 **Ingeniería madrileña durante la Restauración.** (Engineering in Madrid during the Restoration.)
Pilar Corella Suárez.   Madrid: Ayuntamiento, 1994. 104p. bibliog.
(Aula de Cultura; El Madrid de Isabel II).

The Restoration régime in Spain lasted from 1874 to 1931, and this up-to-date study describes the important subject of engineering developments over a fifty-year period in Madrid. The author also wrote *Puentes madrileños en la época isabelina* (Bridges of Madrid during the reign of Isabella II) (Madrid: Ayuntamiento, 1993. 72p.); and *Bibliografía de bibliografías locales* (A bibliography of local bibliographies) (Madrid: Biblioteca Nacional, 1987. 32p.) (q.v.).

308 **Primeros pasos de la luz eléctrica en Madrid y otros acontecimientos.** (The arrival of electric lighting in Madrid and other events.)
José María García de la Infanta.   Madrid: Fondo Natural, 1986. 203p. bibliog.

This work details the development and installation of electric lighting in Madrid (1883) and its effect on people's lives. It also describes other important technological and social advances which took place during this period, such as railways and new factories. Of related interest is the detailed study, *El gas y los madrileños (1832-1936)* (Gas and the Madrilenians) by María del Carmen Simón Palmer (Madrid: Gas Madrid, 1989. 302p.), which describes the introduction of gas to the city in the 1830s and its importance to the city's inhabitants.

309 **Early computer developments in Madrid.**
José García Santemases. *Annals of the History of Computing*, vol. 4, no. 1 (Jan. 1982), p. 31-34.

The author briefly considers early computer developments and related topics at the University of Madrid and the Institute of Electricity and Automatics at the Consejo Superior de Investigaciones Científicas (CSIC – Higher Council of Scientific Research) during the 1950s and 1960s. Analogue and digital systems are discussed as well as international developments. An extensive bibliography on the subject is included in the article.

310 **Interactive science in Madrid.**
*Siemens Review*, vol. 61, no. 4 (July/Aug. 1994), p. 24-25.

This short, illustrated article provides an introduction to Madrid's Acciona Museo Interactivo de la Ciencia (Interactive Museum of Science), which opened in 1993. In addition to interactive exhibitions, screens and experimentation sections, the museum also offers facilities for symposia and laboratories for visiting school classes. It is particularly aimed at stimulating an interest in science in the young.

311 **Parque Tecnológico de Madrid (P. T. M.).** (The Science Park of Madrid.)
Madrid: IMADE, 1987. 56p.

Produced by the city's Institute for Development, this short booklet describes the history and development of, and facilities at, Madrid's science park. Also of interest for the innovation and development of science and technology in Madrid is *Ciencia y tecnología en Madrid* (Science and technology in Madrid) by José Molero and Mikel Buesa (Madrid: Fundación Universidad-Empresa, 1992. 174p.).

**De Madrid al cielo: Planetario de Madrid.** (From Madrid to the heavens: Madrid's Planetarium.)
*See* item no. 61.

**El Observatorio Astronómico de Madrid: Juan de Villanueva, arquitecto.** (The Astronomical Observatory of Madrid: Juan de Villanueva, architect.)
*See* item no. 62.

**Nuevas tecnologías en la industria madrileña.** (New technology in Madrid's industry.)
*See* item no. 227.

**Los primeros cien años del Canal de Isabel II.** (The first hundred years of the Canal of Isabella II.)
*See* item no. 266.

**El Ateneo científico, literario y artístico de Madrid (1835-1885).** (The scientific, literary and artistic Athenaeum of Madrid [1835-85].)
*See* item no. 352.

**Insula.** (Island.)
*See* item no. 485.

**Médicos madrileños famosos: biografías y bibliografías de médicos ilustres, nacidos en Madrid y su provincia.** (Madrid's famous doctors: biographies and bibliographies of illustrious physicians, born in Madrid and its province.) *See* item no. 512.

# Literature

312 **Locos: a comedy of gestures.**
Felipe Alfau, afterword by Mary McCarthy.   Harmondsworth,
England: Viking, 1990. 206p.

Felipe Alfau was born in Barcelona, but emigrated to the United States during the
Second World War, where he studied music and wrote music criticism for a brief
period for *La Prensa* (the Spanish newspaper in New York). Deciding to write in
English because he felt he could not reach a Spanish audience, he completed *Locos* in
1928 and took eight years to find a publisher (Farrar & Rinehart, 1936). After its
publication Alfau gave up writing, and after working in a bank as a translator he
retired in New York City. The interconnected stories that form this novel take place in
an exotic Madrid and feature unforgettable characters, comedy and surrealistic effects.
Each chapter is a complete short story in its own right and, despite Alfau's mock
warning that the characters are mere puppets, the reader discovers 'beneath a more or
less entertaining comedy of meaningless gestures, the vulgar aspects of a common
tragedy'.

313 **Madrid, distrito federal.** (Madrid, federal district.)
Juan Jesús Armas Marcelo.   Barcelona, Spain: Seix Barral, 1994.
275p.

The prize-winning writer set this latest novel in the Spanish capital. He is also a
contributor to both Spanish and Spanish-American newspapers and magazines.

314 **Madrid.**
Azorín, edited by Manuel Lacarta.   Madrid: El Avapiés, 1988. 214p.
bibliog. (Biblioteca Matritense).

Azorín was the pseudonym used by José Martínez Ruiz (1873-1967), one of Spain's
most famous essayists and novelists. The present work has been published in several
editions over the years and represents Azorín's writings on the people and places of
Madrid.

315 **Materiales para escribir Madrid: literatura y espacio urbano de Moratín a Galdós.** (Writings on Madrid: literature in an urban setting from Moratín to Galdós.)
Edward Baker. Madrid: Siglo Veintiuno, 1991. 152p. bibliog. (Lingüística y Teoría Literaria).

Written by a distinguished professor of Spanish literature at the University of Florida, this has become a standard work on Madrid's urban and social settings as described in 18th- and 19th-century works by some of the city's most famous writers. Chapter one examines Moratín's *La comedia nueva o El café* (New drama or The coffee-house) (1792) (Madrid: Espasa-Calpe, 1995. 24th ed.), a satire against what he considered to be the excesses of the Madrid theatre, while chapter two looks at a short newspaper article by Larra about Madrid's public gardens. Chapter three is given over to one of Madrid's greatest 19th-century chroniclers, and one of Spain's leading exponents of the genre known as *cuadros de costumbres* (sketches of manners), Mesonero Romanos. Chapter four is dedicated to popular Madrid novelists during the reign of Isabella II (1833-68), while the concluding chapter is devoted to Galdós's works and, in particular, to his novel, *La fontana de oro* (The golden fountain) (1871), set in Madrid during the early 1820s. Richly detailed, Baker's work is required reading for any serious study of Madrid in literature.

316 **Pérez Galdós, Spanish liberal crusader.**
Hyman Chonon Berkowitz. Madison, Wisconsin: University of Wisconsin Press, 1948. 499p. bibliog.

Despite its age, this remains the fullest biography of Benito Pérez Galdós (1843-1920), the writer who is generally recognized as Spain's greatest novelist after Cervantes, and one of Madrid's most famous residents and chroniclers. Born in the Canary Islands, he arrived in Madrid as a student in 1862 and developed such an immediate and overriding obsession with the city that whenever possible he would go out walking and observe the people and bustling life both on the streets and in the cafés and theatres. Frequently compared to Dickens, Balzac and Dostoevsky, his vast output as a novelist is divided between works chronicling key moments in Spain's political history (his *Episodios nacionales* [National episodes]) and novels on contemporary life (which constitute his greatest achievement). His intimate portrayals of Madrid have never been equalled, and this talent is most clearly exemplified in his epic novel, *Fortunata y Jacinta* (1986-87) (q.v.). Berkowitz (late Professor of Spanish at the University of Wisconsin) minutely dissects the life of this great writer, emphasizing how Galdós constantly strove to inspire the Spaniards with a national conscience and to learn to know themselves. The book also contains a full list of the published works of Galdós, numerous bibliographical references and a full index. Readers wishing to delve deeper into Galdós's work should consult the following: Hensley C. Woodbridge's *Benito Pérez Galdós: a selective annotated bibliography* (Metuchen, New Jersey: Scarecrow Press, 1975); Theodore A. Sackett's *Pérez Galdós: an annotated bibliography* (Albuquerque, New Mexico: University of New Mexico Press, 1968); Sherman H. Eoff's *The novels of Pérez Galdós* (St. Louis, Missouri: Washington University Press, 1954); and Walter T. Pattison's competent biography, *Benito Pérez Galdós* (New York: Twayne, 1975).

317 **Servants and their masters: a novel.**
Fergus Reid Buckley. London: Hodder & Stoughton, 1975. 607p.

Set in Madrid during 1967, the novel has as its theme the relationship between the titled, middle and working classes. The plot circles around a planned sexual scandal which was designed to destabilize Madrid society and which took place at the same time as the Six-Day War between Israel and the Arab states. After its original publication in 1973 (New York: Doubleday) it received mixed reviews. The popular magazines praised its complex plot and characterization, whilst more respected periodicals, although noting the amount of effort and research that went into the book, criticized its cold-blooded and detached approach, and even more scathingly its triteness, self-indulgent prose and pointless inflation of minor facts.

318 **The Madrid writer in Spanish society: 1833-1843.**
Anne Victoria Burdick. PhD thesis, University of California, San Diego, 1983. 358p. bibliog.

Burdick's thesis describes the place of literary activity in Madrid society at the height of the Romantic movement in Spain between 1833 and 1843. She examines the political, social and economic implications of authorship during these years and also analyses the importance of the relationships between the Madrid literary community and Madrid society. A collective biography of 120 active Madrid authors provides the documentation for recreating the pattern of an author's life, his world and what it meant to be a writer in Madrid during the Romantic decade. Her approach throughout is historical rather than literary. In December 1996 a promising historical survey by Michael Ugarte was due to be published: *Madrid 1900: the capital as cradle of literature and society* (University Park, Pennsylvania: Pennsylvania State University Press). The same publisher also planned to publish *Spanish comedy and contexts in the 1620s* by William R. Blue in late 1996, which would consider, amongst other topics, literature and society in 17th-century Madrid.

319 **Cervantes en Madrid: vida y muerte.** (Cervantes in Madrid: life and death.)
Juan Antonio Cabezas. Madrid: Ayuntamiento, 1990. 175p. bibliog.

The author has written prolifically on Madrid's history, and this book presents an authoritative illustrated biography of Spain's most renowned novelist, Miguel de Cervantes Saavedra (1547-1616), author of *Don Quijote* and one of Madrid's most famous inhabitants. He lived on the Calle León, and it is probable that he was buried in the Trinitarian convent on Calle Lope de Vega (a detail made more confusing by the fact that Lope de Vega's old house in Madrid is situated on the Calle Cervantes!). Studies of Cervantes' and Lope's lives and works run into thousands, but readers may find it useful to consult some of the following in the first instance: *Cervantes: a biography* by William Byron (London: Cassell, 1979. 583p. bibliog.); *Cervantes* by Melveena McKendrick (Boston, Massachusetts: Little Brown, 1980. 310p. bibliog.); *Cervantes* by Peter Edward Russell (Oxford: Oxford University Press, 1985. 117p. bibliog.); *Cervantes: en busca del perfil perdido* (Cervantes: in search of a lost profile) by Jean Canavaggio (Madrid: Espasa-Calpe, 1992. 2nd rev. ed.); *Anales Cervantinos* (Cervantes studies) (Madrid: Consejo Superior de Investigaciones Científicas, Instituto de Filología; annual); *Bibliography of Lope de Vega* by Raymond Leonard Grismer (Minneapolis, Minnesota: Burgess-Beckwith, 1965. 2 vols.); and *Nueva biografía de Lope de Vega* (A new biography of Lope de Vega) by Cayetano Alberto de la Barrera y Leirado (Madrid: Atlas, 1973-74. 2 vols.).

320 **The hive.**
Camilo José Cela, translated by J. M. Cohen in consultation with
Arturo Barea.   London: Sceptre, 1992. 215p.

Camilo José Cela Trulock was born in Galicia in 1916, and is one of Spain's greatest writers. His mother was English and his brother is the novelist, Jorge C. Trulock. He has been awarded many prizes, including the Spanish literary prize, The Prince of Asturias, and, in 1989, the Nobel Prize for Literature. Originally published in Buenos Aires as *La colmena* in 1951 (and banned in Spain in the same year), *The hive* (Cela's fourth novel) was first published in English in 1953 and was made into a film in 1982. Set in Madrid in the aftermath of the Spanish Civil War (1943), Cela's masterpiece deals with poets, prostitutes, fools, homosexuals and the poor who frequent Doña Rosa's sordid café. The hundreds of characters shelter, literally and metaphorically, in the café, and disappear as quickly as they appear. The Madrid portrayed is one of misery, rationing and hunger. The characters' grey and sad lives in the cells of the hive are masterfully dissected by Cela, where all the action takes place within a period of three days. The book was received with great critical acclaim upon its publication: 'a riveting portrait of post-Civil War Madrid' (*The Observer*); 'its depiction of everyday life in Madrid after the Spanish Civil War is as shocking today as it must have been to the Spanish censor who banned the book in 1951' (*The Sunday Correspondent*). Two other works by Cela are worthy of mention here for their relevance to Madrid: *Madrid: calidoscopio callejero, marítimo y campestre . . . para el reino y ultramar* (Madrid: urban, rural and maritime kaleidoscope . . . for locals and foreigners) (Madrid: Alfaguara, 1966), a collection of essays and sketches about the city; and *The eve, feast and octave of Saint Camillus of the year 1936 in Madrid*, translated by J. H. R. Polt (Durham, North Carolina: Duke University, 1991), Cela's third novel, first published in 1969, which focuses on the lower classes in Madrid during the early days of the Civil War.

321 **The Maravillas district.**
Rosa Chacel, translated by D. A. Démers, introduction by Susan
Kirkpatrick.   Lincoln, Nebraska; London: University of Nebraska
Press, 1992. 283p. (European Women Writers Series).

Born in Valladolid in 1898, Rosa Chacel spent several years in Italy studying art. Before the Civil War she had acquired a modest literary reputation with her short stories, poetry and novel. After 1939 she went into exile, travelling to Paris, Athens, Geneva and, in 1940, to Rio de Janeiro, where she remained until 1972 when she returned to Spain. Ironically, her fame as a novelist was only fully recognized in 1987 when she was awarded the National Prize for Spanish Letters in recognition of her lifetime achievement. *The Maravillas district* (originally published in Spanish in 1976 as *Barrio de Maravillas*) is the first novel in an autobiographical trilogy, and regarded by critics as her best. Proustian in its use of memory, it traces two girls' discovery of their artistic and intellectual vocations whilst living in a small apartment in a somewhat seedy area of Madrid between 1912 and 1914. Throughout the novel there is strong emphasis on artistic locations in Madrid such as the Prado, the Athenaeum and the Academy of San Fernando.

322 **In the palace of the King: a love story of old Madrid.**
Francis Marion Crawford. London; New York: Macmillan, 1900.
363p.

Francis Crawford (1854-1909) was born in Italy and educated in the United States and England. He had a great gift for languages and travelled extensively in Europe and India. Author of over forty novels, his books were popular and remunerative. His novels depended largely on the complications of plot, but it was their vivid characterization and richness of detail which led to their success, although this has now waned. This novel, a love story set in 16th-century Madrid and centred around the court of Philip II, includes other historical figures of the time such as Don Juan of Austria, Antonio Pérez and the Princess of Eboli. A number of descriptive illustrations accompany the text.

323 **Especial Madrid.** (Madrid special issue.)
*Leer*, no. 73 (summer 1994), whole issue.

The entire ninety-page issue is devoted to a variety of aspects of the city including: Madrid in literature and poetry; books about Madrid; Madrid in the theatre; Madrid in education and philosophy; life and industry in the capital; and Madrid as seen by foreign visitors and writers. The Spanish text is accompanied by a large number of illustrations and photographs.

324 **Europeos en Madrid.** (Europeans in Madrid.)
Madrid: Instituto de Estudios Madrileños, 1992. 12 vols. bibliog.
(Madrid Capital Europea de la Cultura).

Published to coincide with Madrid's year as European Capital of Culture (1992), this series encompasses a wide variety of cultural facets of the city. Each volume contains around fifty pages and is representative of cultural links between Madrid and one of the member states of the European Union. Thus there are volumes on Victor Hugo in Madrid, Rilke in Madrid, *Recuerdos italianos* (Italian recollections), and *Recuerdos ingleses* (English recollections), related to art, literature and culture. Each volume includes illustrations.

325 **La Puerta del Sol.** (The Sun Gate.)
Fernando Fernán Gómez. Madrid: Espasa-Calpe, 1996. 4th ed. 267p.

The author has written several descriptive works on Madrid, and in this novel he uses his extensive knowledge of the city's history and geography to maximum effect. The story centres on a young poor girl, Mariana Bravo, during the years surrounding the Spanish Civil War (1936-39), and her life in, and around, the heart of Madrid, the Puerta del Sol.

326 **Madrid! Madrid!**
Alan E. Fisher. London: Robert Hale, 1980. 192p.

This popular novel tells the story of Spencer, a pilot with the International Brigade during the siege of Madrid in the winter of 1936. The author has taught history and did national service with the RAF.

327 **Madrid y sus literaturas: de la Generación del 98 a la postguerra.**
(Madrid and its literature: from the Generation of '98 to the postwar era.)
Manuel Lacarta.   Madrid: El Avapiés, 1986. 173p. bibliog.

This fascinating study looks at the presence and descriptions of Madrid in the literature of poets, playwrights and novelists over a period of seventy-five years. It examines the changing geography of Madrid without overlooking the history and social conditions of the city. Commencing with the Generation of 1898 (a group of writers connected by their recognition of the inability of the mind to make sense of human existence), Lacarta moves on through the work of Ramón Gómez de la Serna, the poets of the Generation of 1927 and the literature of the Spanish Civil War (1936-39). The concluding chapters discuss Madrid as portrayed in literary works between 1939 and 1975 (the Franco era), and the search by its inhabitants for an identity as defined through its literature and writers.

328 **The monk: a romance.**
Matthew Gregory Lewis, edited with an introduction by Howard Anderson.   London: Oxford University Press, 1973. 455p. bibliog. (Oxford English Novels).

First published in 1796, this work has become a classic amongst gothic novels. The theme of the story is the sexual repression at the heart of asceticism. It recounts the story of Ambrosio, the devout superior of a Capuchin monastery in Madrid, succumbing to the temptations of Matilda, a Devil-inspired wanton who, disguised as a boy, enters the monastery as a novice. The opening chapter sets the scene of Madrid in the days of the Inquisition, although subsequent pages do not offer any great detail on the city. Grove Press (New York) published a reprinted edition in 1993.

329 **Another man's wife.**
Torcuato Luca de Tena, translated by John Marks.   London: Constable, 1965. 309p.

Luca de Tena (b. 1923) is a member of the Spanish Royal Academy and worked as a journalist for the newspaper, *ABC* (q.v.), during the 1950s and 1960s. This prize-winning novel's setting ranges from Madrid to Central Africa, with its central theme being that of desertion.

330 **Madrid en la Literatura.** (Madrid in Literature.)
Madrid: Comunidad, Consejería de Educación y Cultura, 1992- . ongoing.

This series represents an ambitious project by the Community of Madrid to produce a range of anthologies covering all aspects of Madrid as represented in literature. Different volumes are dedicated to specific forms of writing, and thus there are subseries for: *Madrid en la Novela* (Madrid in the Novel) (1992- . 4 vols. already published); *Madrid en el Teatro* (Madrid in Drama) (1994- . 1 vol. already published); *Madrid en la Poesía* (Madrid in Poetry) (1993- . 2 vols. already published); *Madrid en la Prosa de Viaje* (Madrid in Travellers' Accounts) (1992- . 3 vols. already published); and *Madrid en el Texto* (Madrid in Prose) (1995- . 1 vol. already published). Similarly, the 'Clásicos Madrileños' (Madrid Classics) series (Madrid: Comunidad, Consejería de Educación y Cultura; Castalia, 1992- . ongoing) aims to offer a range of classic works which were either written in Madrid or have Madrid as their setting. Almost ten volumes have already appeared, including works by Lope de Vega (*Tres comedias madrileñas* [Three Madrid comedies] [1992. 355p.]); Mesoneros Romanos (*Memorias de un setentón* [q.v.]); Tirso de Molina (plays); Carvajal y Saavedra (eight novels); and Francisco Santos. Other 'classic' works for possible inclusion in the series are: Padre Luis Coloma's two-volume novel, *Pequeñeces* (Trivia) (1890), which created a furore over its satirical attack on the Madrid aristocracy during the first year of the Restoration in 1874; Ayguals de Izco's popular novels (including *La bruja de Madrid* [The witch of Madrid], published in the 1840s), which were read avidly by the Madrid lower classes (he was also founder of the important Madrid printing house, 'Sociedad Literaria'); Pío Baroja's *La lucha por la vida* (The struggle for life), a trilogy first published in 1904 which opened the eyes of a generation to the condition of the poor and underprivileged in Madrid; and Valle-Inclán's trilogy, *El ruedo ibérico* (The Iberian ring) (1927-28), an evocation of life in the Madrid of Isabella II, its court, corruption and social classes.

331 **Time of silence.**
Luis Martín-Santos, translated by George Leeson. New York: Columbia University Press, 1990. 247p. (Twentieth-Century Continental Fiction Series).

Originally published in Spain as *Tiempo de silencio* in 1962, this was Martín Santos's first and only complete novel. Born in Morocco in 1924, a qualified surgeon and psychiatrist, he was killed in a road accident at the age of thirty-nine before completing his second novel, *Tiempo de destrucción* (Time of destruction). Set in Madrid during the late 1940s, *Time of silence* is regarded by many as a 'classic' work of its time, and renowned for its depiction of character and innovative treatment of reality. The author was praised particularly for his observation of the slum environment of Madrid's lower classes, his style of 'dialectic realism' and his mirroring (through Pedro, the protagonist) of the tragic life of Spaniards of all classes in post-war Spain, victimized by science, the Church and their own sexuality. Introducing into Spanish the linguistic complexity of James Joyce's *Ulysses*, Martín-Santos has also been compared to Albert Camus and Jean-Paul Sartre in relation to the 'novel of the absurd'. Specific aspects of Madrid in the novel have been closely studied in: Sheri Long's 'An anatomy of Madrid in Luis Martín-Santos's *Tiempo de silencio*' (PhD thesis, University of California, Los Angeles, 1990); her short article, 'El instituto: Madrid as a structuring device and the poetization of space in "Tiempo de silencio"' in *Selected proceedings of the thirty-ninth annual mountain interstate foreign language conference*, edited by Sixto E. Torres and Carl S. King (Clemson, South Carolina: Clemson University Press, 1991, p. 63-67); Michael Ugarte's article, 'New historicism and the story of Madrid: "Fortunata y Jacinta" and "Tiempo de silencio"' in *Anales Galdosianos*, vol. 25 (1990), p. 45-52; and G. Pérez Firmat's 'Repetition and excess in "Tiempo de silencio"' in *PMLA*, vol. 96 (March 1981), p. 194-209. In Spanish there is the useful publication by Eduardo Galán Font, entitled *El Madrid de 'Tiempo de silencio'* (Madrid: Ayuntamiento, Servicio de Educación, 1991. 42p.).

332 **The 'kidney' of Madrid: the literary image of the Barrio de Lavapiés.**
Thérèse Marie Mirande.   PhD thesis, University of Washington, Seattle, Washington, 1993. 128p. bibliog.

The *barrio* (neighbourhood) of Lavapiés was the centre of Madrid's mediaeval Jewish community, and although pretty run-down today it has a lot of character and is home to Madrid's fringe theatre. Mirande's study looks at the image of the *barrio* in literature through the years. Lope de Vega and Tirso de Molina both referred to it in their plays. Subsequently the area was described and discussed in the works of Ramón de la Cruz, Galdós, Emilio Carrère and Arturo Barea, and in Martín-Santos's *Tiempo de silencio* (q.v.).

333 **Prince of shadows.**
Antonio Muñoz Molina, translated by Peter Bush.   London: Quartet Books, 1993. 196p.

Originally published in Spanish under the title, *Beltenebros* (Barcelona, Spain: Seix Barral, 1989), this psychological thriller is set in the Madrid of the early 1960s. Muñoz Molina is a writer, critic and journalist who contributes regularly to the daily newspapers, *ABC* and *El País* (qq.v.). He has won the Premio Nacional de Literatura (National Prize for Literature) twice with *El invierno en Lisboa* (Winter in Lisbon) in 1982 and *El jinete polaco* (The Polish horseman) in 1992. The present novel tells the story of Darman, a professional killer and political exile hired to return to Madrid and execute a traitor who has betrayed his comrades in the anti-Franco resistance. Madrid's architecture and the dark, glistening streets of the city by night are wonderfully evoked. In 1992 the film of the book was released: directed by Pilar Miró and starring Terence Stamp and Patsy Kensit, it was received by some critics as 'flawed but fascinating', but was particularly praised for the art design and the use of Madrid locations. Muñoz Molina's prolific output also includes *Los misterios de Madrid* (The mysteries of Madrid) (Barcelona, Spain: RBA, 1995. 192p.) in the series, 'Obras Maestros de la Literatura Contemporánea' (no. 25).

334 **The fell of dark.**
James Norman.   London: Michael Joseph, 1960. 288p.

This novel owes something to Arturo Barea's *The clash* (q.v.), as it recounts a story set in the last days of the Civil War (1936-39). At the heart of the tale is Don Luis Sanromán, a great philosopher, whose son and daughter are fighting on the Republican side in Valencia. Although initially set in Madrid, much of the subsequent action takes place in Valencia. The title comes from a poem by Gerald Manley Hopkins.

335 **Cinco escritores y su Madrid: Galdós, Azorín, Baroja, Rubén Darío y Ramón.**
(Five writers and their Madrid: Galdós, Azorín, Baroja, Rubén Darío and Ramón.)
Mario Parajón.   Madrid: Prensa Española, 1978. 174p.

In five separate chapters Parajón discusses the Madrid described by each of the authors in their works. The chapter on Galdós (1843-1920) naturally emphasizes the Madrid that is minutely detailed in *Fortunata y Jacinta* (q.v.). For Azorín (1873-1967), the analysis encompasses his book, *Madrid* (q.v.), and within it the importance of the portrayal of the Prado Museum. Baroja's (1872-1956) trilogy on Madrid's poor and lower classes (*La busca* – The hunt; *Mala yerba* – Bad grass; *Aurora roja* – Red dawn), first published in 1904, is the subject of chapter three. The study of Rubén Darío's (1867-1916) poetry concentrates on Darío's Latin American roots and his views on women in Madrid. The final chapter looks at the works of one of Madrid's greatest and most prolific chroniclers, Ramón Gómez de la Serna (1888-1963): in particular, Parajón considers his histories and descriptions of the Puerta del Sol, Plaza Mayor, Cava Baja, Paseo de la Castellana, Plaza de la Paja and the Rastro (flea market). Unfortunately no index or bibliography is included in this work, which nevertheless remains a standard study of Madrid in literature.

336   **Escritores madrileños.** (Writers of Madrid.)
      Enrique Pardo Canalís.   Madrid: Ayuntamiento; Instituto de Estudios
      Madrileños, 1986. 24p.

This is a brief survey of Madrid's principal writers and updates some of the biographical sketches contained in *Escritores ilustres madrileños: apuntes para un álbum biográfico-literario* (Famous Madrid writers: sketches for a biographical-literary album) by Arturo Viala (Madrid: Tip. de Segundo Martínez, 1879. 79p.).

337   **Troteras y danzaderas.** (Procuresses and dancing girls.)
      Ramón Pérez de Ayala.   Madrid: Castalia, 1991. 430p. (Clásicos
      Castalia; no. 52).

Pérez de Ayala (1880-1962) is regarded as one of the masters of the early 20th-century Spanish novel. First published in 1913, *Troteras y danzaderas* is a *roman-à-clef* on Madrid Bohemian life in 1910. The novel follows the career of Alberto Díaz de Guzmán (Pérez de Ayala's *alter ego*), a young man who suffers from lack of will and aimlessness. It describes the literary world of the poets, the cafés and the boarding-houses in Madrid, and the disillusioned Alberto concludes that Spain has produced only 'procuresses and dancing girls'.

338   **Fortunata and Jacinta: two stories of married women.**
      Benito Pérez Galdós, translated with an introduction by Agnes Moncy
      Gullón.   London: Penguin, 1988. 818p.

Arguably the greatest novel to have come out of 19th-century Spain, this is Galdós's masterpiece. Set in Madrid during the 1870s, it details the life of a spoiled young man from a wealthy middle-class background, and the destructive jealousy of the two women who love him: one his wife, the other his mistress. The main part of the action takes place around the Plaza Mayor, but as the novel unfolds a truly panoramic picture of Madrid emerges, with its developing wealthy suburbs to the north, and the slum dwellings to the south. One of the main attractions for present-day readers of his works is that the city he so vividly describes is still immediately recognizable today, even down to some of the smallest details. Originally published in Spain in 1886-87, the novel has become a classic amongst European literatures and has been translated into a number of languages. A book in Spanish which focuses specifically on the role of the city in the novel is Farris Anderson's *Espacio urbano y novela: Madrid en 'Fortunata y Jacinta'* (The urban setting and the novel: Madrid in 'Fortunata and Jacinta') (Madrid: José Porrúa Turanzas, 1985). Professor Anderson counted over 700 allusions to Madrid place-names in the novel, and through a series of street maps, text, prints and a seventy-page census of Madrid's streets and places, he describes and interprets the wealth of detail about the city contained in the novel. A plethora of articles and critical studies consider Galdós's use of Madrid and its history in his works, including: *Anales Galdosianos* (Galdós Studies) (Ithaca, New York: Cornell University; International Association of Galdós Scholars, 1966- . annual); Geoffrey Ribbans' *Pérez Galdós: Fortunata y Jacinta* (London: Grant & Cutler, 1977); and the specific article by Phyllis Zatlin Boring, 'The streets of Madrid as a structuring device in Fortunata y Jacinta' in *Anales Galdosianos*, vol. 13 (1978), p. 13-22. Two other novels by Galdós are particularly relevant for their Madrid setting. *The spendthrifts* (London: Weidenfeld & Nicolson, 1953) was inspired by life within the Royal Palace, and deals with the months leading up to the flight of Isabella II and her court in 1868. Galdós focuses on the Palace's minor functionaries and specifically on the spendthrift wife of the miserly Bringas. *Miau* (London: Penguin, 1966) is also full of descriptions of, and events in, Madrid during the late 19th century. It is the tragic story of a civil servant, Ramón Villamil, with the title evoking his cries for help as well as referring to the cat-like features of his wife, sister-in-law and daughter. The area around the Plaza de España is particularly well described in the novel.

339 **Madrid.**
Benito Pérez Galdós.    Madrid: Afrodisio Aguado, 1957. 253p.

Galdós's best writings reflected his intimate knowledge of, and love for, Madrid. The present study, which is prefaced by an essay by José Pérez Vidal, is a compilation of his articles published in *La Nación* (a progressive Madrid newspaper) and *El País* (newspaper of Las Palmas, Canary Islands: Galdós's birthplace). The articles selected include those which convey his first impressions of Madrid on his arrival from Las Palmas in 1862. These encompass items on the fiestas, the Manzanares river and walks around the city, all published in 1865. The next section reproduces a paper describing the Madrid of his youth, written fifty years later in 1915. Two final chapters contain some of his writings on music (1865) and his observations on the novel in Spain (1870). The work as a whole provides interesting insights into the author's feelings about the city, and his descriptions of the time are detailed and evocative. It is a pity, however, that the book does not contain a list of further readings or an index. Numerous editions of Galdós's work are available, together with critical studies, but the following are particularly helpful for those looking at Galdós and Madrid: 'Galdós' "pueblo": a social and religious history of the urban lower classes in Madrid, 1885-1898' by Peter Bernard Goldman (PhD thesis, Harvard University, Massachusetts, 1972); *Pérez Galdós: an annotated bibliography* by Theodore A. Sackett (Albuquerque, New Mexico: University of New Mexico Press, 1968); and *Madrid en Galdós, Galdós en Madrid* (Madrid in Galdós, Galdós in Madrid) (Madrid: Comunidad, 1988), a catalogue of an exhibition of his works held in the Palacio de Cristal del Retiro in 1988.

340 **The Flanders panel.**
Arturo Pérez Reverte, translated by Margaret Jull Costa.    London: Harvill, 1994. 295p.

Pérez Reverte is one of Spain's most acclaimed young writers. He has made his career in journalism and television news, but has received international recognition as a novelist. His previous novel, *The fencing master*, was made into a film which was also well received. The present work was a bestseller in Spain and won an award in France. A complex novel of intrigue, it is set in the Madrid art world and is an ingenious crime thriller, with clues embedded both in the details of a 500-year-old painting and a highly sophisticated game of chess.

341 **Bibliografía literaria de Madrid.** (Literary bibliography of Madrid.)
Compiled by Matilde Sagaró Faci. Madrid: Concejalía de Educación,
Juventud, Deportes y Coordinación del Ayuntamiento; El Avapiés,
1993. 352p. bibliog.

This is a very useful and beautifully presented book, which includes photographs,
street plans and illustrations, and a comprehensive bibliography of the authors and
literary texts on Madrid. Five chapters (divided by historical periods) cover Madrid's
principal literary figures, including Cervantes, Lope de Vega, Ramón de la Cruz,
Moratín, Larra, Mesonero Romanos, Pérez Galdós, Unamuno, Baroja, García Lorca
and Cela. The eleven writers are all inextricably linked in one way or another to the
city of Madrid, and each of the chapters considers the writers and their works within
the relevant period of the city's history. The volume also includes a selection of
literary texts on Madrid throughout the centuries. Although certain important writers
are missing (Calderón de la Barca, for example), Sagaró Faci suggested that more
volumes on other writers could follow. A series entitled 'Cuadernos Madrileños'
(Madrid Notebooks), published by the Servicio de Educación del Ayuntamiento de
Madrid, already includes a number of volumes on the same writers with the titles, *El
Madrid de . . .* (The Madrid of . . .). Each includes a bibliography, a selection of
writings and street plans of Madrid.

342 **Madrid underground: a Superintendent Bernal novel.**
David Serafin. London: Collins, 1982. 212p.

David Serafin is the pseudonym of Ian Michael, author of a series of crime novels
whilst Professor of Spanish at the University of Oxford. Bestsellers in Spain, his
books have been critically acclaimed for their attention to detail and realistic
descriptions of Madrid's history, politics and pageantry. Set in Madrid during the run-
up to Spain's first general election for forty-one years (1977), this story combines the
author's extensive knowledge of the city with that of Spanish forensic methods. The
action centres around Madrid's Metro stations (indeed, the station names head each
subsection of the book) where a psychopath is at large. The task of catching the killer
falls to the 'Maigret of Madrid', Superintendent Luis Bernal. The finale takes place on
general election day itself, deep in the Madrid underground network. A plan of the
Metro system is included, which shows the principal stations featured in the story.
Serafin's first crime novel, *Saturday of glory* (London: Collins, 1979) is similarly set
in Madrid, and has been praised by critics for its evocation of Madrid's atmosphere
and as a 'lovingly written guide to much of Madrid'. It was the winner of the Crime
Writers Association John Creasey Award for the best first crime novel of 1979. His
later novel, *Port of light* (London: Collins, 1987), again has Superintendent Bernal as
the protagonist, with the setting switching between Madrid and other locations.

343 **Mariano José de Larra: a directory of historical personages.**
Alvin F. Sherman. New York; Berlin: Peter Lang, 1992. 552p.
bibliog. (American University Studies: Series II, Romance Languages
and Literature, vol. 196).

Born in Madrid (1809), Larra is one of Spain's most famous Romantic writers and
Madrid's most notable essayist and satirist, despite his short life (he committed
suicide in 1837). Considered the founder of Spanish journalism, he wrote under a
number of pseudonyms, but most frequently as 'Fígaro' after the character by
Beaumarchais. His most famous satirical essay, *Vuelva usted mañana* (Come back

tomorrow), attacked procrastination and Spanish bureaucracy, and was the inspiration for the use of the word *mañana* (tomorrow) to denote the delaying attitude perceived by many foreigners as characteristic of the Spanish way of doing things. Many of Larra's other essays and articles shed further light on various aspects of Madrid society and public life. Sherman's scholarly study is the most recent and complete analysis of Larra's sources in literature and history, and is particularly valuable for its extensive and up-to-date bibliography which includes a number of references to articles specifically related to Madrid in Larra's writings. Other works of interest by Larra are *Artículos literarios* (Literary works) (Barcelona, Spain: Plaza & Janés, 1985. 361p.); and his *Artículos de costumbres* (Articles of customs and manners) (Madrid: Espasa-Calpe, 1995. 5th ed. 456p.). For a scholarly analysis of such 'articles' as they appeared before Larra's time, readers should refer to 'The "artículo de costumbres" in the periodicals of Madrid 1700-1808' by Albert Eddy Lyon (PhD thesis, University of Wisconsin, 1929), although it may prove difficult to locate.

344  **Guía literaria de Madrid.** (Literary guide to Madrid.)
José Simón Díaz.  Madrid: Instituto de Estudios Madrileños;
La Librería, 1993-94. 2 vols.

This set contains an extensive selection of writings on all aspects of Madrid from the 16th to the 20th century. With over 1,000 writers included, the work has become one of the most useful and interesting literary studies of the city. Volume one considers the area within the boundaries of the old city walls, and contains 327 extracts from around 160 authors, looking at topics such as nature, the town's inhabitants and the Manzanares river. Volume two moves to the areas outside the walls, including the working-class districts, paying particular attention to spectacles and festivities, and the Rastro and Lavapiés quarters. Both volumes are well indexed. Of related interest is *Geografía literaria de la provincia de Madrid* (Literary geography of Madrid province) by José Fradejas Lebrero (Madrid: Instituto de Estudios Madrileños, 1958. 260p.).

345  **Madrid 1940: memorias de un joven fascista.** (Madrid 1940:
memories of a young fascist.)
Francisco Umbral.  Madrid: Planeta, 1993. 246p.

Born in 1935, Umbral is one of Spain's most talented and prolific (and most-read) writers, and one who writes in a variety of styles (journals, novels, short stories, essays and biographies). Many of his novels are autobiographical and a large number deal with post-Civil War Spain in general, and Madrid in particular. The present novel develops on three levels. Firstly, it recounts the story of a young falangist who arrives in Madrid just after the end of the Civil War in order to make a career in politics or writing. On a second level, the novel recounts the cruelty and repression of the Franco régime in the immediate aftermath of the General's victory. Finally, it directly relates events of the time through the appearance of real-life characters of the period in Madrid, purposely juxtaposing their hectic social life with the torture and murder which were taking place in Madrid's prisons. Other works by Umbral which relate to Madrid include *Amar en Madrid* (To love in Madrid) (Barcelona, Spain: Destino, 1991 [first published in 1977]), which contains a number of descriptions of Madrid's districts, buildings, people, customs and idiosyncrasies; *Retrato de un joven malvado* (Portrait of a young villain) (Barcelona, Spain: Destino, 1986. 2nd ed.), a non-fiction work which presents a graphic portrait of Madrid life in the early 1970s through its world of people, cafés, *pensiones* and streets, while the writer searches for his own identity; *Spleen de Madrid 2* (Madrid's vile humour 2) (Barcelona, Spain: Destino,

1982); *Travesía de Madrid* (Travelling through Madrid) (Barcelona, Spain: Destino, 1974); and *La noche que llegué al Café Gijón* (The night I arrived at the Café Gijón) (Barcelona, Spain: Destino, 1977), which contains some wonderfully evocative descriptions of Madrid.

346  **Trilogía de Madrid: memorias.** (Madrid trilogy: memoirs.)
Francisco Umbral.   Barcelona, Spain: Planeta, 1984. 337p.
(Colección Narrativa; no. 71).

The singularity of Umbral's prose and his richness of style are clearly evident in this trilogy of works. Together they make up an 'autobiography' of Madrid in the 20th century, from Galdós the novelist to Colonel Tejero and the coup attempt of 1981. Descriptions of famous people and places are intermingled with real and imaginary events in Madrid's history. An extensive index of names concludes the volume.

**The new Plaza Mayor of 1620 and its reflections in the literature of the time.**
*See* item no. 105.

**Pedro Calderón de la Barca and Madrid's theatrical calendar, 1700-1750: a question of priorities.**
*See* item no. 403.

**Luis Candelas, el bandido de Madrid.** (Luis Candelas, the bandit of Madrid.)
*See* item no. 426.

**Tertulias of Madrid.**
*See* item no. 433.

**Insula.** (Island.)
*See* item no. 485.

# The Arts

## General

**347  Aproximación al arte de la Comunidad de Madrid.** (An introduction to the art of the Community of Madrid.)
V. Cuevas Fernández, Ramón Hidalgo Monteagudo.   Madrid: Comunidad, Dirección General de Educación, 1995. 196p.

This volume studies the artistic trends within the region of Madrid throughout the centuries, and links them to the political and social developments of the time.

**348  Postales antiguas de Madrid.** (Old postcards of Madrid.)
Reyes García, Ana María Ecija.   Madrid: La Librería, 1994. 4 vols.

Wonderfully evocative of the city and its bygone years, this superb collection of postcards provides an illustrated history of the city between 1900 and 1930. Each card is described and commented upon with regard to the social, political and cultural events of the time. The first three volumes include postcards accompanied by commentaries by inhabitants of the city who were children during the period covered. The fourth volume provides a complete catalogue of the old postcards held in the archives of the Museo Municipal de Madrid. The collection as a whole is a remarkable artistic achievement and is also an extremely useful source of information for researchers and those interested in Madrid's local history.

**349  Guía de jóvenes artistas de Madrid.** (A guide to young artists of Madrid.)
Madrid: Comunidad, Dirección General de la Juventud, 1993. 2 vols.

Resident artists of Madrid and its province are described, together with their work. In volume one handicrafts, design, sculpture, photography and painting are highlighted, whilst volume two concentrates on dance, literature, music, theatre and cinema.

350 **Madrid: art and culture.**
Madrid: Comunidad de Madrid, Consejería de Economía, [s.d.]. 36p.
(Madrid Art and Customs Collection).

Published in the early 1990s, this pamphlet is one of several in a series which is aimed at the English-speaking tourist in Madrid. Available from most Spanish tourist offices and those in Madrid, it provides a useful introductory survey to the arts in the capital, concentrating on the wealth of museums and art galleries. Addresses and opening hours are included, together with a number of colour illustrations and other useful information.

351 **Madrid arts guide.**
Claudia Oliveira Cezar. London: Art Guide Publications, 1989. 109p.
3 maps. (Art Guide Series).

The author resides in Madrid, and at the time of writing this guidebook she was involved in promoting contemporary art in the city. It is a comprehensive guide aimed at both art specialists and travellers in general, and is recommended by a number of important and well-known periodicals such as *The Sunday Times*, *Vogue*, *The Bookseller* and *Art Monthly*. Unfortunately, some of the contents have now become slightly dated and readers would have to double-check facts such as opening times and other data. Nevertheless, this pocket-size guide provides a wealth of facts and details relating to all aspects of the arts in Madrid including: museums; galleries; cultural centres; art critics; art schools; art fairs; palaces and places of architectural interest; and design shops and fashion. There are also over twenty pages providing general background information on Madrid. Well illustrated and lively, as well as informative, the volume includes a number of photographs, illustrations and maps, as well as a plan of Madrid's Metro system.

352 **El Ateneo científico, literario y artístico de Madrid (1835-1885).**
(The scientific, literary and artistic Athenaeum of Madrid [1835-85].)
Antonio Ruiz Salvador. London: Támesis Books, 1971. 186p.
bibliog.

The Ateneo of Madrid was founded in 1820 and was to become one of the great intellectual and cultural institutions of Spain. It became a meeting-place and centre for discussion and debate, particularly in the years leading up to the Second Republic of 1931, and enjoyed a reputation as a centre of Liberal politics. The repressiveness of Ferdinand VII's régime (1813-33) had the effect of stimulating Madrid's intellectual life and the Ateneo devoted itself to the furtherance of the arts and sciences. The original building was soon closed down by the King because of its politics, but on the initiative of Mesonero Romanos and other members of his intellectual circle, it was reopened in 1835 on the Calle del Prado. The present building at no. 21 dates back to the 1880s and boasts a particularly impressive interior, housing one of Spain's largest and finest libraries. It also contains a vast, oval lecture theatre and rows of portraits of some of Spain's greatest intellectuals. Ruiz Salvador's history details the events which led to its foundation, its closure and re-establishment, and its role in Madrid's cultural life. He also wrote a further study of the Ateneo, entitled *Ateneo, dictadura, república* (Athenaeum, dictatorship, republic) (Valencia, Spain: Levante, 1976. 284p.).

353 **Recalling the Golden Age: collections and taste in Madrid, 1833-1868.**
Oscar Enrique Vázquez.   PhD thesis, University of California, Santa Barbara, 1989. 513p. bibliog.

This study analyses the collections and patronage of art during the reign of Isabella II (1833-68). It traces the changing patterns of collection policies of private individuals, the State and the Church, and also provides a comparison of art collections and collecting in France.

**Madrid.**
*See* item no. 9.

**Madrid and Toledo.**
*See* item no. 33.

**Madrid: architecture, history, art.**
*See* item no. 42.

**Art Libraries Journal.**
*See* item no. 448.

**Insula.** (Island.)
*See* item no. 485.

**El Punto de las Artes.** (Arts Focus.)
*See* item no. 501.

# Painting

354 **A corpus of Spanish drawings, vol. 2: Madrid 1600-1650.**
Diego Angulo, Alfonso E. Pérez-Sánchez, translated by Nicholas Wyndham.   London: Harvey-Miller, 1977. 199p. bibliog.

This beautifully produced work presents more than 400 drawings of the Madrid School. The artists concerned were all active in Madrid between 1600 and 1650, and some even go beyond this period. Most of the volume is taken up with the work of Vicente Carducho (1576-1638), Eugenio Cajés (1574-1634) and Antonio de Pereda (1611-78), the most prominent and prolific artists at the Madrid court. All the artists known by name are listed alphabetically with brief biographical sketches and a catalogue of their drawings, grouped broadly by subject matter. They are followed by drawings whose attribution is in doubt, and groups of anonymous drawings. The 443 black-and-white illustrations form the bulk of the work. Several indexes (names, locations and themes) are included as well as an extensive bibliography. Of related interest is *Collections of paintings in Madrid, 1601-1755*, edited by Marie L. Gilbert (Munich; New York: K. G. Saur, 1995. 900p.), another beautifully made guide to the principal collections and individual works.

## 355  The School of Madrid.

Aureliano de Beruete y Moret.  London: Duckworth; New York:
Charles Scribner's, 1909. 288p. bibliog. (The Library of Art).

Translated from the author's original Spanish manuscript by Beatrice Steuart Erskine,
this standard work studies the period of Spanish painting in Madrid after Velázquez
(1599-1660) to the time of its decline under the influence of the Italian artist, Luca di
Giordano (1632-1705). As the author notes, Velázquez gave the impetus to, and
inaugurated, the Madrid School of Painting which lasted from 1623, the year in which
he arrived at court, until the end of the 17th century and the death of Claudio Coello
(1693). Generally speaking, the book covers those painters of the town and the court
who worked during the reigns of the last two Habsburg monarchs of Spain, Philip IV
(1621-65) and Charles II (1665-1700). The painters of the School of Madrid include
Juan Bautista Martínez del Mazo, the Rizi brothers (Juan and Francisco), Juan
Carreño de Miranda, Mateo Cerezo and the illustrious artist, Claudio Coello.
Accessible to the non-specialist, Beruete's work has become an authoritative source
on what was, at the time of writing, a little-known school of painting. It includes
numerous black-and-white illustrations which exemplify each artist's work.

## 356  Velázquez: painter and courtier.

Jonathan Brown.  New Haven, Connecticut; London: Yale University
Press, 1986. 322p. bibliog.

Recognized as one of the world's greatest painters, Velázquez was not only court
painter under Philip IV (1621-65), but also an important court official in his own right.
Brown, a highly respected art historian and author of many works on Spanish art, has
produced in this volume the most comprehensive study in English of Velázquez.
Dissecting the aims and achievements of the artist, he also provides the most detailed
biography, including a full account of his role as court official (a role that occupied an
increasing amount of his time and severely restricted the number of pictures he was
able to paint). Indeed, he emphasizes 'his ambition to be considered both a great
painter and a great gentleman in a court society that held painters in low esteem' as
the central dilemma of Velázquez's career. Lavishly produced and elegantly written, it
includes over 300 magnificent illustrations (many in colour), a list of Velázquez's
paintings and drawings, an extensive bibliography and a highly detailed index.

## 357  Corrado Giaquinto at the Spanish court, 1753-1762: the fresco cycles at the new Royal Palace in Madrid.

Irene Cioffi.  PhD thesis, New York University, 1992. 3 vols.

Corrado Giaquinto (1703-66) was called to the Madrid court in 1753 by Ferdinand VI
to serve as his first painter. Soon after, he was appointed as the head of the Royal
Tapestry Factory of Santa Barbara and as the first director of the newly-established
San Fernando Royal Academy of Fine Arts. His main endeavour during his ten-year
tenure of the post of first painter was his role in the decoration of the Royal Palace, the
building which had been commissioned by Philip V to replace the Alcázar which had
burnt down in 1734. Giaquinto's pre-eminent position in Madrid led to him greatly
influencing painters of the time and succeeding generations of Spanish painters, most
notably Goya. Cioffi's thesis analyses the artist's frescoes for the Royal Palace, with
volume one providing the text, volume two supplying a documentary appendix and
volume three containing illustrations of the frescoes.

358   **Antonio López, painter of Madrid.**
Max Kozloff.   *Art in America*, vol. 81, no. 10 (Oct. 1993), p. 94-101,
p. 157.

Antonio López García (1936- ), ultra-realist painter, sculptor and draughtsman, has been hailed as 'the undisputed master of contemporary Spanish figurative art', but is virtually unknown outside Spain. Nevertheless, he was already painting at the age of thirteen, and after several solo exhibitions in Madrid he was invited to participate in the 1964 Carnegie International, as well as the New York World's Fair. In subsequent years his subjects became more limited and his technique more elaborate, and because of this and periods of self-doubt, it was not unusual for him to work on a painting or sculpture over several years. Kozloff's article looks at the artist's output (which includes cityscapes, domestic interiors and portraits of his own family) at a time when examples of his work were being exhibited at the Reina Sofía Art Gallery. A resident of Madrid, much of his work depicts Madrid cityscapes and skylines, and the article contains a number of colour and black-and-white illustrations of his canvases. López García was the subject of Victor Erice's film, *El sol del membrillo* (The quince tree sun) (1992), which documented his painting technique.

359   **Madrid: el arte de los 60.** (Madrid: art of the 60s.)
Madrid: Comunidad, Dirección General de Patrimonio Cultural, 1990.
445p.

Presents a catalogue of a wide selection of the most prominent artists of a decade which was fundamental to the development of contemporary art. The exhibition took place in May 1990 and marked the inauguration of the Community of Madrid's new Sala de Exposiciones (Exhibition Hall). Of related interest are the exhibition catalogues: *23 artistas: Madrid, años 70* (23 artists: Madrid, the 1970s) (Madrid: Comunidad, Dirección General de Patrimonio Cultural, 1991. 204p.); and *Artistas en Madrid: años 80* (Artists in Madrid: the 1980s) (Madrid: Comunidad, Dirección General de Patrimonio Cultural, 1992. 249p.).

360   **La pintura de la época isabelina en la prensa madrileña.** (Painting
in the Madrid press during the reign of Isabella II.)
Esperanza Navarrete Martínez.   Madrid: Fundación Universitaria
Española, 1986. 139p. bibliog.

This interesting, illustrated study considers the use of art in the Madrid press during the reign of Isabella II (1833-68).

361   **Baroque painting in Madrid: the contribution of Claudio Coello
with a catalogue raisonné of his works.**
Edward J. Sullivan.   Columbia, Missouri: University of Missouri
Press, 1986. 293p. bibliog.

During the period between 1650 and 1700 great artistic activity could be witnessed in Madrid. A number of artists contributed great works to the city's art and architecture in both the religious and secular arenas. Many of the painters of the so-called School of Madrid were not born there, but rather were attracted to the capital by the possibilities of court, ecclesiastical and private patronage. During the 17th century great churches, monasteries and convents were built in Madrid, adorned with elaborate and ambitious schemes of painting and sculpture. Subsequent plans for modernization and urban development in the later 19th and early 20th centuries sadly accounted for the destruction of some of these wonderful buildings. Nevertheless, Sullivan's book focuses on the masters who epitomized the Baroque style in Madrid during the second half of the 17th century. He aims to present the major personalities and styles of the period, whilst concentrating on the greatest artist of the time, Claudio Coello. Indeed, Sullivan's study is the first detailed biographical and critical work in English on Coello and includes an illustrated catalogue of the artist's surviving works. In addition, he examines Coello's principal contribution to the history of late 17th-century art in Spain, the 'Sagrada Forma' altarpiece. An extensive bibliography is included, together with a number of helpful and detailed appendices relating to collections of Coello's paintings.

362 **Goya in the twilight of enlightenment.**
Janis A. Tomlinson.  New Haven, Connecticut; London: Yale
University Press, 1992. 240p. bibliog.

Francisco José de Goya y Lucientes (1746-1828) began his career executing cartoons for the Royal Tapestry Factory (founded by Philip V in 1521) and went on to become one of the most characteristically Spanish artists of all time, and one of the most important figures in the history of European art. Nevertheless, Tomlinson argues that 'the common perception of Goya comprises documented fact and myth, inextricably intermeshed'. In this stimulating study she reviews and revises fundamental beliefs about the artist, and sheds new light on areas of both his life and work. After examining the social history of the times, she discusses some of Goya's most famous works and his relations with his patrons at the Madrid court. Clearly written and beautifully produced, with a wealth of colour and black-and-white illustrations, this remains a standard work for any serious study of Goya. Tomlinson also wrote several other important works on Goya, including: *Francisco Goya y Lucientes 1746-1828* (London: Phaidon, 1994), an authoritative and up-to-date survey of the artist (lavishly illustrated with numerous full-colour plates), concentrating on the range of Goya's works and their social and political context; and *Francisco Goya: the tapestry cartoons and early career at the court of Madrid* (Cambridge, England: Cambridge University Press, 1989), which provides an in-depth critical appraisal and interpretation of a specific area of Goya's work. Numerous texts and catalogues are available on Goya and his life and work in Madrid, but two standard volumes which are particularly accessible to the general reader are: *Goya* by José Gudiol (London: Thames & Hudson, 1966) in the 'Library of Great Painters' series, which contains 127 illustrations with 48 full-colour plates and a selected bibliography; and *Goya: a witness of his times* by Pierre Gassier (London: Alpine Fine Arts Collection, 1985), which provides a thorough biography and study, and similarly includes a large number of colour and black-and-white illustrations and a selected bibliography.

**The cities of Spain.**
*See* item no. 73.

# Museums and art galleries

363　**Artwise Madrid: the museum map.**
New York: Streetwise Maps, 1994.

This glossy, fold-out map highlights the principal art galleries and museums of Madrid, and represents a companion pocket-map to *Streetwise Madrid* (q.v.). Gallery and museum opening hours and entrance charges are provided, and an index of buildings gives full map references. The useful guide also contains a general floor plan of the Prado Museum.

364　**Museum of the Royal Academy of Fine Arts in Madrid.**
Leticia Azcue. *Museum*, vol. 39, no. 3 (1987), p. 201-04.

The San Fernando Royal Academy of Fine Arts was founded in 1752, whilst its museum was officially opened in 1774 – thus making it the oldest art institution in Madrid. Its collection of paintings ranges from the 16th century to the present day. It contains many items from the Spanish School, including works by Goya, Velázquez, Ribera, El Greco and Murillo. Flemish and Italian paintings are well represented, and the museum also houses a valuable collection of plans and drawings such as those of Prado architect, Juan de Villanueva, as well as an interesting collection of rare books. Azcue's article provides a brief, general introduction and includes several interior photographs of the museum.

365　**Boulevard of the arts: Madrid's great museums, Prado, Thyssen, Reina Sofía.**
Madrid: Comunidad de Madrid, Consejería de Economía, [s.d.]. 32p.
(Madrid Art and Customs Collection).

This pamphlet is aimed at the English-speaking tourist in Madrid, and contains information which also appears in a companion volume in the series, entitled *Madrid: art and culture* (q.v.). It describes the history and background of each of Madrid's 'golden triangle' of museums (so called because of their geographical locations). Their principal collections are highlighted and exemplified in numerous colour illustrations. Directions, opening hours and details of entrance fees are also included in the pamphlet, which was produced in the early 1990s and is available from Spanish tourist offices in the UK and in Madrid.

366　**The Prado of Madrid and its paintings.**
Edited by Mia Cinotti, with a foreword by Xavier de Salas y Bosch.
Edinburgh: John Bartholomew & Son, 1973. 118p. (Great Galleries of the World).

The Prado Museum houses the world's richest and most comprehensive collection of Spanish art, as well as masterpieces of other schools of European painting (particularly Italian and Flemish). Charles III (1759-88) commissioned the architect, Juan de Villanueva, to design a natural science museum in 1787. The building was completed and opened in 1819, but as the Royal Museum of Painting, becoming the National Museum of the Prado in 1868 after the exile of Queen Isabella II. Besides art collected by the Habsburg and Bourbon monarchs, the Prado acquired numerous valuable paintings in 1872 which had formerly been kept in the Trinidad Museum in

Madrid. Further notable additions to the collections, as well as to the building itself, have been made over the years. Cinotti's work contains over 100 colour reproductions of the Prado's masterpieces, black-and-white reproductions of other important paintings and a complete catalogue of all the works held there at the time of publication. Aimed at the general reader, the volume also contains a history of the museum, an introduction by its then Director, floor plans and detailed descriptions of all the major works. The Museum itself produces a number of guides (in English and French) for specific artists, including Goya (1985) and Velázquez (1986), which can be purchased by visitors at a small charge. Published by the Amigos del Museo del Prado (Friends of the Prado Museum), each provides an introduction to the artist with descriptions, illustrations and critical analysis of the major works.

367  **The museums of Spain.**
Aurora Fernández Vegue.   Madrid: Secretaría General de Turismo, 1992. 47p. (Arte y Cultura).

This publication is available from Spanish tourist offices and represents a brief introduction to all of Spain's principal museums. Amongst more than forty mentioned, there are short descriptions of around a dozen of Madrid's most famous museums. These include colour photographs and a text outlining each museum's highlights, together with the address and telephone number.

368  **Treasures of the Prado.**
Felipe Vicente Garín Llombart.   New York: Abbeville Press, 1993. 311p.

Numerous treasures have been added since the Prado Museum opened in 1819, and this richly illustrated volume provides an excellent pocket-guide for those seeking to gain an understanding and interpretation of the full range of masterpieces on display. The sections on the various collections (Spanish, Flemish, Italian, French, German and English), together with chapters on the decorative arts and sculpture, each contain a short survey of their history and value followed by beautiful colour prints of the works themselves. An index of the illustrations concludes this useful book. Also of interest is another lavishly illustrated coffee-table book, entitled *The Prado*, by Santiago A. Blanch (New York: Abrams, 1991. 416p.).

369  **Museos de Madrid: guía de Madrid y región.** (Museums of Madrid: a guide to Madrid and its region.)
Lola Garrido, Javier Olivares, Pablo Olivares.   Madrid: Comunidad, Dirección General de Patrimonio Cultural, 1990. 181p.

This useful guide provides information about all Madrid's museums and their collections, together with a short summary of the importance and contents of each.

370  **Museums of Madrid: volume 1, the Prado Museum.**
Juan Antonio Gaya Nuño.   León, Spain: Everest, 1970. 213p. map.

This was one of the first English-language guides to appear on the Prado, and was specifically aimed at tourists visiting the Museum. Although there are now better and easier-to-use works available, this one still represents a standard, well illustrated guidebook. After a brief history of the Museum, a description of the building itself and its collections is provided. Unfortunately, the numerous colour plates are laid out in a rather haphazard manner, and although there is an abridged catalogue of paintings in the Museum appended, there is no separate index for these illustrations. A map of Madrid and a floor plan of the museum (now out of date) are also included. Gaya Nuño has since collaborated with José Alvarez Lopera on the more recent *Museos de Madrid* (Museums of Madrid) (León, Spain: Everest, 1990. 384p.).

371   **The Prado: treasure house of the Spanish royal collections.**
Enriqueta Harris.   London; New York: Studio Publications, 1940.
136p.

Despite its age, this book retains a usefulness due to the clarity of its text and the fact that it appeared shortly after the end of the Spanish Civil War and the outbreak of the Second World War. During this time of conflict the country's art treasures had been in constant danger and many of the Prado's paintings had only just been returned from safe keeping in Geneva. After a short introduction to the Prado's history, Harris provides some background information on the various royal collections from Isabella I (1479-1504) to Ferdinand VII (1813-33), followed by plates illustrating paintings within these collections. Of related interest is *Museo del Prado: catálogo de las pinturas* (The Prado: a catalogue of its paintings) (Madrid: El Museo, 1985. 870p.).

372   **The Prado, Madrid.**
Manuel Lorente, translated from the Italian by Paul Colacicchi.
London: Oldbourne, 1965. 2 vols. (Great Galleries Series).

Originally published in Italy in 1962, this two-volume work chiefly comprises several hundred plates (both in colour and black-and-white) of many of the Prado's most famous masterpieces. All the Museum's major artists are represented and short descriptions are given of each work, together with dates and canvas dimensions. The introduction to volume one provides a clear, concise (four pages) history of the Museum and its collections, whilst the introduction to volume two concentrates (again concisely) on the collection policies of the Spanish monarchs from Isabella I (1479-1504) onwards. At the end of each 150-page volume there is an index of artists, which provides page references for plates of their works. Although there are more up-to-date and comprehensive surveys of the Prado available, Lorente's is still of value to those interested in gaining an insight into the range of paintings held in the Museum including its high concentration of masterpieces.

373   **Guide to the Prado.**
Consuelo Luca de Tena, Manuela Mena, translated by Evelyne
Colchero.   Madrid: Sílex, 1995. 350p. bibliog.

The quantity and quality of the Prado's paintings make it the most important art museum in the world. This detailed, up-to-date guide offers a survey of the full range (nearly 3,000) of works housed there and will be of value to the general visitor and art scholar alike. It lists both the works on show in the exhibition rooms and those that are temporarily kept in the Museum's storerooms. The traditional arrangement divides coverage into schools of painting (which are studied separately) and individual artists and styles. The work as a whole is based on the Prado's latest catalogues, excluding the 19th-century works exhibited in the nearby Casón del Buen Retiro (future editions of this guide are expected to include these paintings). Hugely informative and excellently produced, the guide contains over 200 black-and-white illustrations and 79 colour plates, as well as floor plans and indexes of artists, paintings and illustrations.

The same authors also produced a shorter version of this guide, particularly aimed at tourists, under the title, *The key to the Prado* (Madrid: Sílex, 1993), which contains some beautiful colour illustrations. At the time of writing, remodelling work was in progress in the Prado with the aim of achieving complete air-conditioning and humidity control in an attempt to combat the serious air pollution problem in this area of the city.

374   **Museo Municipal: catálogo de las pinturas.** (The Municipal
      Museum: a catalogue of its paintings.)
      Madrid: Museo Municipal, 1990. 385p.

Founded in 1929, this fascinating museum is particularly important for those interested in the history of Madrid. It contains prehistoric finds, portraits, paintings, designs, engravings, sculptures, plans, coins, ceramics and porcelain. A notably good collection of paintings by famous Madrid artists (e.g. Goya) and artists from elsewhere is housed, as well as wide-ranging collections of writings by two famous Madrid writers, Ramón de Mesonero Romanos and Ramón Gómez de la Serna. The Museum publishes a number of other catalogues, the *Gaceta* (Gazette) and the important journal, *Estudios de Prehistoria y Arqueología Madrileñas* (q.v.).

375   **Museo Nacional de Artes Decorativas.** (The National Museum of
      Decorative Arts.)
      Madrid: Servicio de Publicaciones del Ministerio de Educación y
      Ciencia, 1978. 144p.

This museum (founded in 1912) contains collections of interior decorative arts, in the main Spanish works from the 15th to 19th centuries. It includes examples of carpets, furniture, leatherwork, jewellery, tapestries, ceramics, glass, porcelain and textiles. This illustrated guide provides a useful introduction to the Museum's collections and complements the book of the same title by María Dolores Enríquez Arranz (Madrid: Patronato Nacional de Museos, 1961. 143p.). The Museum's library holds approximately 12,000 volumes of related interest.

376   **Prado, Madrid.**
      Anna Pallucchini et al.   Montreal: Newsweek, 1968. 171p. bibliog.
      (Great Museums of the World).

Translated from the original Italian edition (Milan: Mondadori, 1968), this magnificently illustrated work presents the Museum's most important and memorable works of art from Spain, Italy, Flanders, Germany, France and Holland. It also includes: an introduction by the Prado's director; text commenting on the historical and artistic significance of the works and their artists; and indexes of illustrations and names. This coffee-table book is particularly helpful and accessible to the general reader.

377   **Guide Prado Museum.**
      Alicia Quintana Martínez.   Madrid: Aldeasa, 1994. 149p.

One of a series of guides commissioned by the Prado, this volume has been translated into several languages for the benefit of tourists. Beautifully illustrated in colour, it describes both the building itself, architecturally, and the wealth of paintings held within. Quintana also wrote *Museo de Prado guide: quick visit* (Madrid: Aldeasa, 1994. 79p.) which provides a more concise guide for the passing tourist.

378 **A royal patrimony: the Prado Museum and Spanish history.**
Jan Read. *History Today*, vol. 26, no. 8 (Aug. 1976), p. 489-98.
This short, illustrated article provides an interesting and readable survey of the history of the Prado Museum and the role of Spain's monarchs in contributing to its collections. As well as highlighting certain dates in the Prado's history, the article also illustrates how individual rulers viewed the arts, and details various aspects of the royal collections. The illustrations which accompany the text are taken from paintings hanging in the Museum.

379 **A basic guide to the Prado.**
José Rogelio Buendía. Madrid: Sílex, 1993. 298p.
Beautifully illustrated and comprehensively indexed, this guide covers all periods of the Museum's collections and is subtitled 'a view of the museum according to styles'. It contains 181 illustrations of which 100 are in colour. The author also wrote *La Ermita de San Antonio de la Florida: historia e itinerario artístico* (The hermitage of San Antonio de la Florida: a history and artistic itinerary) (Madrid: Ayuntamiento, 1992. 94p.), a guide to the neo-classical chapel built by Felipe Fontana for Charles IV between 1792 and 1798. The chapel is most famous as being the burial-place of Goya and for the unique frescoes he painted there in 1798, which many consider to be amongst his finest works. An English-language study relating to these is Enrique Lafuente Ferrari's *The frescoes in San Antonio de la Florida in Madrid: historical and critical study* (New York: Skira, 1955. 149p.).

380 **The Prado.**
Francisco Javier Sánchez Cantón, translated from the French by James Cleugh. London: Thames & Hudson, 1971. rev. ed. 261p. (The World of Art Library).
Sánchez Cantón was Assistant Director (1922-60) and subsequently Director of the Prado (1960-68), and was responsible for many large-scale changes and improvements. A historical background to the Museum is followed by vivid and expert descriptions and analyses of its masterpieces from Spanish, Italian, Flemish, German, French and Dutch schools of the 14th to 18th centuries. Hundreds of colour and black-and-white illustrations complement the text. A number of other important studies and descriptions have been written of the Prado, including *The Prado*, edited by José Antonio de Urbina (London: Scala in association with Sotheby, 1988), a catalogue of its paintings; *Great paintings from the Prado Museum* by Harry B. Wehle, foreword by F. J. Sánchez Cantón (London: Thames & Hudson, 1964), which provides a very useful introduction to the Prado and its collections; and *Masterpieces of the Prado Museum*, with an introduction by Fernando Alvarez de Sotomayor (London: Faber & Faber, 1948), which contains numerous colour plates and descriptions of the Prado's most famous paintings. Sánchez Cantón is also author of *Spanish drawings; from the tenth to the nineteenth century* (London: Studio Vista, 1965), which includes selections from the works of Goya, El Greco and Velázquez amongst others.

381 **The Museo Thyssen-Bornemisza, Madrid: a comprehensive display of quality.**
Robin Simon. *Apollo*, vol. 136, no. 370 (Dec. 1992), p. 354-55.
The Thyssen-Bornemisza Museum opened on 10 October 1992, after Spain had secured the art treasures of Baron Hans Heinrich Thyssen-Bornemisza against

153

counter-bids from London and other major cities. The collection originally came to Spain on a nine-and-a-half-year loan, but subsequent negotiations led to a purchase agreement for the 775 paintings being concluded in June 1993. Madrid's offer to house the collection in the Palacio de Villahermosa was a highly influential factor in the Baron's decision. Converted into offices in the 1960s, the architect Rafael Moneo was able to supply a new interior which cost over twenty million pounds. The collection itself includes works from virtually every major figure in the history of western art, from Goya to Andy Warhol. Simon's short article provides a helpful introduction to the Museum and the importance of its collection. A number of architectural studies of the Museum have appeared, including Penny McGuire's article, 'Transformation in Madrid: the Villahermosa Palace in Spain' (*The Architectural Review*, vol. 194, no. 1,168 [June 1994], p. 23-27), which through brief descriptions and a number of colour photographs illustrates how the architect, Moneo, transformed the Palace's interior into an elegant and carefully-lit gallery; and Colin Davies's 'Palace treasures: Thyssen-Bornemisza Museum, Madrid, Spain' (*Architecture*, vol. 83, no. 1 [Jan. 1994], p. 70-77), which illustrates the excellence of Moneo's design. Also of interest is *Thyssen-Bornemisza Museum* (Barcelona, Spain: Lunwerg, 1992), which provides a catalogue of the Museum's collection.

382 **Madrid modern.**
Marcia E. Vetrocq. *Art in America*, vol. 79, no. 2 (Feb. 1991), p. 122-26, p. 160.

This short, well illustrated article provides a useful introduction to Madrid's Centro de Arte Reina Sofía (full name – Museo Nacional Centro de Arte Reina Sofía), a magnificent visual arts centre and officially a national museum. Originally, the building was the Hospital of San Carlos, commissioned by Charles III and designed by Francesco Sabatini. Built between 1776 and 1781, it remained a hospital until 1965, and it was only in 1977 that work began on its conversion into a multi-purpose museum, exhibition centre and cultural centre. It first opened in 1986, but its permanent collection of contemporary art was not in place until 1990. At the same time its modern interior was matched externally by the addition of bold glass lifts on either side of the entrance, which form a striking contrast to the great expanses of 18th-century brick. In 1992 the Centre acquired its greatest attraction, Picasso's 'Guernica'. Its superb gallery and exhibition spaces make it one of the best venues in Europe for temporary art exhibitions and other cultural activities. However, its permanent contemporary Spanish art collection has been criticized for its patchy representation of individual artists with few of their major works. In response, an active acquisitions policy has been adopted that is going some way to enhancing the display of Spanish art and creating a growing collection of works by foreign artists as well.

**Interactive science in Madrid.**
*See* item no. 310.

**Madrid: art and culture.**
*See* item no. 350.

# Palaces and treasures

**383  A palace for a king: the Buen Retiro and the court of Philip IV.**
Jonathan Brown, John Huxtable Elliott.   New Haven, Connecticut;
London: Yale University Press, 1980. 296p. bibliog.

The Palace of the Buen Retiro (Good Retreat) was created initially as a small annexe
to the royal apartment attached to the church of San Jerónimo (Saint Jerome) in the
Retiro Park to the east of Madrid. It quickly became a huge complex of palatial
buildings, centred on a courtyard presided over by a statue of Philip IV on horseback
(designed by Velázquez and now in the Plaza de Oriente – Eastern Square). In 1632
Philip IV's great minister, the Count-Duke of Olivares, presented the King with the
keys to the new palace residence. Olivares' aim in commissioning the palace was to
emphasize the importance of the monarchy he served, and in fact Louis XIV of France
took the idea as his model for the palace at Versailles. The Retiro in reality served two
purposes: the first was to provide a place of retreat and recreation for the King (Philip
IV was particularly interested in the court theatre); and the second was to create an
ideal setting for the King to act as a great patron of the arts. The full splendour of the
Buen Retiro lasted little more than a century, as the Bourbon monarchs had no great
liking for it. Most of the palace was destroyed in 1812-13, during the Napoleonic
Wars, and the only two sections remaining today are the Casón del Buen Retiro and
the Museo del Ejército (Army Museum) (both close to the Prado, and housing
wonderful art collections and military memorabilia respectively). Elliott (one of the
most respected historians on Spain) and Brown (a renowned art historian who has
written numerous works on Spanish artists) have vividly reconstructed the political
life and spectacle of the Habsburg court and the artistic grandeur of the Palace through
an expertly integrated history of the Palace's construction and occupation. They also
provide a fascinating insight into the characters of Philip IV and the protagonist of
their book, his minister, Olivares. Beautifully illustrated, it also contains a number of
appendices and an extensive bibliography and index.

**384  Royal palaces of Spain: a historical and descriptive account of the
seven principal palaces of the Spanish kings with 164 illustrations.**
Albert F. Calvert.   London: John Kane, The Bodley Head, 1909.
271p. (The Spanish Series).

Calvert's fascinating series of works on Spain provides a rich and detailed survey of
the country's artistic and architectural heritage. As with his other classic volumes
(including one on Madrid [q.v.]), this book comprises text followed by copious
illustrations and reproductions of pictures. Besides a chapter on the Royal Palace of
Madrid, there are also chapters describing El Escorial, La Granja, El Pardo, Aranjuez,
Miramar and El Alcázar (Seville). What is so praiseworthy about Calvert's work is
that he manages to encompass both historical and artistic detail in a clear and concise
way, thus ensuring that the book remains readable and interesting despite its age. El
Escorial (Philip II's monastery-palace) has provoked much writing over the centuries.
One of the best and most detailed studies of its architectural history is George
Kubler's *Building the Escorial* (Princeton, New Jersey: Princeton University Press,
1982); and Mary Cable's *El Escorial* (London: Reader's Digest Association, 1971) is
also worth consulting as it contains beautiful photographs of the Escorial and its
treasures.

385 **The Royal Palace, Madrid.**
Juan Gualberto López Valdemoro y Quesada (Conde de las Navas).
Barcelona, Spain: Hijos de J. Thomas, 1914. 68p. (Art in Spain; no. 4).

This splendid book was produced under the patronage of the Hispanic Society of America. Its forty-eight illustrations and brief, descriptive text provide a fascinating guide to the Royal Palace and its art treasures. Now something of a collector's item because of its age, the attraction of the book lies principally in the historical value of its text and the illustrations of the Royal Palace at the beginning of the 20th century. Another interesting work is Eugenia Montero's *Los secretos del Palacio Real de Madrid* (The secrets of the Royal Palace of Madrid) (Madrid: El Avapiés, 1991. 158p.), which looks at the history, anecdotes and myths surrounding the Palace, as well as considering its artistic value.

386 **Philip IV and the decoration of the Alcázar of Madrid.**
Steven N. Orso. Princeton, New Jersey: Princeton University Press, 1986. 320p. bibliog.

The original *Al-qasr* (from the Arabic, meaning 'the castle', absorbed into Spanish as *alcázar*) was one of a string of Moorish watchtowers, and was built around 875. Although captured by Alfonso VI of Castile in 1086, little is known of its history before the Habsburg accession except that the Kings of Castile had used it as one of the temporary residences for their itinerant courts. Located on the western edge of Madrid, its walls overlooked a steep precipice below which lay the Campo del Moro (Moor's Field), so named after 1109 when Moslem forces besieged the Alcázar. In approximately 1360 King Pedro the Cruel (1357-67) had it rebuilt, and a turning-point in its history came in 1537 when Charles V ordered the expansion of the old mediaeval structure. Work continued under Philip II and took on new importance after he selected Madrid as his permanent capital. In 1734 the Alcázar was destroyed by fire, and the Royal Palace now stands on its site. Orso's excellent study is primarily concerned with the changes which were made both to the Alcázar's façades and to its interior decoration under Philip IV (1621-65). He closely examines the public and private chambers within the King's household, and demonstrates how the vast collections of paintings, sculptures and other furnishings mirrored regal splendour and royal ideals. The work includes nearly 100 illustrations of plans, paintings and sculptures, and a number of appendices.

387 **El Palacio del Ministerio de Justicia y sus obras de arte.** (The Palace of the Ministry of Justice and its works of art.)
Virginia Tovar Martín. Madrid: Ministerio de Justicia, 1986. 335p. bibliog.

The huge Palacio de Justicia (Palace of Justice), now seat of the Spanish Supreme Court, lies just to the north of the Palacio de Buenavista (Buenavista Palace) and the Banco de España (Bank of Spain). Formerly the Convento de las Salesas (Salesian Convent), built in 1750-58, it was taken over by the State in 1870. Its refined, classical baroque exterior contrasts sharply with the art nouveau decor of the Palacio Longoria (Longoria Palace) just a few streets away. The present work describes the architectural significance of the building and the artistic merit of its many art treasures.

388 **Philip IV and the 'Golden House' of the Buen Retiro: in the tradition of Caesar.**
Barbara von Barghahn. New York; London: Garland, 1986. 2 vols. bibliog. (Outstanding Dissertations in the Fine Arts).
Based on the author's doctoral thesis, 'Pictorial decoration of the Buen Retiro Palace during the reign of Philip IV' (PhD thesis, New York University, 1979), this scholarly study looks at Philip IV's decoration of the complex of palatial buildings located in the royal park to the east of Madrid. In particular she details the architecture of the Golden House (now the Casón del Buen Retiro) and the paintings which adorned it. Volume one presents the text of the work, whilst volume two includes plates of illustrations and notes. Of related interest is another von Barghahn two-volume study on the art collections and art patronage of earlier Spanish kings: *Age of gold, age of iron: Renaissance Spain and symbols of monarchy: the imperial legacy of Charles V and Philip II. Royal castles, palace-monasteries, princely houses* (Lanham, Maryland; London: University Press of America, 1985. 2 vols.); and her earlier study, entitled *Philip IV of Spain, his art collection at the Buen Retiro Palace, a Hapsburg 'Versailles'* (Lanham, Maryland; London: University Press of America, 1980).

**Madrid: the Royal Palace.**
*See* item no. 64.

# Decorative arts

389 **Spanish arms and armour: being a historical and descriptive account of the Royal Armoury of Madrid.**
Albert F. Calvert. London: John Lane, The Bodley Head, 1907. 390p. (The Spanish Series).
This impressive collection of suits of armour contains numerous elaborate pieces, including armour for dogs and horses. Although catalogued in numerous Spanish works, the collection had been subjected so many times to the influences of fire, removal and rearrangement that no single-volume catalogue was available until Calvert provided this historical record of the armoury and its treasures. Nearly 150 pages of text present the reader with a detailed study of the collection, its history and significance, together with specific descriptions and analyses of individual pieces of armour and weaponry. Almost 250 black-and-white plates of the exhibits illustrate the narrative and highlight the artistic detail of the collection.

390 **The Spanish royal tapestries.**
Albert F. Calvert. London: John Lane, The Bodley Head, 1921. 344p. (The Spanish Series).
Represents the first English-language work to record the very valuable and highly interesting collection of tapestries kept in the Royal Palace in Madrid. The collection had been steadily accumulating since the 13th century, with the famous Tunis Tapestries being designed and woven by Dutch and Flemish artists and weavers under

the direction of Charles I (1516-56). The practice of weaving was only introduced into Spain in the first quarter of the 17th century, and it was not until 1721 that the Real Fábrica de Tapices (Royal Tapestry Factory) was founded. Many of the fabrics were designed by Goya and owed their existence to the interest displayed by Charles III (1759-88) in the products of the looms. Calvert's study follows the same format as his other volumes in the series, with chapters covering the history of the art of tapestry weaving, the founding of the royal collection, and Gothic and Renaissance tapestries. The major part of the book is given over to 277 black-and-white plates reproducing many of the tapestries in the collection. The Royal Tapestry Factory is now an uninspiring building which is still a going concern, where the dyeing and weaving is carried out much as it was when it was founded. For an illustrated history of the factory, readers should consult *Real Fábrica de Tapices 1721-1971* (The Royal Tapestry Factory 1721-1971) by Enrique Iparaguirre and Carlos Dávila (Madrid: G. R. S. A., 1971. 128p.).

391 **Aproximación a la escultura religiosa contemporánea en Madrid.**
(Introduction to contemporary religious sculpture in Madrid.)
María Teresa González Vicario. Madrid: Universidad Nacional de Educación a Distancia, 1987. 622p. bibliog.

Religious sculpture has always been very important in Spain generally, and in Madrid there are some wonderful examples of old and modern masterpieces. This up-to-date work provides a detailed survey and analysis of contemporary sculptors and their works. Other related studies which may be of interest are: *Madrid mira a sus estatuas* (Madrid looks at its statues) by Antxon Hernández and Antonio Ruiz Barbarín (San Sebastián, Spain: Promoción Moda, 1992. 219p.); and *Estatuas ecuestres de Madrid* (Equestrian statues of Madrid) by Antonio Soroa y Pineda (Madrid: Ayuntamiento; Instituto de Estudios Madrileños, 1970. 48p.).

392 **French decoration in Spain: Parisian style shapes the Bartolomé March Palacete in Madrid.**
Nicholas Shrady, photography by José Luis Pérez. *Architectural Digest*, vol. 50, no. 1 (1993), p. 96-101.

Short and well illustrated, this article describes the residence of the art collector and financier, Bartolomé March. In particular, it emphasizes the style of the Paris firm of Jansen's interior designs and the decoration of the house which is situated in the centre of Madrid.

**Fuentes de Madrid.** (Fountains of Madrid.)
*See* item no. 66.

**Templo de Debod.** (Temple of Debod.)
*See* item no. 67.

**Museo Nacional de Artes Decorativas.** (The National Museum of Decorative Arts.)
*See* item no. 375.

# Music and dance

393  **Gottschalk in Madrid: a tale of ten pianos.**
Clyde W. Brockett.  *Musical Quarterly*, vol. 75 (fall 1991),
p. 279-315.

Louis Moreau Gottschalk (1829-69) was the first American pianist to achieve
international recognition and the first American composer to use Latin American and
Creole folk themes and rhythms. Son of an English-German father and an aristocratic
Creole mother, he was a child prodigy on several instruments. This article looks at his
highly successful concert tour in Madrid in 1851. Brockett notes how Queen Isabella
II (1833-68) and the Spanish court had been eagerly awaiting his visit, and goes into
minute detail about various aspects of the composer's stay there. Gottschalk's Madrid
programmes were filled with premières of original music or fantasies built on themes
by other composers. The article captures the excitement surrounding his salon, court
and public concerts, the influence of the city on his musical compositions and the wide
coverage his tour of the capital received in the Madrid press. It also contains a number
of illustrations and extracts from both the press of the day and his musical scores.

394  **Aesthetics, politics and opera in the vernacular: Madrid 1737.**
Donald Curtis Buck.  *Opera Quarterly*, vol. 10 (spring 1994),
p. 71-91.

This short article considers the role of opera in 18th-century Madrid society and its
relationship to social and political events of the time.

395  **Y Madrid se hizo flamenco.** (And Madrid took up flamenco.)
Antonio Escribano Ortiz.  Madrid: El Avapiés, 1990. 221p. bibliog.
(Colección Avapiés, no. 32).

Interestingly titled, this valuable study gathers together documents, facts and oral
histories to illustrate the history of flamenco in Madrid from the 17th century to the
present day. A social as well as artistic history, it also contains a selection of
biographical sketches of the most famous proponents and aficionados of flamenco. Of
related interest is *Flamenco en el Madrid del siglo XIX* (Flamenco in 19th-century
Madrid) by Arie C. Sneeuw (Córdoba, Spain: Virgilio Márquez, 1989. 69p.).

396  **La Orquesta Sinfónica de Madrid.** (The Madrid Symphony
Orchestra.)
Carlos Gómez Amat, Joaquín Turina Gómez.  Madrid: Alianza, 1994.
264p. bibliog. (Alianza Música, vol. 68).

The Madrid Symphony Orchestra was founded in 1903, and its most famous musical
director, the violinist, Enrique Fernández Arbos, was appointed in 1905 and stayed for
thirty years. He dominated the pre-war period so much that the orchestra became
known as the Arbos. After his retirement, several attempts were made to revive the
orchestra's fortunes, but it was not until 1981 that it finally recovered from its post-
war decline. That year saw its controversial appointment as resident orchestra at the
Teatro de la Zarzuela, a move strongly opposed by the city's two other principal
orchestras, the Orquesta Nacional de España (the Spanish National Orchestra) and the
Orquesta y Coro de RTVE (the Orchestra and Choir of Spanish State Broadcasting).

Nevertheless, it has convincingly justified the vote of confidence and no longer has a musical director but an artistic committee, an arrangement which has added to its success. The present book provides a clear, chronological survey of the Orchestra's history, its high points and low points, and famous individuals who have been connected with it.

397 **Music and musicians at the Escorial, 1563 to 1665.**
Michael John Noone.   PhD thesis, Cambridge University, England, 1989. 522p. bibliog.

Noone's thesis examines Latin liturgical music at the royal monastery of El Escorial. He reconstructs the Escorial's musical repertoire through a close study of musical manuscripts. The work contains a wealth of information on the musicians and their performances, including detailed biographies of some seventy-two musicians. The dates of the study span the foundation of El Escorial through the reigns of Philip II (1556-98) and Philip III (1598-1621) up to the end of the reign of Philip IV (1621-65). The text covers about 150 pages, whilst the bulk of the work is made up of appendices of illustrations and musical scores.

398 **Música en Madrid.** (Music in Madrid.)
Edited by José Ramón Encinar.   Madrid: Consorcio para la Organización de Madrid Capital Europea de la Cultura, 1992. 207p.

Published to coincide with Madrid's role in 1992 as European Capital of Culture, this book surveys all aspects of the music scene in the city. A monthly guide of the same title is also available for those wishing to keep up to date with musical events and concerts.

399 **The Spanish symphony in Madrid from 1790 to 1840: a study of the music in its cultural context.**
Jacqueline Andrea Shadko.   PhD thesis, Yale University, Connecticut, 1981. 2 vols. bibliog.

This thesis (664p. in total) discusses the origin of the symphony in Madrid in the late 18th century and traces its development through the first four decades of the 19th century. Shadko highlights the three establishments where orchestras assembled in Madrid for public or private performances: the Royal Palace; salons in the residences of noble patrons of music; and theatres. She then goes on to discuss the music itself and its possible influences. The work is extensively illustrated and includes some musical scores.

400 **El Madrid del cuplé: crónica de un siglo.** (The Madrid of the cabaret song: chronicle of a century.)
Juan Villarín.   Madrid: Comunidad, Consejería de Educación y Cultura, 1990. 292p. bibliog.

Not an early version of the karaoke, the *cuplé* was imported from France just over a century ago, and was performed to popular acclaim in music halls and theatres. Its appeal grew (particularly in the pre-Civil War period), and the *cuplé* developed with famous protagonists uniting and performing classic revue-style songs. Villarín's book provides a full and detailed history of the form, includes biographical sketches of famous artists, and is beautifully presented and illustrated.

401 **Practicing flamenco guitar in Madrid, Spain: an event-centered study of accompaniment and accompanists in guitar lessons and dance classes.**
William Jones Wheeler.   PhD thesis, Indiana University, 1993. 212p. bibliog.

Accompanied by an audio-cassette, this detailed study is based on the author's fieldwork with flamenco guitar accompanists in Madrid. He concentrates on some specific learning and teaching contexts where guitarists, dancers and singers learn, practise and experiment with flamenco. Musical events are also discussed, and the work includes transcribed excerpts of specific musical compositions and interactions, emphasizing the role of the guitarist in each.

**Dancer in Madrid.**
*See* item no. 134.

**Historia del Teatro Real como sala de conciertos, 1966-1988.** (A history of the Teatro Real as a concert hall, 1966-88.)
*See* item no. 407.

**Madrid en Música.** (Musical Madrid.)
*See* item no. 498.

# Theatre

402 **The reconstruction of a Spanish Golden Age playhouse, El Corral del Príncipe, 1583-1744.**
John Jay Allen.   Gainesville, Florida: University Presses of Florida, 1983. 129p. bibliog. (A University of Florida Book).

Subject of a number of studies, the Corral del Príncipe was one of only two permanent public theatres (the other being the Corral de la Cruz) in Madrid for more than a century and a half, from the time of the earliest plays of Lope de Vega until long after the death of Calderón de la Barca (1681). The present-day Teatro Español stands on the site where the Príncipe was built in 1583. Allen's fascinating study reconstructs the Príncipe and illustrates a working model down to the smallest details. Painstaking in his research, the author is to be congratulated for dealing with such a complex subject in a clear and interesting way. His text is enhanced by excellent illustrations, line-drawings, photographs and tables. A final chapter compares the Príncipe with the playhouses of London during the same period.

403 **Pedro Calderón de la Barca and Madrid's theatrical calendar, 1700-1750: a question of priorities.**
Donald Curtis Buck.   *Theatre Survey*, vol. 25, no. 1 (1984), p. 69-81.

Calderón de la Barca (1600-81) was one of the leading dramatists of the Spanish 'Siglo de Oro' (Golden Age). He developed the themes and techniques of the other genius of dramatic art of the period, Lope de Vega (1562-1635), and his plays are notable for their philosophical content, their skilful plotting and their dramatic effectiveness. Buck's interesting study is concerned with the popularity of his plays in relation to the number of plays performed, the number of days they held the stage and the amount of money earned by the productions. With a large amount of statistical data included, the article sheds a great deal of light on Madrid's theatres during the first half of the 18th century, and is a useful adjunct to the works of Varey and Shergold (qq.v.).

404 **Theatrical productions in Madrid's Cruz and Príncipe theaters during the reign of Felipe V.**
Donald Curtis Buck.    PhD thesis, University of Texas, 1980. 437p. bibliog.

This thesis explores the social environment in which theatrical productions were staged at the Cruz and Príncipe theatres during the reign of the first Bourbon king of Spain, Philip V (1700-24). It covers not just the social context but also administration, the theatre companies and the theatrical productions. In particular, it focuses on: the financial relationship between the Ayuntamiento (town council) and the theatre companies; the critical influence of theatre administration on the productions; and the general direction taken by the theatre in Madrid during the first half of the 18th century. Other works of interest include: *Teatro y sociedad en el Madrid del siglo XVIII* (Theatre and society in 18th-century Madrid) by René Andioc (Madrid: Castalia, 1988. 572p.); and *El teatro en Madrid 1583-1925: del Corral del Príncipe al Teatro del Arte; exposición febrero-marzo 1983* (Madrid theatre 1583-1925: from the Corral del Príncipe to the Teatro del Arte; exhibition February-March 1983) (Madrid: Ayuntamiento, 1983. 62p.).

405 **Entertainments in the little theatres of Madrid 1759-1819.**
Ada M. Coe.    New York: Hispanic Institute, 1947. 144p. map. bibliog.

Most of the books and articles written about the history of Madrid's theatre entertainment have concentrated on the capital's three principal theatres, the *coliseos* of La Cruz, El Príncipe and Los Caños del Peral. However, performances in small theatres or amusement halls were extremely popular during the 18th and early 19th centuries, and were regularly advertised in the daily newspapers. Coe's fascinating study 'is an attempt to interpret the press notices published during the sixty years between the date (1759) of the first advertisement of these popular public entertainments . . . and 1820'. In Madrid stage shows were particularly popular, and these little theatres provided entertainment for the large number of people who could not afford the higher prices charged in the *coliseos*. The variety of entertainments discussed and analysed is great, ranging from scientific shows with magic lanterns, automatons and other machinery to puppet shows, shadow pictures and sleight-of-hand tricks. Other sections look at actors, music and ticket prices with appendices providing: an alphabetical list of the entertainments presented in the little theatres of Madrid; a repertory of dramatic works in chronological order; street addresses of little theatres; and a map of Madrid with the location of the theatres. Unfortunately, the book lacks an index, although the contents pages are quite detailed.

406  **La escena madrileña entre 1918-1926: análisis y documentación.**
(The Madrid stage between 1918-1926: analysis and documentation.)
Dru Dougherty, María Francisca Vilches de Frutos.   Madrid:
Fundamentos, 1990. 525p. bibliog.

The authors have painstakingly researched theatre in Madrid over a nine-year period,
and the study includes a full checklist of the plays produced in the city between the
dates specified. They planned on producing at least one more volume which would
analyse the plays between 1926 and 1931, but at the time of writing it had still not
been published. Their unpublished research project, 'Historia del teatro madrileño
entre 1900-1936: texto y representación' (A history of the Madrid stage between 1900
and 1936: text and performance) forms the basis for these works, and they also co-
authored the article, 'Eugene O'Neill in Madrid, 1918-1936' in *The Eugene O'Neill
Review*, vol. 17, no. 1/2 (spring 1993), p. 157-64. Of related interest is the Spanish
study, *Estrenos teatrales en Madrid de las últimas décadas* (Theatrical opening nights
in Madrid over the last decades) by Crisógono García (Madrid: Grupo Libro 88, 1992.
371p.).

407  **Historia del Teatro Real como sala de conciertos, 1966-1988.**
(A history of the Teatro Real as a concert hall, 1966-88.)
Antonio Fernández Cid.   Madrid: Instituto Nacional de las Artes
Escénicas y de la Música, 1991. 414p. bibliog.

Situated to the east of the Plaza de Oriente, Madrid's Theatre Royal is the city's opera
house and has undergone major refurbishment and renovation over the past few years.
This book gives a detailed history of the building and its role in the culture of the city.
It also includes twenty-eight pages of illustrations. Of related historical interest is
*Teatro musical español en el Madrid ilustrado* (Spanish musical theatre in enlightened
Madrid) by Eduardo Huertas Vázquez (Madrid: El Avapiés, 1989. 245p.).

408  **A documentary survey of theater in the Madrid court during the
first half of the eighteenth-century.**
Colin Bayley Johnson.   PhD thesis, University of California, Los
Angeles, 1974. 345p. map. bibliog.

Johnson's investigation focuses on the organization of theatre in Madrid, including its
funding and development. Amongst the areas studied are the festivals for court
occasions and the architecture and scenic development at the Theatre of Caños del
Peral and the Coliseo of the Buen Retiro. Numerous appendices are included,
containing statistical data and reprinted 18th-century documents.

409  **Cincuenta años de teatro en Madrid.** (Fifty years of theatre in
Madrid.)
Ana Mariscal.   Madrid: El Avapiés, 1984. 146p.

The author attempts to provide the reader with a general overview and history of
Madrid's theatre since the 1930s. A number of distinct aspects of the subject are
covered, including comic actors of the 1930s; theatre during the Civil War;
commercial theatre of the 1940s; theatre in Madrid, 1945-60; and individual
playwrights (e.g. Federico García Lorca, Alejandro Casona, Lauro Olmo and Ana
Diosdado) and plays (e.g. *Bodas de sangre* and *Yerma*). Detailed and authoritative,
the work includes a number of illustrations, including one of the author who is one of

Spain's most famous actresses and film directors. Born in Madrid in 1925, she has appeared in over forty films and was a professor at the Spanish Film Institute between 1955 and 1961.

410 **The bureaucratization of the Madrid theater: government censorship, curfews and taxation (1868-1925).**
Nancy Jane Hartley Membrez. *Anales de la Literatura Española Contemporánea*, vol. 17, nos. 1-3 (1992), p. 99-123.

'From 1868 to 1874, the theater enjoyed an unprecedented freedom under the Republican administration, but that ended with the first Conservative government of the Bourbon Restoration'. Thus, in 1875 censorship of theatres and newspapers was re-established, with the government actively involving itself in the rapidly expanding theatre industry. Membrez's clear and well documented article analyses how, over a period of fifty years, government intervention in the form of censorship, curfews and taxation played a major role in the destiny of the Madrid theatre industry, and ultimately led to the dismantling of many of the smaller theatres. At the same time, she points out that government intervention also led to the introduction of several beneficial laws regarding the employment of minors, building safety and security, and the payment of royalties. Nevertheless, she concludes that spiralling ticket prices, regulation of hours of performance and censorship between 1900 and 1925 'made life difficult for the theater industry and the patrons'. Indeed, the theatre entered a period of prolonged crisis in the 1920s from which only a few of the principal theatres emerged unscathed.

411 **The mass production of theater in nineteenth-century Madrid.**
Nancy Jane Hartley Membrez. In: *The crisis of institutionalized literature in Spain.* Edited by Wlad Godzich, Nicholas Spadaccini. Minneapolis, Minnesota: Prisma Institute, 1988, p. 309-56. bibliog. (Hispanic Issues, no. 3).

The author is a respected writer and researcher on Spanish theatre, cinema and women's studies. Her chapter in the present work forms the appendix to the volume and considers, on a broad level, the whole range of theatres which were growing up in 19th-century Madrid. The rapid expansion of theatres in the city during this period had numerous repercussions, not just for the playwrights and audiences but also for the area of social differences and social transition generally. Membrez considers, in particular, the importance of the café-theatres and the *teatro por horas* (theatre by the hour).

412 **The 'teatro por horas': history, dynamics and comprehensive bibliography of a Madrid industry, 1867-1922 ('género chico', 'género ínfimo' and early cinema).**
Nancy Jane Hartley Membrez. PhD thesis, University of California, Santa Barbara, 1987. 1,357p. bibliog.

This huge study provides a fascinating analysis of the *teatro por horas* (theatre by the hour) of Madrid, whereby astute theatre producers staged the same short, one-act play at regular intervals throughout the day, thus increasing their box-office receipts by replacing their audiences every hour. The text of the thesis is divided into four main parts. Part one traces the re-emergence of popular theatre in Madrid during the revolutionary atmosphere of the late 1860s. Parts two and three look at the mass production of theatre and the dynamics of the *género chico* – the one-act play at the heart of theatre production during this period. Part four charts the decline of the *género chico* between 1898 and 1915, the metamorphosis of the *teatro por horas* between 1898 and 1922, and the crisis in the theatre brought about by the introduction of the cinema and increasing government taxation and regulation. Numerous illustrative appendices and an excellent comprehensive bibliography are also included. For an up-to-date Spanish survey of the subject, readers should refer to *El teatro por horas en Madrid 1870-1910* (The 'teatro por horas' in Madrid 1870-1910) by María Pilar Espín Templado (Madrid: Instituto de Estudios Madrileños, 1995).

413   **The urban and architectural environment of the 'corrales' of Madrid: the Corral de la Cruz in 1600.**
Thomas Middleton.   PhD thesis, University of California, Los Angeles, 1976. 284p.
Describing the urban and architectural environment of Madrid's public yard theatres (*corrales*), this interesting study explains how that environment influenced the selection, in 1579, of the site of one of the two permanent *corrales*, the Corral de la Cruz. The author also discusses the background to the *corrales* generally in Madrid, in relation to the rapid growth of the city between 1561 and 1656, and the consequent urban problems and housing and building regulations. The neighbourhood of the *corrales* in the parish of Santa Cruz (near the Puerta del Sol) is described, and the history of the construction of the Corral de la Cruz is traced. The work is well illustrated and includes floor plans of the theatre and a reconstruction of how it probably looked in 1600.

414   **Teatro español e iberoamericano en Madrid 1962-1991.** (Spanish and Latin American theatre in Madrid 1962-91.)
Juan Mollá, selected and introduced by Luis T. González del Valle. Boulder, Colorado: Society of Spanish and Spanish-American Studies, 1993. 204p. (Publications of the Society of Spanish and Spanish-American Studies).
Represents a selection of 140 articles on theatre productions in Madrid, written by the Valencian poet, Juan Mollá, a great theatre-lover and critic. The articles originally appeared in the Barcelona magazine, *El Ciervo* (The Deer), and illustrate the range of productions in Madrid during three decades. Themes, performances, actors and technical aspects of the plays and productions are all critically appraised, but in such a way as to be accessible to the non-specialist. Interspersed with the critiques (which range from five or six paragraphs to two or three pages) are short sections discussing the principal points of interest in Madrid's theatre-world for each year of the period covered. Productions which are critically surveyed include ten by Valle-Inclán and works by Buero Vallejo, García Lorca, Miguel Delibes, Jorge Díaz and Carlos Fuentes, as well as classic Golden Age plays.

415  **The National Theater in mid-nineteenth century Spain, and the curious project to destroy a block of houses facing the Teatro Español.**
Michael Schinasi.  In: *Resonancias románticas: evocaciones del romanticismo hispánico en el sesquicentenario de la muerte de Mariano José de Larra.* (Romantic repercussions: evocations of hispanic romanticism on the 150th anniversary of the death of Mariano José de Larra.)  Edited by John R. Rosenberg.  Madrid: José Porrúa Turanzas, 1988, p. 195-205. bibliog.

Although relatively short, this is a fascinating chapter on Madrid's most beautiful theatre. The site has housed a theatre ever since 1583, when the Corral del Príncipe witnessed performances of many of Lope de Vega's works. It was replaced by the Teatro Español in 1745, and subsequent to theatre reforms in 1849 was nominated as the newly created National Theatre (a position which it retained for just over two years). The project to destroy a block of houses as part of the development of the National Theatre ultimately could not be completed until 1859. The present-day Teatro Español (located on the eastern side of the Plaza Santa Ana) now presents mainly 20th-century Spanish drama and international classics. For a detailed study of the original Corral del Príncipe theatre, readers should refer to John J. Allen's *The reconstruction of a Spanish Golden Age playhouse, El Corral del Príncipe, 1583-1744* (q.v.). The rest of Rosenberg's book may also be of interest as all the chapters (English and Spanish) relate to Madrid's famous essayist, Mariano José de Larra, and include some examination of various aspects of Madrid as portrayed in Larra's writings.

416  **Los corrales de comedias de Madrid: 1632-1745 – reparaciones y obras nuevas, estudio y documentos.** (The 'corrales de comedias' of Madrid: 1632-1745 – repairs and alterations, a study with documents.)
N. D. Shergold.  London: Tamesis, 1989; Rochester, New York: Boydell & Brewer, 1990. 335p. bibliog. (Colección Támesis, Serie C: Fuentes para la Historia del Teatro en España, no. 10).

This tenth volume in the important series of documents relating to the history of the theatre in Spain presents an analysis and documentary evidence of the expenses incurred in the maintenance and repair of Madrid's two principal *corrales* (theatres) of the time, the Cruz and the Príncipe. The information provided in the documents sheds light on a fascinating area of Madrid's theatre history and adds significantly to what is known about the physical aspects of the *corrales de comedias.* They also convey a vivid picture of daily vicissitudes, the struggle to survive changes in taste and popularity, and eventual decline and disrepair. A companion volume appeared in 1995 (as volume twenty of the same series), written by Charles Davis with the assistance of J. E. Varey, entitled *Los corrales de comedias y los hospitales de Madrid: 1574-1615, estudio y documentos* (The 'corrales de comedias' and the hospitals of Madrid: 1574-1615, a study with documents). It represents the first part of a two-volume edition of the surviving theatrical documents from the archives of the old Madrid hospitals, founders of the capital's playhouses. It includes documents relating to contracts of sale, account books, information on the acting companies, the construction of the theatres and the early stages of the theatre business in Madrid. Like these two volumes, most of the volumes in the same series are indispensable sources of information on the Madrid theatre. For example, volumes 3-6 and 11-12 (published between 1971 and 1995) provide analysis and documents relating to theatres and plays in Madrid between 1600 and 1745; volumes 7-8 (published in 1972 and 1995 respectively) cover the subject of puppet shows and other popular entertainments in Madrid between 1758 and 1840; volume 9 (published in 1988) considers plays performed in Madrid between 1603 and 1709; volume 13 (published in 1987) is a study with documentary sources on the letting and renting of Madrid playhouses between 1587 and 1719; and volume 16 (published in 1992) sheds light on the account books of the Madrid playhouses between 1706 and 1719. Readers wishing to consult a short study in English of modifications and repairs to the Corral del Príncipe should refer to Varey and Davis's article, 'The Corral del Príncipe in 1609' in the *Bulletin of Hispanic Studies*, vol. 70, no. 1 (Jan. 1993), p. 53-63.

417    **El Coliseo de la Cruz: illustrations from the Archivo Municipal de Madrid.**
Phillip Brian Thomason.    *Bulletin of Hispanic Studies*, vol. 70, no. 2 (April 1993), p. 237-47.

The Coliseo de la Cruz represented Madrid's first modern public theatre. Constructed in 1737, it was notable not only for its longevity (it was demolished in 1859), but also for the outstanding theatrical productions which took place there. Using architectural drawings from Madrid's Municipal Archives, Thomason illuminates the history of this important theatre and provides the missing architectural link between the Coliseo and its predecessor, the Corral de la Cruz. For detailed examinations of both theatres readers could usefully refer to: Thomas Middleton's unpublished thesis, 'The urban and architectural environment of the "corrales" of Madrid: the Corral de la Cruz in 1600' (q.v.); and Thomason's own PhD thesis (University of Kentucky, 1987), *The Coliseo de la Cruz: Madrid's first enclosed municipal playhouse (1737-1859)* (Ann Arbor, Michigan: University Microfilms International, 1989. 351p.).

418    **Popular entertainment in Madrid, 1758-1859: a survey.**
J. E. Varey.    *Renaissance and Modern Studies*, vol. 22 (1978), p. 26-44.

The author is one of the most prolific and respected writers on the history of Spanish theatre. In this article he presents a thoroughly entertaining general survey of popular entertainment in Madrid over a period of 100 years. It is a very useful text for those wishing to gain a broad view of the subject and unable to meet the challenge offered by the full-scale analyses (in Spanish) of Madrid's theatres and plays in the series, 'Fuentes para la Historia del Teatro en España' (q.v.). Varey looks at a number of entertainments offered by the little theatres of Madrid together with puppet shows, open-air performances, the circus, acrobats, automata and phantasmagoria. Those wishing to read further on the subject could usefully refer to: Ada M. Coe's *Entertainments in the little theatres of Madrid 1759-1819* (q.v.); Varey's own two-part article, 'Notes on English theatrical performers in Spain' in *Theatre Notebook*, vol. 8 (1954), p. 28-39 and vol. 10 (1956), p. 74-79 (which looks at the origins of the circus in Madrid); and another two-part article by Varey, 'Robertson's phantasmagoria in Madrid, 1821' in *Theatre Notebook*, vol. 9 (1955), p. 89-95 and vol. 11 (1957), p. 82-91.

419    **A theatre in Madrid.**
Ivor Waters, Mercedes Waters.    In: *Fragments of Spain.*    The Authors.    Chepstow, Wales: Moss Rose Press, 1987, p. 28-35.

The book as a whole represents a 'different' kind of book on Spain, and was printed in a limited edition. It gives a strange and fascinating account of everyday events as witnessed by a couple who spent a great deal of time in Spain during the 1950s. This chapter recounts the wonderful story of a remarkable theatre called Curva de Zésar, which was formerly sited on a piece of waste ground by the Manzanares river (its official address was 'facing no. 26 Antonio López Street'). It was named 'Caesar's Curve' as a symbol of the roundabout way in which its proprietor hoped to achieve his ambition of being acknowledged as a great playwright: in fact, Zésar was often referred to as the Shakespeare of the Manzanares and the theatre became an institution in Madrid, despite not being supported. Unfortunately, his theatre lay in the path of a proposed motorway, and in the early 1960s it was demolished.

420  **Theatre in Madrid: the difficult transition to democracy.**
      Phyllis Zatlin Boring. *Theatre Journal*, vol. 32, no. 4 (Dec. 1980),
      p. 459-74.
The author has written a number of articles on various aspects of contemporary Spanish theatre as well as studies of individual playwrights. In this one, she studies the Madrid theatre since the death of Franco (1975) and tries to explain why the post-Franco period has been one of confusion for playwrights and theatre-goers alike. Although her analyses are now more relevant as a historical survey of the theatre during the first five years of democracy in Spain, her article also discusses how tradition still greatly influences society and theatre. Despite the relaxation of censorship, many traditional theatre-goers were unprepared for, and unwilling to pay to see, new avant-garde theatre which contained nudity and anti-religious, anti-Franco or anti-army sentiments. Contemporary Madrid theatre has borne out her conclusion that 'the future of the stage will largely mirror the path taken by Spanish society as a whole'.

**The theatre in Madrid during the Second Republic: a checklist.**
*See* item no. 526.

**An index to the 'Teatro Español' collection in the 'Biblioteca de Palacio'.**
*See* item no. 537.

# Cinema

421  **Almodóvar's city of desire.**
      Marvin D'Lugo. *Quarterly Review of Film and Video*, vol. 13, no. 4
      (1991), p. 47-65.
Almodóvar moved to Madrid (to work as a clerk at the Spanish telephone service) in the early 1980s and was a potent force in *la movida madrileña* (Madrid movement) with its blend of style, attitude and excess. His early films depict Madrid during that period, and he became known as the 'Warhol of La Mancha'. This article provides a detailed critical analysis of this depiction in his cinematic work. The author argues that the city can be seen as an image or symbol of a cultural force that challenges traditional values and moral institutions such as the family, the Catholic Church and the law. A respected critic of Spanish cinema, D'Lugo is also author of *The films of Carlos Saura: the practice of seeing* (Princeton, New Jersey: Princeton University

Press, 1991. 274p.). Readers could also usefully refer to the recent article by Nuria Triana Toribio, entitled 'Almodóvar's melodramatic mis-en-scène: Madrid as a setting for melodrama' in *Bulletin of Hispanic Studies*, vol. 73, no. 2 (April 1996), p. 179-89. For more extensive and wide-ranging critical studies of Almodóvar's work, readers should consult Gwynne Edwards' *Indecent exposure: Buñuel to Almodóvar* (New York: Manon Boyers, 1994. 240p.), and Paul Julian Smith's *Desire unlimited: the cinema of Pedro Almodóvar* (q.v.). Almodóvar's eleventh feature film, *La flor de mi secreto* (The flower of my secret) was released in January 1996 to critical acclaim. It is a sober, more austere piece which includes references to Madrid and retains Almodóvar's stunning visual style.

422 **Los primeros veinticinco años de cine en Madrid, 1896-1920.**
(The first twenty-five years of cinema in Madrid, 1896-1920.)
Josefina Martínez. Madrid: Filmoteca Española, 1992. 263p.

Cinema was born a hundred years ago in 1896, and Spanish cinema has attracted a good deal of international attention over the intervening years. In Madrid, going to the cinema is a serious business. Massive cinemas line the Gran Vía, and their hand-painted publicity hoardings remain one of the sights of the city. A new studio complex to the west of Madrid at Pozuelo (the Ciudad de la Imagen – City of Images) opened for business at the end of 1994, and there were plans to open a film school there in late 1996. The Filmoteca Española is Madrid's official film theatre (founded in 1953) and its collection of 20,000 titles was transferred to the Ciudad de la Imagen in 1994. Martínez's excellent book provides a fascinating insight into Madrid's early cinema history.

423 **Desire unlimited: the cinema of Pedro Almodóvar.**
Paul Julian Smith. London; New York: Verso, 1994. 169p. bibliog.
(Critical Studies in Latin American and Iberian Cultures).

With Franco's death in 1975, and the end of forty years of authoritarian rule, a new age dawned and a transformed Madrid exploded into life with the *movida madrileña*, whereby the city and its people were able to express their love of life and living. The *movida* is often associated with certain figures, particularly artists, as the city's art scene expanded enormously in a short period of time. Pedro Almodóvar rapidly rose to fame as one of the country's leading film directors, with much of his work illuminating the vibrant atmosphere of 1980s Madrid. Since shooting his first film in 1974 (whilst at the same time performing with his own pop-rock band), he has become Spain's most outrageous and flamboyant export. Smith's well presented book explores Almodóvar's life and work against the background of modern Madrid and important political and social questions. It represents the first full-length English-language study, and includes a useful bibliography, a thorough analysis of his films and a number of illustrations of still photographs from the films. Readers might also be interested in reading Almodóvar's own quirky writings in *The Patty Diphusa stories and other writings*, translated by Kirk Anderson (London: Faber & Faber, 1991. 155p.), which is full of the frenetic atmosphere of 1980s Madrid; and *The films of Pedro Almodóvar* by Nuria Vidal, translated by Linda Moore and Victoria Hughes (Madrid: Ministerio de Cultura, Instituto de la Cinematografía y las Artes Audiovisuales, 1988. 326p.). Another recently published work is *Almodóvar on Almodóvar* by Frederic Strauss (London: Faber & Faber, 1995. 187p.). Strauss (editor of the respected magazine, *Cahiers du Cinéma*) conducts a series of in-depth interviews with Almodóvar, covering his career but little more. In addition, the illustrations are visually uninspiring and the filmography does not include short films or his television works.

# Customs and Folklore

424 **Guía de las fiestas de la Comunidad de Madrid.** (Guide to the festivals of the Community of Madrid.)
A. Aguado Bonet, M. Martín Castillo. Madrid: Comunidad, 1991. 328p.

Madrid is the scene of festivals, fairs, saints' days and traditional fiestas virtually every other day throughout the year. A particular feature of the city's various celebrations is the importance afforded to popular traditions and the way in which old and new are integrated in fiesta programmes to involve people from all age groups. The most traditional celebrations are the down-to-earth local street festivals or *verbenas* which reach a peak with 'La Paloma' (The Dove) in August (in the La Latina district). The current book is an extensive, illustrated study of the city's festivals and those held in other towns in the region.

425 **From Madrid to purgatory: the art and craft of dying in sixteenth-century Spain.**
Carlos M. N. Eire. Cambridge, England: Cambridge University Press, 1995. 571p. maps. bibliog. (Cambridge Studies in Early Modern History).

This is the first full-length study of Spanish attitudes towards death and the afterlife during the Counter-Reformation. The first section of the book (250 pages) is given over to the study and analysis of the death rituals requested in Madrid testaments. Wills and other legal documents from the Archivo Histórico de Protocolos (Historical Archives of Protocols), the depository for all Madrid wills, have been closely scutinized by Eire, and the section as a whole provides a fascinating insight into social customs and religious beliefs in 16th-century Madrid. Maps, statistical tables and figures support the text and, although scholarly, it is written in such a style as to be accessible to the general reader. Of related interest is *Ritos funerarios en el Madrid medieval* (Funeral rites in mediaeval Madrid) by Leonor Gómez Nieto (Madrid: Al-Mudayna, 1991. 119p.), another fascinating study of death, wills, the cost of burial, masses and ceremonies, and other customs. It includes a wealth of statistical data and is a very useful source of information regarding the social history of the period.

170

426  **Luis Candelas, el bandido de Madrid.** (Luis Candelas, the bandit of Madrid.)

Antonio Espina García.  Madrid: Espasa-Calpe, 1996. 260p.

Luis Candelas Cagigal (1806-37) has become one of Madrid's most famous folklore characters, and the city's most renowned bandit. As a child he worked as a carpenter and then as a bookseller. He was first arrested in 1824 for robbery and sent to prison in Málaga. He escaped and moved to Madrid where he committed a large number of robberies. It was here that he became both infamous with the authorities and a legendary figure to the common people. His ability to escape from the scenes of crimes and prison cells thwarted officers of the law, whilst the fact that he never harmed or killed anyone during the course of his robberies (from the wealthy) made him a folk hero and subject of popular songs and stories of the time. Initially he worked alone, but later joined the outlaw gang of Francisco Villena. In 1831 he again escaped from prison but was eventually captured, imprisoned and executed by the garrotte in 1837, having been convicted of over forty crimes. His life was the subject of the 1926 film, *Luis Candelas o el bandido de Madrid* (Luis Candelas or the bandit of Madrid), directed by Armando Estivalis. Espina García (1894-1972) spent much of his writing life on biographies, but was also a journalist and novelist. This excellent study of the life of Candelas was originally published in 1929.

427  **Leyendas de Madrid: mentidero de la villa.** (Legends of Madrid: gossip shop of the town.)

Reyes García, Ana María Ecija.  Madrid: La Librería, 1994. 192p. bibliog. (Madrid de Bolsillo, no. 6).

This interesting little book provides the reader with a general understanding of the legends, traditions and customs of Madrid over the years. It also discusses the history of the city's streets and daily life throughout the centuries. The subtitle relates to Habsburg Madrid's *mentideros* – literally, 'pits of lies' or gossip-mills, where people came to catch up on the latest news, scandals and rumours (the Puerta del Sol being the best example). Other relevant works on the subject include: *Leyendas y anécdotas del viejo Madrid* (Legends and tales of old Madrid) by Francisco Azorín García (Madrid: El Avapiés, 1983-90. 2 vols.); and José María de Mena's *Leyendas y misterios de Madrid* (q.v.).

428  **Love customs in eighteenth-century Spain.**

Carmen Martín Gaite, translated by María G. Tomsich.  Berkeley, California; Los Angeles; Oxford: University of California Press, 1991. 204p. bibliog.

A translation of the original Spanish edition published in 1972 (Madrid: Siglo Veintiuno de España), this work investigates marriage customs, courtship and social customs generally, but most of the examples included relate specifically to Madrid. In particular, it focuses on the code whereby noblemen allowed their wives to become friends with a member of the opposite sex. The male friend who frequented the lady's house was never to overstep the limits of platonic love, although in practice this may not always have been the case. The wife and 'friend' were allowed to sit together enjoying a whispered conversation. The study then broadens to encompass the significance of this custom to the 18th-century woman in terms of the perception of herself, her relationships with members of the opposite sex, and her environment. The author has made use of archival documents and literary texts to explore the roots of this custom, the terms used to describe it and how both men and women reacted to the 'whispering code of love'. Of related interest is *Amores y amoríos en Madrid* (Lovers and love affairs in Madrid) by José Montero Alonso (Madrid: El Avapiés, 1984. 174p.).

429 **Leyendas y misterios de Madrid.** (Legends and mysteries of Madrid.)
José María de Mena. Barcelona, Spain: Plaza y Janés, 1995. 13th ed. 288p. bibliog.

First published in 1989, this excellent study evokes the rich and fascinating history and traditions of Madrid. In a thoroughly entertaining style the author recounts the legends of the city and stories of famous people, including the playwright Calderón de la Barca, the bandit Luis Candelas and the engineer who wanted to convert Madrid into a sea port! The book contains over thirty pages of illustrations. Mena also wrote *Episodios históricos de Madrid* (Historical episodes of Madrid) (Barcelona, Spain: Plaza y Janés, 1993. 323p.), a wide-ranging exploration of important incidents in the city's past.

430 **Fiestas y tradiciones madrileñas.** (Festivals and traditions of Madrid.)
Pedro Montoliú Camps. Madrid: Sílex, 1990. 418p. bibliog.

This prize-winning book is the result of fifteen years research on the social customs and traditions of Madrid and is arranged as a festive calendar of the city, month by month. Other works of related interest include *Las ferias de Madrid* (Carnivals of Madrid) by Antonio Neira de Mosquera (Madrid: Almatabú, 1984. 188p.), a facsimile of the original 1845 edition; and *Fiestas populares del ciclo de primavera en la Comunidad de Madrid* (Popular springtime festivals in the Community of Madrid) by Consolación González Casarrubios (Madrid: C. E. Y. A.C., 1993. 304p.), a descriptive study of the rituals and celebrations which are held in Madrid and surrounding towns in the spring of each year. The same author also wrote *Calendario de fiestas populares de la Comunidad de Madrid* (Calendar of popular festivals of the Community of Madrid) (Madrid: Comunidad, Consejería de Cultura, 1991. 186p.). Another interesting article on this subject (despite its age) is 'Las fiestas populares de Madrid' by Miguel Herrero García in *Revista de la Biblioteca, Archivo y Museo*, vol. 23 (1954), p. 329-64.

431 **Oficios tradicionales en Madrid.** (Traditional crafts of Madrid.)
Madrid: Diputación Provincial de Madrid, 1982. 3 vols.

The three volumes in this set describe different traditional crafts of the city: *La cestería* (Basket-making) by Adoración Calle Rodríguez; *La churrería* (The fritter stall) by Matilde Cuevas de la Cruz and Juan Manuel Benítez Benítez; and *La forja* (The forge) by María de los Angeles Morcillo.

432 **Costumbres y devociones madrileñas.** (Customs and devotions of Madrid.)
Pedro de Répide. Madrid: Librería de la Viuda de Pueyo, 1914. 202p.

This old classic describes the customs, traditions and religious observances of the people of Madrid, offering a fascinating historical insight into religious practices and piety in the city. A similar historical approach is taken in José del Corral's

*Transformación de las costumbres madrileñas en tiempos de Carlos III* (Changes in Madrid's customs during the reign of Charles III) (Madrid: Ayuntamiento; Instituto de Estudios Madrileños, 1988. 27p.).

### 433 Tertulias of Madrid.
Madrid: Comunidad de Madrid, Consejería de Economía, [s.d.]. 36p.
(Madrid Art and Customs Collection).

A *tertulia* is an intellectual get-together or informal gathering of friends to discuss a particular topic. A deeply-rooted Spanish custom, the true literary *tertulia* began with the appearance of cafés in the early 19th century, although many believe that the term itself came into use during the 17th century, when it simply referred to the theatre and its spectators. By all accounts, the first open *tertulia* in Madrid took place in the Café Príncipe, in the street of the same name, in the 1830s and was attended by Romantic writers such as Larra, Espronceda and Bretón de los Herreros. Ramón de Mesonero Romanos, one of Madrid's most famous literary characters and observer of its customs and manners, gives a graphic account of the meetings in his excellent autobiography, *Memorias de un setentón, natural y vecino de Madrid* (q.v.). The legendary figure of Madrid, Ramón Gómez de la Serna (1888-1963) (affectionately known as 'Ramón') presided over the famous *tertulia* at the Café Pombo which was attended, in the years leading up to the Civil War, by such figures as Buñuel and García Lorca. Author of over a hundred books, it is often said that his best ideas went up in smoke and coffee fumes. The true *tertulia* tradition failed to survive the Civil War, although aspects of it can be seen in Cela's novel, *La colmena* (The hive [q.v.]) which describes a few days in and around the Café Gijón during 1943. The present pamphlet, aimed at the English-speaking tourist, provides an illustrated historical overview of Madrid's 'golden years' of the *tertulia* during the 19th century. Emphasis is placed on the life and work of Pérez Galdós, and their relevance to the *tertulia*, and in particular on his first novel, *La fontana de oro* (The golden fountain), the name of a Madrid café famous for its *tertulia*. The study concludes with a look at the *tertulia* in contemporary Madrid society, although it is generally acknowledged that despite recent efforts at revival, it has been overtaken by political freedom and television. For those interested in reading more on the *tertulia*, see also E. M. Williams's PhD thesis, 'The development of the literary tertulia' (Cornell University, Ithaca, New York, 1935), which may prove difficult to obtain; *Las tertulias de Madrid* (The *tertulias* of Madrid) by Antonio Espina García (Madrid: Alianza, 1995. 272p.); and *Aquellas tertulias de Madrid* (Those *tertulias* of Madrid) by Mariano Tudela (Madrid: El Avapiés, 1984. 180p.).

**Memorias de un setentón, natural y vecino de Madrid.** (Memoirs of a seventy-year-old, born and bred in Madrid.)
*See* item no. 118.

# Food and Drink

434  **Ayer y hoy de la gastronomía madrileña.** (Madrid's cuisine, past and present.)
José del Corral.  Madrid: El Avapiés, 1987. 212p. bibliog.

Madrid's most typical and best-known specialities are hearty winter dishes. The classic dish is the *cocido madrileño* (Madrid stew). Others, such as garlic soup and lentil stews, also feature strongly. The most distinctively Madrilenian dishes are the offal dishes, *callos* (tripe), *orejas* (pigs' ears) and *sesos* (brains). This illustrated study, by one of Madrid's most respected and prolific historians, looks at the ways in which the Madrilenians have fed and watered themselves through the centuries. It considers the Arab influence on cooking and typical Madrid dishes, and selects and describes some of the city's restaurants. The book also contains a selection of recipes that are most representative of the period under discussion.

435  **Comer en Madrid.** (Eating in Madrid.)
Carlos Delgado, Nagore Azurmendi.  San Sebastián, Spain: Donostia, 1995. 193p. bibliog. (Guía Gastronómica).

This well presented gastronomic history of Madrid looks at a variety of aspects of food and cooking in the city. Besides the general historical overview, the book also contains a guide to restaurants, regional cuisine, cooking in *tabernas* (taverns) and a selection of recipes. Readers could also usefully refer to: *Cocina madrileña* (Madrid cooking) (Madrid: Susaeta, 1990. 87p.), which is primarily a photographic compilation of recipes; *Platos típicos de Madrid* (Typical dishes of Madrid) by Magdalena Alperi (Oviedo, Spain: Naranco, 1974. 142p.); *Gastronomía madrileña* (Madrid cuisine) by Joaquín de Entrambasaguas Peña (Madrid: Instituto de Estudios Madrileños, 1954. 49p.); *Comer en Madrid* (Eating in Madrid) by Ana Lorente (Madrid: Dédalo, 1979. 159p.); *Dining, drinking in Madrid* by Frank E. Howell in collaboration with Santiago F. Fernández (Madrid: Artes Gráficas Luis Pérez, 1970. 62p.); and *La cocina típica de Madrid* (Typical cooking of Madrid) by Manuel Martínez Llopis and Simone Ortega (Madrid: Alianza; Comunidad, 1987. 451p.), which presents a history of the origin of certain dishes together with their recipes.

436 **Diez siglos de cocina en Madrid: de los mesones de ayer a los restaurantes de hoy.** (Ten centuries of cooking in Madrid: from the inns of yesteryear to the restaurants of today.)
Lorenzo Díaz. Barcelona, Spain: Folio, 1994. 199p. bibliog.

Díaz is an expert in the field of the history of Madrid's eating and drinking establishments. In this excellent, well illustrated book he examines the gastronomy of the city from mediaeval times up to the present day. His clear text is enhanced by some wonderful anecdotes and interesting asides.

437 **Madrid: tabernas, botillerías y cafés, 1476-1991.** (Madrid: taverns, refreshment stalls and cafés, 1476-1991.)
Lorenzo Díaz. Madrid: Espasa-Calpe, 1992. 383p. bibliog.

This is a beautifully-illustrated history of some of Madrid's most famous refreshment establishments. Divided into sections, Díaz's book considers the various buildings, their history and their place in Madrid society of the period. He also wrote *Madrid: bodegones, mesones, fondas y restaurantes: cocina y sociedad, 1412-1990* (Madrid: Espasa-Calpe, 1991. 2nd ed. 349p.) which, following the same format, looks at aspects of these establishments in Madrid's society and gastronomic history. Of related interest are: *Tabernas de Madrid* (Taverns of Madrid) by Luis Agromayor (Barcelona, Spain: Lunwerg, 1991. 133p.); and *Vinos de Madrid* (Wines of Madrid) (Madrid: Comunidad, Dirección General de Agricultura y Alimentación, 1993. 160p.).

438 **Madrid: a living city of gastronomy.**
Madrid: Municipal Tourist Board, 1988. 68p. maps.

As a cosmopolitan city, Madrid has a wide range of international cuisine represented in over 3,000 restaurants. This short, useful guide is specifically designed for the English-speaking tourist or visitor to the city, and attempts to provide a brief, but representative, overview of the range of food available. Restaurants are listed by district in alphabetical order, with details including their addresses, telephone numbers, opening hours and specialities. Other sections list restaurants with shows, wine bars and a classification of restaurants according to the type of cuisine on offer.

439 **Biografía del restaurante Lhardy.** (Biography of the Lhardy restaurant.)
Julia Mélida Labaig. Madrid: Libros y Revistas, 1948. 181p.

Lhardy is the classic Franco-Spanish restaurant, founded in 1839, and credited with introducing French *haute cuisine* into the culinary repertoire of Madrid. Its founder, Emile Lhardy, was supposedly enticed to the city by the author of *Carmen* (Prosper Mérimée) who told him that there was no decent restaurant in the city. Noted for its history, décor and very expensive food, it is nonetheless possible to at least glimpse this Madrid institution whilst sampling the more reasonably-priced *tapas* rather than eating in the restaurant itself. Similarly, *Taberna del Alabardero: 1974-1984, diez años de historia* (The Taberna del Alabardero: 1974-84, ten years of history) (Madrid: Taberna del Alabardero, 1985. 106p.) represents a descriptive history of the tavern which was the first of several wine bars and restaurants founded by Fray Luis de Lezama, a well-known Madrid personality who manages to combine the life of a priest with that of a highly successful entrepreneur. Originally a sculptor's studio, this particular *taberna* was converted by Lezama into a cosy imitation of a turn-of-the-century tavern. More recently, Lezama has written his own illustrated version of the tavern, *Historias y recetas de mi taberna* (Tales and recipes of my tavern) (Madrid: PPC, 1995. 390p.).

**Oficios tradicionales en Madrid.** (Traditional crafts of Madrid.)
*See* item no. 431.

# Sport and Recreation

440 **Golf: a conflicting recreational activity in the Madrid autonomous area (Spain).**
M. P. Aramburu, R. Escribano. *Landscape and Urban Planning*, vol. 23, nos. 3-4 (June 1993), p. 209-20.
Leisure and recreational activities have become more and more important to a growing number of Spaniards. In Madrid, golf has become one of the most popular sports and there are currently around thirty golf courses in the Autonomous Community of Madrid, with plans already proposed to build another twenty. The authors describe the difficulties faced by local government authorities in approving or rejecting such plans when they have only a relatively short period of time to reach a decision. Tourist and business sector interests are considered, and the article sets out to determine how to classify the territory into zones of greater or lesser compatibility for the construction of golf courses. Planning models, maps and environmental projections designed by the authors enable planners to determine more accurately the suitability of land for the siting, construction and maintenance of golf courses.

441 **Toros en Madrid.** (The bullfight in Madrid.)
María Celia Forneas. Madrid: Pirámide, 1994. 206p. bibliog. (Biblioteca Práctica).
This entertaining, illustrated history of the bullfight in Madrid covers a variety of topics. Facts and tales combine to provide a clear and interesting guide which is particularly aimed at the new aficionado. Chapters discuss the bullring, the bulls, the bullfighters, the public and the bullfighting calendar. Some of the most helpful and informative works of many written on this subject include: *Madrid en el toreo* (Madrid and the bullfight) (Madrid: Unión de Abonados Taurinos de Madrid, 1994. 320p.); *Los toros en Madrid* (The bullfight in Madrid) by Alvaro Martínez-Novillo González (Madrid: Turner, 1992. 250p.); *Madrid y los toros* (Madrid and the bullfight) by Julio Gómez de Salazar y Alonso (Madrid: Centro de Estudios Gómez de Salazar, 1987. 2 vols.); and *Los toros en Madrid: pabellón de la Comunidad de Madrid, Expo '92* (Bullfighting in Madrid: the pavilion of the Community of Madrid, Expo '92) (Madrid: Comunidad, Consejería de Educación y Cultura, 1992. 250p.), a beautifully illustrated catalogue of the exhibition held at Expo '92 in Seville.

442 **Guía de las instalaciones deportivas de la villa de Madrid.** (Guide to the sports facilities of Madrid.)
Madrid: Instituto Municipal de Deportes, 1991. 199p.

In recent years Spanish sportsmen and women have achieved great international success in a variety of sports including athletics, tennis, cycling, golf and rally driving. This success has spurred others to get involved in sport, and in central Madrid there is now great demand for fitness and sports facilities. This useful guide lists the different sports venues and centres which are available (both public and private) in the city. For a brief selection of the larger centres, readers should refer to the *Time Out Madrid guide* (q.v.). A similar, more extensive guide is also available for the Autonomous Community of Madrid area, entitled *Guía de instalaciones deportivas públicas de la Comunidad de Madrid* (Guide to the public sports facilities of the Community of Madrid) (Madrid: Comunidad, Servicio de Documentación y Publicaciones, 1994. 320p.). Another work of related interest is *Ocio, ecología y juventud* (Leisure, ecology and youth) by Andrés Dochao (Madrid: Comunidad, Dirección General de Juventud, 1986. 61p.) which considers young people's involvement in sport and recreational activities in the Madrid region.

443 **The Real Madrid book of football.**
Edited by Ramón Melcón, Stratton Smith. London: Souvenir Press, 1961. 143p.

The city of Madrid boasts two famous football clubs, Real Madrid and Atlético Madrid. Real Madrid are the most successful, having won the European Cup six times (although the last time was in 1966), and have a fanatical following of supporters, 80,000 of whom are regularly drawn to the hugely impressive Santiago Bernabéu stadium (capacity 105,000), named after the club's founder and long-time chairman. The present work provides a fascinating insight into the club and its players at a time when they had just become World Club Champions. This was the era when Alfredo di Stefano, Ferenc Puskas and Francisco Gento were members of the team and Don Santiago Bernabéu was club president. All of these and more make contributions to the book, which also contains a number of illustrations. Melcón also wrote *Historia del Real Madrid club de fútbol, 1902-1950* (A history of Real Madrid football club, 1902-50) (Madrid: Ediciones Deportivos, 1950. 112p.). A more recent, multi-volume publication, entitled *Real Madrid, leyenda viva* (Real Madrid, a living legend) (Madrid: Marca, 1991. 15 vols.), published by one of the country's leading sports dailies, presents an illustrated encyclopaedic history of the club and its achievements.

444 **Historia del Casino de Madrid y su época.** (A history of the Madrid Casino and its era.)
José Montero Alonso. Madrid: The Author, 1971. 226p.

The author is a prolific writer on Madrid, and in this comprehensive history of the Casino he considers its place in 19th-century society and its role in the politics and battles of the time (it was used as a battleground during the Carlist War). He also wrote a shorter study under the title, *El Casino de Madrid* (The Madrid Casino) (Madrid: Ayuntamiento; Instituto de Estudios Madrileños, 1973. 25p.).

445    **Orígenes del deporte madrileño.** (The origins of sport in Madrid.)
       Madrid: Comunidad, Dirección General de Deportes, 1987- . vol. 1- .
Although it is intended to continue to publish volumes in this series, at the time of
writing only this first volume (346 pages) had appeared. It is a collection of fourteen
articles on sporting activity in Madrid between 1870 and 1936, covering topics such as
people's preoccupation with physical exercise, and the history of the sporting press. It
is well illustrated with photographs from the period.

446    **Historia del Atlético de Madrid.** (A history of Atlético Madrid.)
       Juan Carlos Remón.    Bilbao, Spain: Martín de Retana, 1971. 235p.
'El Atléti' are the other big football club of Madrid, alongside Real Madrid.
Traditionally, they are a more working-class club than Real and are nicknamed
*colchoneros* (mattress-men) because of their striped shirts. They have tended to be
overshadowed by their Madrid rivals, who have an impressive collection of
silverware, but their fortunes have improved recently under their controversial
president, Jesús Gil y Gil, and they deservedly won the league and cup double in the
1995-96 season. Other books of related interest are: *Historia del Club Atlético de
Madrid: el ayer y el hoy del Atlético de Madrid* (A history of Atlético Madrid: past
and present) (Madrid: Ediciones Deportivas, 1950. 97p.); and a more up-to-date multi-
volume work, *Atlético de Madrid*, by Pedro Sardina Arthous, J. M. García Zamorano
and Javier García Garrido (Madrid: Universo, 1991. 20 vols. [400p.]).

447    **Las Ventas, cincuenta años de corridas.** (Las Ventas, fifty years of
       bullfighting.)
       Madrid: Diputación Provincial, 1981. 566p. bibliog.
The Plaza de Toros de las Ventas is the Mecca for the bullfight and its aficionados in
Madrid. Building was completed in 1929 and the bullring opened to the public in
1931. The arena can now hold more than 22,000 spectators. Alongside the bullring is
the Museo Taurino (Bullfighting Museum), which is full of memorabilia and
information relating to the history of the bullfight in the city. The *corrida* (bullfight)
season runs from May to October, and out of season Las Ventas proves popular as a
concert arena because of its terracing, and attracts international names. This extensive
work provides a full history of the bullring and includes illustrations and interesting
tales alongside the factual information. Other studies which should be of interest are:
*Historia de la plaza de toros de Madrid (1874-1934)* (A history of Madrid's bullring)
by Rafael Hernández (Madrid: Prensa Española, 1955. 416p.); *Madrid, cátedra del
toreo, 1931-1990* (Madrid, home of the bullfight, 1931-90) by José Luis Suárez-
Guanes (Madrid: Espasa-Calpe, 1990. 718p.), a massive history of bullfighting in the
city; and *Plaza de toros de Madrid (y otros lugares donde se corrieron)* (Bullrings of
Madrid [and other places where they fought]) by Francisco López Izquierdo (Madrid:
El Avapiés, 1985. 212p.), a detailed history of the *plazas* (bullrings) from earliest
times until the opening of Las Ventas.

**As.** (Ace.)
*See* item no. 469.

**Marca.** (Score.)
*See* item no. 475.

# Libraries and Archives

**448   Art Libraries Journal.**
*Art Libraries Journal*, vol. 15, no. 3 (1990), whole issue.

Five out of the six articles in this fifty-one-page issue are devoted to art libraries in Madrid. Written in Spanish, they do, however, include English-language abstracts. The first paper looks at the documentation of Spain's artistic heritage, emphasizing the importance of the Biblioteca Nacional (National Library), whilst the second presents a bibliography of bibliographies of Spanish art, with most of the entries being held in either the Biblioteca Nacional or the ISOC (Instituto de Información y Documentación en Ciencias Sociales y Humanidades – Institute for Information and Documentation in the Social Sciences and Humanities) library in Madrid. The remaining articles centre on Madrid's art libraries, both offering an overview of the various fine arts libraries, and describing in detail the Centre for Historical Studies library and that of the Institute for the Preservation and Restoration of Cultural Treasures. Those wishing to refer to a complete guide to art libraries in Madrid should consult the *Guía de las bibliotecas de arte de Madrid* (Directory of the art libraries of Madrid) (Madrid: Universidad Complutense, 1989). This includes the libraries of those historic institutions dedicated to art teaching (academies and universities) and to the collection and preservation of works of art (museums). It also includes national, academic, public and other kinds of general art libraries.

**449   Libraries and archives of Madrid.**
James W. Cortada.   *Journal of Library History*, vol. 9, no. 2
(April 1974), p. 176-86.

Cortada's article provides an interesting introduction to the principal libraries and archives in Madrid, some of which are amongst the oldest in the world. They include the Biblioteca Nacional (National Library), the Archivo Histórico Nacional (National Archives), the Hemeroteca (Newspaper Library) and the library of the Real Academia de la Historia (Royal Academy of History). For a brief reference guide to Madrid's archives (dated but still helpful), readers could refer to *Breve guía de los principales archivos de Madrid* (A short guide to the principal archives of Madrid) by Antonio Matilla Tascón (Madrid: Gráf. Benzal, 1960. 16p.).

450 **Information science in the Universidad Autónoma de Madrid: developments with the times.**
Emilia Currás. *Education for Information*, vol. 11, no. 3 (Sept. 1993), p. 205-15.
Founded in 1968, the Autonomous University of Madrid has nearly 2,000 teachers and over 32,000 students. Currás describes the development of the study of information science whilst relating it to the history of the department which has been dedicated to documentation or information science over the years (the library school). After a brief introduction she considers: the early days (1969-73); the period of consolidation (1973-77); times of change and activity (1978-84); and the period 1985-93. The twin roles of teaching and research are strongly emphasized throughout.

451 **Bibliotecas de Madrid.** (Libraries of Madrid.)
Pedro González Blasco. Madrid: Ediciones SM, 1984. 118p.
Reasonably up to date, this guide contains information on Madrid's National Library, and public, university and special libraries. For listings of the principal libraries, along with their addresses and collections, readers should refer to the section entitled 'Spain' in *World guide to libraries* (Munich; London; New York; Paris: K. G. Saur, 1995, 12th ed., p. 557-76); and similarly, the section on Spain in the *World guide to special libraries* edited by Helmut Optiz and Elisabeth Richter (Munich; London; New York; Paris: K. G. Saur, 1994. 3rd ed. 2 vols.).

452 **Information for equality: the Documentation Center of the Women's Institute in Madrid.**
Suzanne Hildenbrand. *Wilson Library Bulletin*, vol. 68, no. 7 (March 1994), p. 45-47.
This short article presents an interesting and non-specialist account of the documentation and information centre of the Instituto de la Mujer in Madrid. After a brief description of the categories of women's collections available in Europe, Hildenbrand concentrates on the Institute's documentation centre (which is a government agency), describing its staff, collections and databases, the development of a thesaurus for Spanish women, and the centre's plans for the future. Amongst its many publications, the Institute's quarterly periodical, *Mujeres* (Women), is particularly important in the field of Spanish women's studies.

453 **Nueva guía de las bibliotecas de Madrid.** (A new guide to the libraries of Madrid.)
María Isabel Morales Vallespín et al. Madrid: ANABAD, 1979. 350p.
Including information on the collections, opening hours and other details, this volume represents a standard guide to over 250 libraries in Madrid.

454 **Breve historia de la Hemeroteca Municipal de Madrid, 1918-1968.**
(A brief history of Madrid's Municipal Newspaper Library, 1918-68.)
Federico Carlos Sainz de Robles. Madrid: Ayuntamiento, 1968.
1 vol.

Madrid has several newspaper libraries, the Hemeroteca Municipal, the Hemeroteca Nacional (National Newspaper Library) and the newspaper library of the Complutense University. The Municipal Newspaper Library was founded in 1918 and is housed in the beautifully-restored Cuartel Conde-Duque. It contains an immense stock of the press published in Madrid and many titles from the rest of Spain. The present study provides a thorough history of its development over half a century and could be read in conjunction with *Hemeroteca Municipal de Madrid: su vida y su quehacer, 1940-1967* (The Municipal Newspaper Library of Madrid: its history and function, 1940-67) by Eulogio Varela Hervías (Zaragoza, Spain: [s. n.], 1969. 308p.) which represents a history and catalogue of the library. Madrid's recently-modernized National Newspaper Library holds collections of virtually every periodical published in Spain over the last 150 years, as well as a comprehensive daily stock of the modern Spanish press. For an up-to-date work on the Complutense University's newspaper library, readers should refer to *La hemeroteca de la BUC: una solución de futuro* (The newspaper library of the BUC: its future development) by Javier Gómez López (Madrid: Universidad Complutense, Rectorado, 1994. 64p.), which contains development plans for the library and is updated periodically.

455 **Guía de los archivos de Madrid.** (Guide to the archives of Madrid.)
Prologue by Francisco Sintes y Obrador. Madrid: Dirección General de Archivos y Bibliotecas, 1952. 592p. bibliog. (Guías de Archivos y Bibliotecas).

Virtually all the official, ecclesiastical and individual societies' archives are included in this guide to archival sources in Madrid. Each of the 150 entries contains a brief description of the building along with its history, followed by data relating to the organization and classification of the holdings, their preservation and cataloguing, and a bibliography of further reading on the archive where appropriate. Numerous invaluable collections are included, such as: the Ayuntamiento; the various academies and national institutes; ministries; the Royal Palace; museums; churches; and theatres. The following year a similar guide was published for Madrid's libraries, entitled *Guía de las bibliotecas de Madrid* (Guide to the libraries of Madrid) (Madrid: Dirección General de Archivos y Bibliotecas, 1953. 556p.).

# Mass Media

## The book trade

456 **La feria de libros de la Cuesta de Moyano.** (The book fair of the Cuesta de Moyano.)
Madrid: Ayuntamiento, 1986. 199p. bibliog. (Colección Cuadernos, no. 4).

Madrid's famous book fair on the Cuesta de Claudio Moyano (alongside the railings marking the southern edge of the Jardín Botánico, opposite Atocha railway station) is a long row of restored turn-of-the-century bookstalls selling both new and second-hand books. It is open daily and represents a permanent version of the annual Madrid book fair, a major international event held in the Retiro Park. The present work contains a compilation of extracts on the history of Madrid's book fairs and is well illustrated. Of related interest is *Libros y librerías en la Puerta del Sol (1587-1825)* (Books and bookshops in the Puerta del Sol) by Francisco Vindel Angulo (Madrid: Imp. Góngora, 1950. 31p.), another well illustrated history of the book trade in an area which was once the centre for bookselling in the city.

457 **Madrid for its own sake.**
Herbert R. Lottman. *Publishers Weekly*, vol. 236, no. 11 (15 Sept. 1989), p. 82-87.

Although this article is based on events in Madrid's publishing industry at the end of the 1980s, it nevertheless provides a useful starting-point for anyone looking to gain a general overview of the industry and its principal publishing houses. Lottman looks at how the publishers were undergoing a period of change, both in their areas of interest and in their ownership, with more and more take-overs by other European publishing companies. Lottman is a prolific writer on the subject, and another article of related interest is his 'Madrid as marketplace' in *Publishers Weekly*, vol. 239, no. 17 (6 April 1992), p. 33-36, which takes a general look at publishing in Spain as well as the industry in Madrid and Barcelona.

458 **The book trade in Ibarra's Madrid.**
Diana M. Thomas. *Library*, vol. 5, no. 4 (Dec. 1983), p. 335-58.
Joaquín Ibarra y Marín (1725-85) is recognized as being the most outstanding Spanish printer of modern times, and the man who established Madrid's ascendancy as the printing centre of Spain. He himself was the son of a printer, and between the time he set himself up as a printer in Madrid in 1749 and his death in 1785, more than 2,500 books had come from his press. Thomas's article considers a variety of aspects of Madrid's book trade during the years Ibarra worked in the city. She covers trade associations, laws, and the major changes which took place at the time. Although brief and by necessity selective, the article is useful in providing a general overview of the book trade in Madrid at this time and Ibarra's important role in its development.

459 **Pedro Rodríguez and the wooden printing press in Madrid.**
Diana M. Thomas. *Library*, vol. 4, no. 1 (March 1982), p. 65-70.
This short, interesting article discusses the importance of the wooden printing press designed by Pedro Rodríguez and built by him in Madrid in 1792. The press received much critical acclaim at the time but, as the author concludes, the age of the wooden press in Spain was drawing to an end. An illustration of the pieces and mechanisms of the press is included in the article. For a classic Spanish-language work readers should refer to *Historia de la imprenta en Madrid* (A history of printing in Madrid) by Carlos del Rivero (Madrid: Ayuntamiento, 1935. 118p.).

460 **The Royal Company of Printers and Booksellers of Spain:
1763-1794.**
Diana M. Thomas. Troy, New York: Whitston, 1984. 198p. bibliog.
In general, little has been written on publishing and the book trade in Spain, yet the country was not slow in establishing printing centres widely in the incunabula period. The Royal Company of Printers and Booksellers of Spain played a crucial part in the reorganization and resurgence of the Spanish book trade in the second half of the 18th century. Thomas's well researched and clearly-presented study illuminates the issues which faced the Company, and the power it held within the Madrid book trade. It played a central role in regulating and redirecting the funds from members' licences to finance the expansion of Madrid's book trade and, as Thomas concludes, 'justified the faith of its members and the support of Charles III'. Besides sections dealing with the book trade in Madrid, the company's history, organization and operation, the book also contains appendices which provide detailed information relating to book-trade personnel, and expenditure and production. Thomas is also author of an interesting article, 'Printing privileges in Spain: Nebrija's Latin grammar as a source of income in eighteenth-century Madrid' in *Publishing History*, vol. 5 (1979), p. 105-26.

**Impresos madrileños de 1566 a 1625.** (Madrid's printed works from 1566 to 1625.)
*See* item no. 516.

**Bibliografía madrileña de los siglos XVI y XVII.** (Bibliography of Madrid for the 16th and 17th centuries.)
*See* item no. 522.

# The press

461 **Prensa obrera en Madrid 1855-1936.** (The workers' press in Madrid 1855-1936.)
Edited by S. Castillo, Luis Enrique Otero Carvajal. Madrid: Revista Alfoz; CIDUR; Consejería de Cultura, 1987. 762p. bibliog.

The papers contained in this huge volume were originally presented at the Second Conference on Madrid History. All aspects of the workers' and trade-unions' press are discussed and the result sheds a great deal of light on the working-class mentality and social behaviour during the eighty-year period.

462 **Eléments de caractérisation de la presse madrilène pour les jeunes à la fin du XIXème siècle (1870-1885).** (Characteristic features of the Madrid press for children at the end of the 19th century [1870-85].)
Gisèle Cazottes. *Iris*, vol. 2 (1987), p. 1-38.

The first Spanish publication for children appeared in Madrid in 1798, simply titled *Gaceta de los Niños* (Childrens' Gazette). It lasted only two years, and it was not until 1840 that other titles for children started to appear in the capital. In this illuminating survey Cazottes looks at the specific characteristics of magazines for children published in Madrid during the second half of the 19th century, including their use of language, their function (particularly in education) and their readership. The development and advances made in the graphic arts, together with the appearance of the middle class and the fight against illiteracy, greatly influenced the growth of these magazines. Fascinating facts and figures are scattered throughout the text and the analysis is clear and detailed, but it is a shame that the article does not include any illustrative examples of some of the magazines. However, in her notes at the end, Cazottes provides a comprehensive list of magazine titles, together with details of publication dates, coverage, size and price.

463 **La crisis de la prensa diaria: la línea editorial y la trayectoria de los periódicos de Madrid.** (The crisis of the daily press: editorial direction and the development of the newspapers of Madrid.)
Concha Edo. Barcelona, Spain: Ariel, 1994. 208p. bibliog. (Ariel Comunicación).

The author provides a clear picture of the Madrid daily press and, in particular, analyses the reasons why so many daily newspapers have such a short existence, both on a national level in Madrid (*El Independiente*, *El Sol* and *Claro*) and regionally in Barcelona (*El Observador* and *Nou Diari*). She examines the relationship between editorial principles and a newspaper's collapse, and evaluates the importance of the actual content of newspapers together with other factors which sell the papers. After sections which explain a little about Spain's press laws (Ley de Prensa, 1966), and the press during the transition to democracy after Franco's death (1975), Edo concentrates on Madrid's dailies in the 1990s including *El Mundo*, *El País*, *Diario 16*, *Ya* and *ABC* (qq.v.).

464    **Prensa local madrileña, 1970-1980.** (The local Madrid press, 1970-80.)
       Antonio Ruiz del Arbol.    Madrid: Comunidad, Consejería de Gobernación; Consejería de Cultura y Deportes, 1987. 357p. bibliog.

This extensive survey considers the social, political and cultural factors which influenced Madrid's local press (together with the editorial policies) during the decade which saw the demise of the Franco régime and the rebirth of democracy in Spain.

465    **Revistas femeninas madrileñas.** (Madrid's women's magazines.)
       María del Carmen Simón Palmer.    Madrid: Ayuntamiento; Instituto de Estudios Madrileños, 1993. 36p.

Written by a specialist in Madrid studies, this short survey provides a good overview and analysis of the different women's magazines and journals published in the city. She also compiled the excellent reference work, *Escritores españoles del siglo XIX: manual bio-bibliográfico* (Spanish writers of the 19th century: a bio-bibliographical handbook) (Madrid: Castalia, 1991. 834p.) which contains nearly 5,000 references.

466    **Madrid newspapers 1661-1870: a computerized handbook based on the work of Eugenio Hartzenbusch.**
       Alison Sinclair.    Leeds, England: W. S. Maney, 1984. 964p. map.
       (Compendia, vol. 11).

During the 18th and 19th centuries the most important Madrid newspaper was the famous *Diario* (Daily). First published in 1758, its contents reflected the spirit of the times. It underwent several name changes and lapses in publication until it finally became known as *Diario de Madrid* (Madrid Daily) in 1788. In 1808 it became the political organ of the French invaders, but was suspended in the same year in favour of the *Gaceta de Madrid* (Madrid Gazette) (q.v.). It survived until December, 1918 when it finally ceased publication. Its files are an inexhaustible and fascinating mine of information concerning the life, customs, fashions and tastes of the Madrilenians, and the social and economic reforms of the times. Sinclair's huge study is based upon Juan Eugenio Hartzenbusch's *Apuntes para un catálogo de periódicos madrileños desde el año 1661 al 1870* (Notes for a catalogue of Madrid newspapers from 1661 to 1870) (Madrid: [s.n.], 1894). Hartzenbusch compiled these notes when he was working in the Biblioteca Nacional in Madrid, and his painstaking research was a mammoth effort to record and catalogue all the Madrid newspapers of the period, most of which are now held in the Hemeroteca Municipal of Madrid (Madrid Municipal Newspaper Library). The principal aim of Sinclair has been to render accessible mos' of the material contained in Hartzenbusch's work (supplemented from additiona sources) in order to present as complete a survey as possible of Madrid newspapers fo those conducting research either into the nature of the Spanish press itself, or relate( topics. Hartzenbusch's catalogue has 2,345 entries, and Sinclair's handbook contain not only these, but also an alphabetical list of printers, printers' addresses, and : wealth of other information on such topics as prices, paper sizes, illustration frequency of publication and current library holdings for the Hemeroteca, Bibliotec Nacional and the British Library. An appendix sheds a little more light on Madrid' earliest newspaper. Those wishing to pursue their study of the Madrid press beyon 1870 should consult *La presse périodique madrilène entre 1871 and 1885* (Th Madrid periodical press between 1871 and 1885) by Gisèle Cazottes (Montpelie France: Université Paul Valéry, Centre de Recherche sur les Littératures Ibériques ( Ibéro-Americaines Modernes, 1982).

# Broadcasting

467  **TM-3: factores diferenciadores de una televisión autonómica.**
(TM-3: the distinguishing features of an autonomous television
station.)
Eusebio Moreno Mangada.    Madrid: Universidad Complutense, 1990.
373p. bibliog.

Until the 1980s Spain had only two state-run television channels. Regional channels
sprang up at the beginning of the decade, but it has only been since the broadcasting
laws were liberalized and private channels made their appearance in 1989 that any
semblance of choice has emerged. Like other autonomous regions, Madrid has its own
television station (TeleMadrid) which is upbeat and energetic, and is particularly good
for local news and live football. The present book presents a good, wide-ranging study
of the television station, its history and development.

# Newspapers, Magazines and Periodicals

## Newspapers

### 468  ABC.
Madrid: Prensa Española, 1905- . daily.

Old-fashioned and staunchly conservative, the leading monarchist newspaper maintains strong contact with the establishment and contains news on business, the economy, culture and sport, as well as foreign relations and policy. Circulation nationally reaches 320,000 (140,000 in Madrid) and it is one of the major newspapers which can be readily obtained outside the region of publication. The arts supplement which appears on Mondays is particularly well regarded. Despite the fact that newspaper kiosks offer a vast array of newspapers and magazines, only around ten per cent of the population nationally buy a daily paper (higher in cities like Madrid). Low literacy rates are in part due to the fact that Spain is a country with a poor popular reading tradition and that there are few popular newspapers with a sufficiently wide circulation, as in other European countries. Most of the big kiosks around the Puerta del Sol, Gran Vía, Calle Alcalá and the Castellana have a wide selection of foreign newspapers, and the *International Herald Tribune* and many British dailies arrive on the day of publication.

### 469  As. (Ace.)
Madrid: Semana, 1967- . daily/weekly.

This is one of the leading sports papers, with a daily circulation figure of 165,000 nationally (49,000 in Madrid) and 215,000 for the weekly edition (60,000 in Madrid). All sports are covered, but most attention and space is devoted to Madrid's two major football teams, Real and Atlético.

### 470  Cinco Días. (Five Days.)
Madrid: Gerencia de Medios, 1979- . daily.

A business and economic daily, this publication has a national circulation of around 30,000 (including 12,000 in Madrid).

471   **Diario 16.** (Daily 16.)
      Madrid: Información y Revistas (Grupo 16), 1976- . daily.
This independent newspaper includes a weekly colour supplement (*Gente*) and has a circulation figure of around 75,000 nationally (48,000 in Madrid), which marks a drop of over thirty per cent on the 1992 figure of 110,000. It looks and reads like a middle-of-the-road version of *El Mundo* (q.v.), but its sports coverage is particularly good.

472   **Expansión.** (Expansion.)
      Madrid: Grupo Recoletos, 1986- . daily.
This is a business/economic daily, which has a circulation of 15,000 in Madrid.

473   **La Gaceta de los Negocios.** (Business Gazette.)
      Madrid: Grupo Zeta, 1989- . daily.
Relatively new, this paper targets the Madrid business and financial sector. It has a national circulation figure of 60,000 (nearly 10,000 in Madrid).

474   **La Información de Madrid.** (Information of Madrid.)
      Madrid: Proprensa, 1994- . daily.
This is Madrid's only specifically local newspaper and contains district-by-district round-ups, which take precedence over national and international news. It has a bright, clean layout and comprehensive daily venue and events listings.

475   **Marca.** (Score.)
      Madrid: Grupo Correo, 1938- . daily.
The most important daily sports paper, *Marca*, has a circulation figure of around 300,000 nationally (102,000 in Madrid), and is one of the top four best-selling dailies in the country (with *ABC*, *El Mundo* and *El País* [qq.v.]), demonstrating how seriously Spaniards take sport. It covers all sports, but concentrates on football (particularly the Madrid clubs of Real and Atlético). During the 1950s and 1960s newspapers in Spain devoted practically no space to political news and even less to local and national news. Cultural, religious and, in particular, sports news were given much more prominence, a fact which accounts for the success of sports newspapers like *Marca* and *As* (q.v.).

476   **El Mundo (del Siglo Veintiuno).** (The World [in the 21st Century].)
      Madrid: Unidad Editorial, 1989- . daily.
The popularity of this newspaper continues to grow despite its relatively short existence. Fiercely critical of the González government and responsible for unearthing the numerous corruption scandals of recent years, it will be interesting to see the approach it takes towards Aznar's new government. Its layout and clarity of news coverage has made it a major rival to the established independent leading daily, *El País* (q.v.). Its sports coverage is good and the weekend magazine (*Revista*) boasts a wonderful style, despite its sometimes lightweight content. On Thursdays it publishes *Metrópoli* (Metropolis), free with the paper, which includes an exhaustive films listing as well as reviews of new releases, and the week's films on television.

477   **El País.** (The Nation.)
      Madrid: El País, 1976- . daily.

The country's biggest-selling paper, *El País* is an independent liberal newspaper which is particularly strong on international news coverage, and provides an informative daily Madrid supplement. The Friday edition includes the arts and entertainment pull-out section, *Tentaciones* (Temptations), which features in-depth analysis of current fashions, and arts and entertainment listings for Madrid and the provinces. On Sundays the newspaper comes with a glossy general-interest magazine, *El País Semanal* (The Nation Weekly). The paper has a circulation figure of around 410,000 (163,000 in Madrid). Since 1982 it has been printed simultaneously in Barcelona, and at the end of 1984 it began publishing a microform edition with subject and chronological indexes. In 1996 it became accessible via the Internet.

478   **Ya.** (Now.)
      Madrid: Editorial Católica, 1935- . daily.

This Catholic, right-wing daily is currently struggling to survive amidst industrial disputes and falling circulation (25,000 nationally, including 21,000 in Madrid). One of the principal underlying reasons for its massive slump in circulation is the fact that the Catholic Church's influence and authority have simultaneously waned over the years since Franco's death in 1975.

**Catálogo de las publicaciones periódicas madrileñas presentadas por la Hemeroteca Municipal de Madrid en la Exposición Internacional de Prensa de Colonia, 1661-1930.** (A catalogue of Madrid periodicals displayed by Madrid's Municipal Newspaper Library at the Cologne International Press Exhibition, 1661-1930.)
*See* item no. 532.

**Catálogo de publicaciones periódicas de la biblioteca de la Universidad Complutense.** (Catalogue of the periodicals held in the Complutense University library.)
*See* item no. 535.

# Magazines

479   **Actualidad Económica.** (Economic News.)
      Madrid: Punto Editorial, 1958- . weekly.

This influential magazine covers business and economic affairs and has a circulation figure of approximately 40,000, principally in Madrid.

480    **Cambio 16.** (Change 16.)
Madrid: Información y Revistas (Grupo 16), 1972- . weekly.
Spain's most widely-read news and current affairs magazine provides reliable information on political, economic and social affairs and has a circulation of around 110,000. Sister publication of *Diario 16* (q.v.), it has a bright and lively style and some excellent reporting. The publishing group and proprietors, Group 16, took their name from a group of sixteen people who founded the magazine at a time of growing political change in Spain.

481    **Ciudadano.** (Citizen.)
Madrid: Ediciones Triángulo, 1978- . monthly.
This publication represents Spain's leading consumer magazine (the equivalent of *Which?*) and includes a wealth of facts, news and surveys. Its circulation is approximately 70,000.

482    **Diez Minutos.** (Ten Minutes.)
Madrid: Gráficas Espejo, 1951- . weekly.
A long-established, general-interest magazine, this represents part of the country's *prensa del corazón* (press of the heart), which gives 'beautiful people' the opportunity to show off their wealth and families. It has a circulation of around 400,000.

483    **Epoca.** (Epoch.)
Madrid: PCM Promoción y Comunicación de Medios, 1985- . weekly.
This general news and information magazine concentrates on politics and business and has a circulation figure of approximately 100,000.

484    **¡Hola!** (Hello!)
Madrid: Hola, 1944- . weekly.
Another of Spain's most popular general-interest weeklies, this is the magazine which gave rise to the *prensa del corazón* (press of the heart). Its unchanging format and style have been successfully exported to France and to Britain in the shape of *Hello!* It has been dubbed the 'bible of bad taste' and 'is dedicated to ensuring that the rich stay famous and the famous stay rich' (Robert Elms, *Spain: a portrait after the general* [London: Mandarin Paperbacks, 1994. 252p.] – which also contains a sharp and witty analysis of contemporary Madrid). The magazine's huge circulation is around 800,000.

485    **Insula.** (Island.)
Madrid: Insula, 1946- . monthly.
In 1955, when Spanish philosopher and writer, José Ortega y Gasset, died, the Ministry of Information and Tourism issued an edict outlining coverage of his death and restricting newspapers to 'three articles relating to the death of Ortega y Gasset: a biography and two commentaries'. *Insula* exceeded the authorized number of pages in issues devoted to the writer, and was consequently closed down. However, in 1957 it reappeared, covering the arts, literature and science, and has a current circulation of about 6,000.

486 **Interviú.** (Interview.)
Madrid: Grupo Zeta, 1976- . weekly.

Usually described as a 'male-interest' magazine due to its glossy pin-ups, this publication occasionally carries some hard-hitting if rather sensationalist reporting. Although more concerned with nudes than news, it has a strong following and a circulation approaching 225,000.

487 **Mercado.** (Market Place.)
Madrid: Grupo Editorial Mercado, 1980- . weekly.

Company directors and financial advisers in Madrid tend to be the principal readers of this respected economic and business information periodical. It has a circulation of about 30,000.

488 **El Mundo Financiero.** (Financial World.)
Madrid: El Mundo Financiero, 1946- . monthly.

This long-established magazine is aimed at executives, chambers of commerce, bankers, directors and other top managers in the city. Written in both English and Spanish, it covers finance, economics, investment, industry and technology. It has a circulation of about 15,000.

489 **Muy Interesante.** (Very Interesting.)
Madrid: G. & J. España, 1981- . monthly.

A popular scientific news magazine, this covers a range of topics including aeronautics, medicine, botany, astronomy, mathematics, history and all aspects of popular science and technology. Its popularity is reflected in its circulation figure of close to 300,000.

490 **Pronto.** (Here and Now.)
Madrid: Publicaciones Heres, 1972- . weekly.

This general-interest magazine, targeted at women in their thirties, enjoys a circulation figure approaching one million.

491 **Semana.** (This Week.)
Madrid: Semana, 1942- . weekly.

One of the country's most popular weeklies, this illustrated general-interest magazine has a circulation figure of around 370,000.

492 **Tiempo.** (Time.)
Madrid: Grupo Zeta, 1982- . weekly.

This general information magazine has become one of the most popular weeklies in Spain. It includes some good reporting, but like its sister publication, *Panorama* (Grupo Zeta. weekly), it is more light-hearted than *Cambio 16* (q.v.). It also enjoys a respectable readership in the United Kingdom (students and teachers of Spanish). The magazine mixes politics with economics, general-interest and current affairs, but also includes numerous photographs of the rich, famous and influential. More recently, the number of pages taken up with these, together with slightly more sensationalist reporting, has tended to detract from its established approach. Circulation, nationally, is around 185,000.

493　**Tribuna.** (Tribune.)
Madrid: Tribuna de Ediciones de Medios Informativos, 1988- .
weekly.
With an emphasis on politics and business, this popular weekly has a circulation of
approximately 95,000.

# Listings magazines

494　**En Madrid.** (In Madrid.)
Madrid: Ayuntamiento, Patronato Municipal de Turismo, 1981- .
monthly.
This 'what's on?' guide is produced for visitors to the city and has parallel English
and Spanish text. It provides a monthly listings guide for ballet, concerts, conferences,
sports, exhibitions, fairs, music, children, opera and theatre, as well as a range of other
helpful information. Illustrated, it also contains a good map of the city.

495　**Enjoy Madrid.**
Madrid: Nuevas Alternativas Turísticas, 1994- . bimonthly.
Aimed at tourist visitors to Madrid, this is more than a simple listings magazine. Each
issue contains a standard range of information relating to: transport, galleries and
museums, places of interest, events and festivities, culture, hotels, sport and leisure,
eating and drinking, nightlife and shopping. Complementing this information are maps
and illustrations and an updated calendar of events in the city. The text is presented in
parallel Spanish and English.

496　**Guía de Madrid.** (Guide to Madrid.)
Madrid: Información y Prensa, 1988- . weekly.
Every Friday *Diario 16* (q.v.) publishes this free listings guide for the city. It follows a
standard format covering cinema, theatre, art and culture, food and drink, nightlife,
television, videos and music.

497　**Guía del Ocio.** (Leisure Guide.)
Madrid: Trisiansky, 1976- . weekly.
Published every Thursday and sold in the city's kiosks, this 150-page pocket-sized
leisure guide offers comprehensive cinema, arts and entertainments listings. In
addition there are regular sections on sport, festivals, television, nightclubs, bars,
children's entertainment (from the aquarium to puppet shows) and reviews of books.

498　**Madrid en Música.** (Musical Madrid.)
Madrid: Ignacio Martín, 1994- . monthly.
A mixture of listings, interviews and articles, this magazine provides a full and
detailed guide to all the important musical events in the city, from blues and jazz to
classical. It also includes a review section for new books and recordings.

499  **Madrid y sus Servicios.** (Madrid and its Services.)
Madrid: Información Empresarial, 1994- . monthly.

This is not a full listings guide as such, but a magazine which mixes articles with small-ads (cars, accommodation, offices, jobs and services) and television and cinema listings. Packed with advertisements and information, its layout could be improved. Similarly, *Segundamano* (Secondhand) is an expanded small-ads magazine that appears three times a week on Mondays, Wednesdays and Fridays. It is the first stop for anyone flat-hunting and also advertises a wide range of goods. Adverts can be placed free-of-charge at any of its many offices around the city.

500  **Periódico Inmobilario.** (Property Newspaper.)
Madrid: Commodity Traders, 1992- . fortnightly.

Primarily consisting of advertisements for renting and selling flats and offices, this paper also contains an editorial and articles which deal with the housing market in, and urban development of, Madrid.

501  **El Punto de las Artes.** (Arts Focus.)
Madrid: Comunicación y Cultura, 1986- . weekly.

This newspaper looks at the whole range of arts and exhibitions in Madrid and the rest of Spain, and provides details and listings. It also contains international, people, and music and dance sections.

**El Mundo (del Siglo Veintiuno).** (The World [in the 21st Century].)
*See* item no. 476.

**El País.** (The Nation.)
*See* item no. 477.


# Other periodicals

502  **Alfoz: Madrid, Territorio, Economía y Sociedad.** (Alfoz: Madrid, Land, Economy and Society.)
Madrid: Centro de Investigaciones y Documentación Urbana y Rural, 1983-94. bimonthly.

Although this publication has now ceased to appear, it still remains a very useful source of information on issues relating to the urban development of the city and Community of Madrid.

503  **Boletín del Museo Arqueológico Nacional.** (Bulletin of the National Archaeological Museum.)
Madrid: Museo Arqueológico Nacional, 1983- . annual.

The National Archaeological Museum is one of Madrid's oldest museums (established in 1867) and traces the evolution of human cultures from prehistoric times up to the

15th century. Some of its most interesting displays come from the area around Madrid itself, such as the 4,000 year-old neolithic campaniform (bell-shaped) pottery bowls found just north of the city at Ciempozuelos. The ground floor of the Museum holds its most prized possession, the Iberian sculpture of the *Dama de Elche* (Lady of Elche), an enigmatic figure whose true gender and identity remains a mystery. In the front garden of the Museum, steps lead underground to a reproduction of the renowned Altamira cave-paintings of Cantabria. As the actual caves have been closed to visitors in order to preserve and conserve the paintings, the Museum's reproductions are the closest most people can get to the real thing. Unfortunately, items and relics in the Museum are labelled in Spanish only. The Museum's *Bulletin* provides information on its acquisitions, organization and plans for the future.

504 **Boletín Oficial del Estado.** (Official Gazette.)
Madrid: Ministerio de la Presidencia, 1939- . daily.
The Spanish state's official gazette began life in 1661 as the *Gaceta de Madrid* (Madrid Gazette). It was founded on the advice of Philip IV's secretary, Pedro Fernández del Campo, who had encouraged the creation of a government publication similar to those that existed in Paris and other European capitals. It went through some changes of name (*Gaceta Nueva* [New Gazette], *Gaceta Ordinaria de Madrid* [Current Madrid Gazette]) until in 1697 it was definitively named *Gaceta de Madrid* (Madrid Gazette). It soon became extremely popular, and under Charles III (1759-88) it developed into the official organ for the dissemination of government information. Up to this time it had appeared weekly, but in 1788 it began to appear twice a week on Tuesdays and Fridays. In 1837 it became the *Boletín Oficial Nacional* (Official National Bulletin) in which all official decrees and reports had to be included. It started to appear on a daily basis in 1909 and its various sections were formally structured to give it a uniform appearance. During the course of the Civil War (1936-39) its name was changed in the nationalist zone to its present title. Since 1995 summaries of the contents of each issue of the *Boletín* have been made available electronically on the World Wide Web (URL: http://www.boe.es). It is also worth noting that the Comunidad de Madrid publishes its own official gazette, the *Boletín Oficial de la Comunidad de Madrid* (Official Bulletin of the Madrid Community) (Madrid: Comunidad de Madrid, Secretaría General Técnica, 1983- . daily [except Sundays]), as does the Madrid Assembly with its *Boletín Oficial de la Asamblea de Madrid* (Official Bulletin of the Madrid Assembly) (Madrid: Asamblea de Madrid, 1983- . weekly) and the *Diario de Sesiones de la Asamblea de Madrid* (Daily Bulletin of the Sessions of the Madrid Assembly) (Parliamentary Report of the Assembly of Madrid) (Madrid: Asamblea de Madrid, 1983- . irregular).

505 **En Directo.** (Live.)
Madrid: Cámara Oficial de Comercio e Industria, 1989- . monthly.
This useful publication contains details and dates relating to meetings, trade fairs and talks, and is an important source of information for the business and industrial sectors in Madrid. Other regular sections give information relating to courses, new publications and useful addresses.

506 **La Farola.** (Street Light.)
Barcelona, Spain: El Periódico de la Precariedad, 1994- . fortnightly.

Spain's newspaper of the homeless and unemployed is published in Barcelona but is distributed widely in Madrid, with its contents reflecting the capital's social problems of homelessness and unemployment. Articles and letters form the bulk of the publication. The vendors receive seventy-five per cent of the sale price which, compared with similar publications in other European countries, is generous (Britain's *Big Issue* offers fifty per cent).

507 **Revista de la Universidad Complutense.** (Journal of the Complutense University.)
Madrid: Universidad Complutense, 1972-86. annual.

Although this journal is no longer published, it remains a rich source of information, not just on the University but on Madrid generally. It began life in 1869 as the *Boletín de la Universidad de Madrid* (1869-70), which became the *Revista de la Universidad de Madrid* (1873-77) and continued as the *Boletín de la Universidad de Madrid* (1929-31), the *Anales de la Universidad de Madrid* (1932-36) and the *Revista de la Universidad de Madrid* (1940-72). Copies of all these titles are available in the Biblioteca Nacional (National Library).

**Estudios Geográficos.** (Geographical Studies.)
*See* item no. 14.

**Anuario de prehistoria madrileña.** (Yearbook of Madrid prehistory.)
*See* item no. 77.

**Estudios de Prehistoria y Arqueología Madrileñas.** (Studies in the Prehistory and Archaeology of Madrid.)
*See* item no. 80.

**Anales del Instituto de Estudios Madrileños.** (Annals of the Institute of Madrid Studies.)
*See* item no. 85.

**Anuario Económico y Financiero.** (Economic and Financial Yearbook.)
*See* item no. 208.

**Madrid as a business centre: Financial Times survey.**
*See* item no. 220.

# Encyclopaedias, Directories and Biographical Dictionaries

## Encyclopaedias

508 **Madrid.**
Edited by Antonio Bonet Correa.    Madrid: Espasa-Calpe, 1979-80.
5 vols. maps. bibliog.
One of the best reference sources for Madrid, this huge, glossy publication spans over 2,000 pages. Each volume considers a particular district of the city and provides an informative and reliable text, amply supported by numerous colour illustrations.

509 **Enciclopedia de Madrid.** (Encyclopaedia of Madrid.)
Edited by Vicente Giner.    Madrid: Giner, 1988-89. 3 vols. bibliog.
This up-to-date reference encyclopaedia covers over 2,000 pages and contains numerous black-and-white illustrations. Compiled by respected specialists, the work focuses on the buildings and arts of the city. Volume one describes and analyses historic monuments, fountains and tombstones; volume two concentrates on all aspects of the city's civil architecture; and volume three considers the folk-songs of Madrid.

510 **Gran enciclopedia de Madrid, Castilla-La Mancha.** (Great encyclopaedia of Madrid, Castile-La Mancha.)
Edited by José Luis Morales y Marín.    Zaragoza, Spain: Unión Aragonesa del Libro, 1982-88. 12 vols. maps. bibliog.
Although encompassing the Community of Madrid, this extensive survey also contains a wealth of detail on all aspects of the city itself.

# Directories

511 **Madrid Práctico.** (Practical Madrid.)
Madrid: Espasa-Calpe, 1990- . annual. (Guías Espasa).

Subtitled 'the 3000 best addresses for living, spending and enjoying yourself – the indispensable guide for saving time and money', this handy guide runs to over 600 pages each year, and offers tips, bargains and insights for anyone living in, or visiting, the capital.

**Guía del Comercio y de la Industria de Madrid.** (Guide to Commerce and Industry in Madrid.)
*See* item no. 223.

**Guía de la comunicación de la Comunidad de Madrid.** (Guide to communications in the Community of Madrid.)
*See* item no. 235.

**Bibliotecas de Madrid.** (Libraries of Madrid.)
*See* item no. 451.

**Nueva guía de las bibliotecas de Madrid.** (A new guide to the libraries of Madrid.)
*See* item no. 453.

**Guía de los archivos de Madrid.** (Guide to the archives of Madrid.)
*See* item no. 455.

# Biographical dictionaries

512 **Médicos madrileños famosos: biografías y bibliografías de médicos ilustres, nacidos en Madrid y su provincia.** (Madrid's famous doctors: biographies and bibliographies of illustrious physicians, born in Madrid and its province.)
José Alvarez Sierra.   Madrid: El Siglo Médico, 1934. 261p. bibliog.

The author wrote a number of studies on medicine and health in Madrid. This biographical dictionary provides details of the most famous physicians of Madrid, together with a list of works written by, and about, them. Other related books by this author include: *Historia de la medicina madrileña* (A history of medicine in Madrid) (Madrid: Editorial Universitaria Europea, 1968. 181p.); and *Los hospitales de Madrid de ayer y de hoy* (q.v.).

513   **Madrid: cien madrileños ilustres.** (Madrid: one hundred famous
      Madrilenians.)
      José del Corral.   Madrid: Espasa-Calpe, 1980. 100p.

This illustrated biographical study includes details on some of the city's most
important and interesting characters from different periods of its history. Other older
works of related interest include: *Hijos de Madrid, ilustres en santidad, dignidades,
armas, ciencias y artes* (Sons of Madrid, famous for their saintliness, dignity, military
achievement, science and art) by José Antonio Alvarez y Baena (Madrid: [s.n.], 1789-
91. 4 vols.); *Diccionario biográfico matritense* (Biographical dictionary of Madrid) by
Luis Ballesteros Robles (Madrid: Ayuntamiento, 1912. 702p.); and *Diccionario
histórico, político, topográfico, genealógico, bibliográfico y de costumbres de Madrid
hasta 1780* (Historical, political, topographical, genealogical, bibliographical and
anthropological dictionary of Madrid up to 1780) by Basilio Sebastián Castellanos
(Madrid: [s.n.], 1780. 1 vol.).

514   **Who's who in Spain: 1994.**
      Edited by John C. Dove.   Zürich, Switzerland: Who's Who in Spain,
      1994. 2,050p. (Sutter's International Red Series).

Reflecting the growing interest in Spain and its economic, political, industrial and
cultural figures, this revised and expanded edition (from the 1992 edition) contains
around 9,000 biographies and over 4,000 company profiles. It is the only English-
language biographical dictionary available for Spain, and the data on individuals
includes occupation, career, address, awards, publications and hobbies.

**Alcaldes de Madrid.** (Mayors of Madrid.)
*See* item no. 202.

**Pérez Galdós, Spanish liberal crusader.**
*See* item no. 316.

**Cervantes en Madrid: vida y muerte.** (Cervantes in Madrid: life and death.)
*See* item no. 319.

**Escritores madrileños.** (Writers of Madrid.)
*See* item no. 336.

**Bibliografía literaria de Madrid.** (Literary bibliography of Madrid.)
*See* item no. 341.

**Y Madrid se hizo flamenco.** (And Madrid took up flamenco.)
*See* item no. 395.

# Bibliographies

## General

515 **Bibliografía de bibliografías locales.** (Bibliography of local bibliographies.)
Madrid: Biblioteca Nacional, 1987. 32p.

This short bibliography includes references to the principal local bibliographies, and can be purchased from the National Library.

516 **Impresos madrileños de 1566 a 1625.** (Madrid's printed works from 1566 to 1625.)
Yolanda Clemente San Román. Madrid: Universidad Complutense, 1992. 1,248p.

This massive work was originally presented as the author's doctoral thesis at the Universidad Complutense. It is a staggeringly comprehensive bibliographical survey of the output of the Madrid presses over a period of nearly sixty years.

517 **Manual bibliográfico de estudios españoles.** (A bibliographical guide to Spanish studies.)
Fernando González Ollé. Pamplona, Spain: Ediciones Universidad de Navarra, 1976. 1,375p.

Despite its age, this mine of information on all subjects relating to Spain remains a valuable source. It includes many references on a whole range of subject areas for Madrid, from art to football clubs, with entries primarily in Spanish but also in English and French. Reference is made to over 30,000 works covering twenty-two subject areas, each closely subdivided with chronological and geographical subsections where appropriate. It is easy to use due to its excellent author and subject indexes, detailed table of contents and numerous cross-references. Unfortunately, it does not include the names of publishers, but only cites the place of publication.

518  **Libros sobre Madrid, 1992: catálogo.** (Books on Madrid, 1992:
a catalogue.)
Madrid: La Librería, 1992. 120p.

The publisher is one of the two bookshops in the city (El Avapiés being the other)
specializing in the field of Madrid studies. This expanded catalogue of books about the
city was published to coincide with Madrid's role as European Capital of Culture in
the same year. A work of related interest is *Libros sobre Madrid y provincia* (Books
about Madrid and province) (Madrid: Instituto Nacional del Libro Español, 1982.
101p.).

519  **Bibliografía de Madrid y su provincia.** (A bibliography of Madrid
and its province.)
José Luis Oliva Escribano.  Madrid: Instituto de Estudios Madrileños,
1967-69. 2 vols. (Biblioteca de Estudios Madrileños, nos. IX, X).

Although now very dated, this excellent work represents the first full-scale
bibliographical study of all aspects of Madrid city and province. It was first published
in 1958-59 (Madrid: El Libro Español. 2 vols.), again in two volumes, although it was
originally intended to produce a third volume containing references to illustrations and
pictures of Madrid in books and periodicals. This third volume never materialized, and
the two published volumes cover books and manuscripts, and periodical articles
respectively. The compiler, Oliva Escribano, spent years researching his entries from
the catalogues of all the major libraries of Madrid, and each entry includes an
abbreviation of the library which houses that particular work. Volume one contains
5,425 references organized in alphabetical order by author, whilst volume two has
7,304 entries and a complete index for both volumes.

520  **Manual del librero hispanoamericano: bibliografía general
española e hispanoamericana desde la invención de la imprenta
hasta nuestros tiempos, con el valor comercial de los impresos
descritos.** (Handbook for the bookseller of Latin American
publications: a general bibliography of Spanish and Latin American
publications from the invention of printing to the present, including the
commercial price of the listed works.)
Antonio Palau y Dulcet.  Barcelona, Spain: Librería Palau; Oxford:
Dolphin, 1948-78. 2nd ed. 28 vols.

Originally published in Barcelona between 1923 and 1927 in seven volumes, this
revised and expanded edition is the most complete bibliography of Spanish-language
publications from the beginning of printing to the 20th century. It remains a rich
source of information for material on Madrid amongst its total of 321,827 references,
which are often accompanied by corresponding library locations. The twenty-eight
volumes are arranged in alphabetical order by author, or under title for anonymous
works. In 1981 an index to the set began to appear and was completed in 1987,
compiled by Agustín Palau Claveras: *Indice alfabético de títulos-materias,
correcciones, conexiones y adiciones del Manual del librero hispanoamericano de
Antonio Palau y Dulcet* (Ampurias, Spain: Palacete Palau y Dulcet; Oxford: Dolphin,
1981-87. 7 vols.). As its title states, it represents a full index of titles and subjects, and
includes corrections, references and addenda.

521 **Bibliografía madrileña: obras bibliográficas de carácter general.**
(Madrid bibliography: bibliographical works of a general nature.)
Ramón Paz.   Madrid: Ayuntamiento, 1946. 40p.

Still useful, despite its age, this bibliography of bibliographies lists a number of general bibliographical publications on Madrid. The author also compiled *Bibliografía madrileña* (Madrid bibliography) (Madrid: Ayuntamiento, 1948. 54p.), and a similar work with the same title in collaboration with Isidro Montiel (Madrid: Ayuntamiento, 1950. 34p.).

522 **Bibliografía madrileña de los siglos XVI y XVII.** (Bibliography of Madrid for the 16th and 17th centuries.)
Cristóbal Pérez Pastor.   Amsterdam, Netherlands: Gérard Th. Van Heusden, 1970-71. 3 vols.

Originally published as *Bibliografía madrileña o descripción de las obras impresas en Madrid* (Madrid bibliography or description of works printed in Madrid) (Madrid: Imp. del Asilo de Huérfanos del S. C. de Jesús, 1891-1907. 3 vols.), this comprehensive work details the output of Madrid's presses from: 1566-1600 (vol. 1); 1601-20 (vol. 2); and 1621-25 (vol. 3).

523 **Bibliografía de Madrid.** (Bibliography of Madrid.)
María Teresa Rodríguez, María Luisa Martínez Conde.   Madrid: La Librería, 1994. 445p.

The specific aim of this work was to update the pioneering work of Oliva Escribano's *Bibliografía de Madrid y su provincia* (q.v.). Supported by the Fundación Amigos de Madrid (Friends of Madrid Foundation), this admirable volume contains 5,230 unannotated bibliographical references and is now established as the standard bibliographical work in Spanish on the city of Madrid. Although the work is wide-ranging, with most of the entries compiled from the holdings of the five biggest libraries in Madrid (including the Biblioteca Nacional), it does not include references to periodical articles, nor does it contain material relating to law. The subject areas covered are: reference works (bibliographies, biographies, encyclopaedias and dictionaries); travellers' accounts; customs; history; religion; education; science and technology; Madrid in literature; dialectology; arts; libraries, museums and archives; book trade; society and population; health; politics and government; commerce and industry; economy; town planning; transport and communications; agriculture, flora and fauna; sport and recreation; and food and drink. Within each section the entries are organized alphabetically by author (or by title). The volume is completed by an author index and a detailed subject index, each referring the reader to the relevant item number in the text. As so many works have 'Madrid' as their title, the authors felt it unhelpful to include a title index. Despite the inevitable gaps and omissions, it is a fine work, and the authors are to be congratulated on producing such a substantial and well-organized bibliography. It will prove an invaluable source of information for researchers, students and those curious about aspects of Madrid for many years to come.

524 **Aproximación a la bibliografía sobre la Comunidad de Madrid.**
(An introductory bibliography on the Community of Madrid.)
Miguel Angel Torremocha. *Educación y Biblioteca*, no. 55
(March 1995), p. 64-66.

This short, up-to-date compilation provides a useful starting-point for references on various aspects of the Autonomous Community of Madrid, including the province and city. The article lists nearly 200 books on Madrid divided into the following sections: general; history; art, architecture and urban development; geography; flora and fauna; the city of Madrid; customs and literature; economy; and local history.

# Subject

525 **Guía de fuentes documentales para la historia urbana de Madrid:**
**1940-1980.** (A guide to documentary sources on the urban history of
Madrid: 1940-80.)
Carmen Gavira. Madrid: Instituto de Información y Documentación
en Ciencias Sociales, 1984. 365p. maps.

Written specifically to facilitate the work of students, researchers, administrators and local government officials interested in the recent history of Madrid, this very useful bibliography contains references to over 3,000 documents relating to the demographic, social, urban and administrative history of the city and Autonomous Community of Madrid. Clearly set out and thorough in its coverage of sources, it includes: a general survey of Spain during the forty-year period; a chronology of Madrid's urban, political, economic and planning history during the same period; the bibliography itself (including books, reports, laws, periodical articles and conferences); indexes (by subject, geographical location and author); and appendices listing libraries and information centres consulted, bibliographies on Spain in general and Madrid in particular, the local press and Madrid dailies between 1936 and 1980.

526 **The theatre in Madrid during the Second Republic: a checklist.**
Michael D. McGaha. London: Grant & Cutler, 1979. 105p. (Research
Bibliographies and Checklists, no. 29).

The purpose of this chronological list is to provide as complete a record as possible of the plays performed in Madrid from the proclamation of the Second Republic (14 April 1931) to the outbreak of the Civil War (18 July 1936). The data have been compiled from the theatre pages of the Madrid daily newspapers of the period, supplemented by information from additional sources. The 1,258-item list is followed by an index of authors, translators, adaptors and titles. A select bibliography of the Spanish theatre in the period 1931-36 is appended to the introduction.

527 **Contribuciones documentales a la historia de Madrid.**
(Documentary contributions to the history of Madrid.)
Agustín Millares Carló. Madrid: Instituto de Estudios Madrileños,
1971. 249p. (Biblioteca de Estudios Madrileños, no. XIII).

The author has written widely on various aspects of Madrid's history, and this fascinating study contains extracts from a number of documents from the archives of the Ayuntamiento. It also includes a list of the incunabula held in the Biblioteca Municipal, together with helpful indexes to the material. It has become a valuable source of information for researchers of primary historical texts for Madrid. Of related interest is the catalogue of an exhibition of historical works on Madrid, entitled *Mil libros en la historia de Madrid* . . . (A thousand books on the history of Madrid . . .), organized by El Consultor de los Ayuntamientos et al. (Madrid: Comunidad de Madrid; El Consultor de los Ayuntamientos, 1993. 261p.).

528 **Reseña bibliográfica y documental en las áreas de trabajo, industria y comercio en la Comunidad de Madrid.** (A bibliographical and documentary report on the subjects of work, industry and trade in the Community of Madrid.)
Madrid: Comunidad, Secretaría General Técnica, 1986. 234p.

Based on the Community's own publications programme, this work includes everything that they had published (up to 1986) in the fields of labour, industry and commerce. Similarly, in the following year they published *Reseña bibliográfica y documental en el área de turismo de la Comunidad de Madrid* (A bibliographical and documentary report on the area of tourism in the Community of Madrid) (1987. 310p.).

529 **Fuentes para la historia de Madrid y su provincia: tomo 1, textos impresos de los siglos XVI y XVII.** (Sources for the history of Madrid and its province: volume 1, printed texts of the 16th and 17th centuries.)
Compiled by José Simón Díaz. Madrid: Patronato 'José Mª. Quadrado' del CSIC; Instituto de Estudios Madrileños, 1964. 461p. (Biblioteca de Estudios Madrileños, no. VIII).

Established in the early 1950s, the instigator and co-publisher of this work, the Instituto de Estudios Madrileños (Institute of Madrid Studies), has been instrumental over the years in producing a wide range of publications covering all aspects of Madrid. Its erudite Secretary, José del Corral, has himself written hundreds of books, pamphlets and articles on Madrid. The Institute's library provides an excellent range of browsable material for the interested visitor. The present work is a fascinating compilation of between sixty and seventy literary texts, printed in the 16th and 17th centuries, which are useful primary sources of historical information for Madrid. Ten are reproduced in their entirety, whilst the others represent extracts from complete works. Authors represented include Juan López de Hoyos, Alonso de Castillo Solorzano and Francisco Bernardo de Quirós. Useful name, topographic and subject indexes are also provided for easy location of material on specific aspects of Madrid. Only volume one was published in what was intended to be a multi-volume study covering a whole range of texts and documents relating to Madrid. Simón Díaz has written numerous books on Madrid, including the imposing two-volume *Guía literaria de Madrid* (q.v.); *Libros madrileños de los siglos de oro* (Madrid books of the Golden Age) (Madrid: Instituto de Estudios Madrileños, 1953. 36p.); *Bibliografía madrileña* (Madrid bibliography) (Madrid: Ayuntamiento, 1951. 19p.); and *Cien escritores madrileños del siglo de oro: notas bibliográficas* (One hundred Madrid writers of the Golden Age: bibliographical notes) (Madrid: Instituto de Estudios Madrileños, 1975. 160p.).

530 **Bibliografía básica de arquitectura en Madrid: siglos XIX y XX.**
(A basic bibliography of architecture in Madrid: 19th and 20th centuries.)
Angel Urrutia Núñez.   Madrid: Universidad Autónoma, 1991. 67p.

Published as a supplement to the annual review of the University's Department of History and Theory of Art, this work provides an excellent starting-point for those interested in the theory and development of Madrid's contemporary architecture. The author also wrote *Arquitectura doméstica moderna en Madrid* (Modern domestic architecture in Madrid) (Madrid: Universidad Autónoma, 1988. 214p.).

**Early computer developments in Madrid.**
*See* item no. 309.

**Bibliografía literaria de Madrid.** (Literary bibliography of Madrid.)
*See* item no. 341.

**The 'teatro por horas': history, dynamics and comprehensive bibliography of a Madrid industry, 1867-1922 ('género chico', 'género ínfimo' and early cinema).**
*See* item no. 412.

**Art Libraries Journal.**
*See* item no. 448.

**Revistas femeninas madrileñas.** (Madrid's women's magazines.)
*See* item no. 465.

**Madrid newspapers 1661-1870: a computerized handbook based on the work of Eugenio Hartzenbusch.**
*See* item no. 466.

**Médicos madrileños famosos: biografías y bibliografías de médicos ilustres, nacidos en Madrid y su provincia.** (Madrid's famous doctors: biographies and bibliographies of illustrious physicians, born in Madrid and its province.)
*See* item no. 512.

**Diccionario histórico, político, topográfico, genealógico, bibliográfico y de costumbres de Madrid hasta 1780.** (Historical, political, topographical, genealogical, bibliographical and anthropological dictionary of Madrid up to 1780.)
*See* item no. 513.

# Library catalogues

531 **Anuario Bibliográfico.** (Bibliographical Yearbook.)
Madrid: Biblioteca Regional de Madrid, 1992- . annual.

Originally published quarterly as the *Boletín Interno del Centro de Documentación para la Historia de Madrid* (Internal Bulletin of the Documentation Centre for the History of Madrid) (Madrid: C. D. H. M., 1990-91), and *Boletín Bibliográfico* (Bibliographical Bulletin) (1991-92), this publication provides bibliographic references for books and articles in the 'Madrid Collection' of the Biblioteca Regional of Madrid. The collection covers a wide range of subjects, including art, science, literature and history. It also includes all the periodical publications which are held in the library.

532 **Catálogo de las publicaciones periódicas madrileñas presentadas por la Hemeroteca Municipal de Madrid en la Exposición Internacional de Prensa de Colonia, 1661-1930.** (A catalogue of Madrid periodicals displayed by Madrid's Municipal Newspaper Library at the Cologne International Press Exhibition, 1661-1930.)
Compiled by Antonio Asenjo Pérez. Madrid: Ayuntamiento, 1932.
1 vol.

This illustrated catalogue lists and describes the most important newspapers held by the city's newspaper library, beginning with the *Gaceta de Madrid* (q.v.) first published in 1661. Asenjo also wrote *La prensa madrileña a través de los siglos: apuntes para su historia desde el año 1661 al de 1925* (The Madrid press through the centuries: notes on its history from 1661 to 1925) (Madrid: Ayuntamiento, 1933. 78p.).

533 **Catálogo de la Biblioteca Municipal de Madrid.** (Catalogue of Madrid City Library.)
Edited by Carlos Cambronero. Madrid: Biblioteca Municipal, 1902.
536p.

This catalogue represents an excellent source of historical information on Madrid and covers a variety of different subject areas.

534 **Catálogo de manuscritos de la Real Academia Española.** (Catalogue of the manuscripts of the Spanish Royal Academy.)
Madrid: La Academia, 1991. 502p.

Founded in 1713, Spain's first official academy had as its objective the cultivation and improvement of the national language (Castilian). To that end it produced a dictionary which would distinguish the words and phrases employed by the best Spanish writers from the slang and colloquial terms to be excluded from good writing. Its authoritative *Diccionario de la lengua española* (Dictionary of the Spanish language) was first published in 1780, and reached its 21st edition in 1994. The Academy's other current duties include the sponsoring of authoritative classic texts, and the present catalogue provides a fascinating reference source for some of the most important and valuable Spanish manuscripts held in the Academy's library.

535 **Catálogo de publicaciones periódicas de la biblioteca de la Universidad Complutense.** (Catalogue of the periodicals held in the Complutense University library.)
Compiled by Cecilia Fernández Fernández et al. Madrid: Editorial Complutense, 1993. 2 vols.

Spanning 1,100 pages, this listing details all the journal and newspaper holdings of the University library.

536 **Colección de documentos sobre Madrid.** (A collection of documents on Madrid.)
Compiled by Angela González-Palencia Simón. Madrid: Instituto de Estudios Madrileños; Archivo de Protocolos de Madrid, 1953. 741p. (Biblioteca de Estudios Madrileños, vol. 3).

Represents an extensive bibliographic and documentary survey of the Archivo de Protocolos de Madrid (Archive of the Protocols of Madrid), and a catalogue of its works.

537 **An index to the 'Teatro Español' collection in the 'Biblioteca de Palacio'.**
Karl C. Gregg. Charlottesville, Virginia: Biblioteca Siglo de Oro, 1987. 155p. (Biblioteca Siglo de Oro, no. 7).

The library of the Royal Palace in Madrid was founded in 1760 and contains over quarter of a million printed works, incunabula, manuscripts, music and rare editions dating from the 16th century, as well as engravings and drawings. The Teatro Español (Spanish Theatre) collection in the library is held in twenty-five identically-bound volumes. The present work provides a short descriptive listing of the works included in these tomes. The index is arranged in alphabetical order by title, and is followed by appendices which list, for all the indexed works: volume contents; sources; numbered editions; date of printing; place of printing; printers, publishers and booksellers; and authors.

**Libros sobre Madrid, 1992: catálogo.** (Books on Madrid, 1992: a catalogue.)
*See* item no. 518.

**Contribuciones documentales a la historia de Madrid.** (Documentary contributions to the history of Madrid.)
*See* item no. 527.

# Theses

538 **Tesis Doctorales de la Universidad Complutense de Madrid.**
(Doctoral Theses of the Complutense University of Madrid.)
Madrid: Editorial de la Universidad Complutense, 1977- . annual.
2 vols.

Originally published as part of the *Revista de la Universidad Complutense* (q.v.), this annual, two-volume publication can be consulted in the University library. Of related interest is the *Catálogo de las tesis doctorales manuscritas existentes en la Universidad de Madrid* (Catalogue of the manuscript doctoral theses held in the University of Madrid) (Madrid: Universidad Central, 1952. 36p.), which offers a fascinating insight into topics investigated in some of the older theses.

# Indexes

There follow three separate indexes: authors (personal and corporate); titles; and subjects. Title entries are italicized and refer either to the main titles, or to other works cited in the annotations. The numbers refer to bibliographical entry rather than page numbers. Individual index entries are arranged in alphabetical sequence.

## Index of Authors

Eire, C. M. N. 425
Elliott, J. H. 383
Elms, J. 46
Elms, R. 484
Enríquez, E. V. 149
Enríquez Arranz, M. D. 375
Entrambasaguas Peña, J. de 435
Eoff, S. H. 316
Epton, N. C. 3
Equipo de Investigación Sociológica 175
Equipo Giens 146
Equipo Madrid de Estudios Históricos 114
Erskine, B. S. 89, 355
Escribano, R. 440
Escribano Ortiz, A. 395
Espín Templado, M. P. 412
Espina García, A. 426, 433
Esgueva, M. 149
Estébanez Alvarez, J. 210
Evans, L. 36
Ezquiaga, I. 245

## F

Farndale, N. 29
Feito Crespo, S. 214
Fernán Gómez, F. 4, 325
Fernández, J. 299
Fernández, S. F. 435
Fernández Alba, A. 62
Fernández Alvarez, M. 107
Fernández Arbos, E. 396
Fernández Arriba, E. A. 104
Fernández Cid, A. 407
Fernández de la Mora, G. 10
Fernández de los Ríos, A. 37
Fernández Durán, R. 233
Fernández Fernández, C. 535
Fernández García, A. 90
Fernández Nieto, B. E. 200

Fernández Polanco, A. 270
Fernández Pombo, A. 38
Fernández Quintanilla, P. 161
Fernández Vegue, A. 39, 367
Ferrer, S. 202
Figueroa, J. 257
Fisher, A. E. 326
Fishman, R. M. 243
Flores, C. 275
Flynn, J. P. 193
Fodor, Eugene 29
Fonteriz, L. de 128
Ford, R. 72
Forneas, M. C. 441
Fradejas Labrero, J. 344
Franco Rubio, G. A. 150
Fuenmayor Gordón, P. de 197
Fuente, L. de la 176
Fundación Amigos de Madrid 54

## G

Galán Font, E. 331
Gallero, J. L. 162
García, C. 406
García, R. 91, 348, 427
García, S. 211
García Alvarez, M. 251
García Ballesteros, A. 139
García de la Infanta, J. M. 308
García Garrido, J. 446
García Gutiérrez, P. F. 66, 292
García Martín, A. 204
García-París, M. 284
García Pastor, A. 232
García Quintas, M. A. 262
García Sainz, C. 244
García Sanjuán, A. 200
García Santemases, J. 309
García Zamorano, J. M. 446
Garín Llombart, F. V. 368
Garrido, L. 369
Gassier, P. 362
Gavira, C. 14, 204, 525
Gaya Nuño, J. A. 370

Gea Ortigas, M. I. 5, 68, 91, 289
Gentilli, L. 75
Gibbons, J. L. 163
Gil Huerres, A. 221
Gilbert, M. L. 354
Gilmour, D. 6
Giménez Romero, C. 144
Giner, V. 509
Godzich, W. 411
Goldman, P. B. 339
Gómez Amat, C. 396
Gómez de Aizpurua, C. 284
Gómez de Salazar y Alonso, J. 441
Gómez de la Serna, R. 63, 69, 118
Gómez Iglesias, A. 201
Gómez López, J. 454
Gómez Moreno, M. 94
Gómez Nieto, L. 425
Gómez Santos, M. 238
González Alonso, S. 254, 262
González Bernáldez, F. 262
González Blasco, P. 451
González Calbet, L. 221
González Casarrubios, C. 430
González del Valle, T. 414
González Ollé, F. 517
González-Palencia Simón, A. 536
González Serrano, P. 66
González Vicario, M. T. 391
González-Yanci, M. P. 147, 234
Gosling, S. 45
Gregg, K. C. 537
Grismer, R. L. 319
Guardia, C. de la 186
Gudiol, J. 362
Guerrero Mayllo, A. 101
Gunther, R. 243
Gutiérrez Solana, J. 57
Gutkind, E. A. 263
Guerra de la Vega, R. 64, 293
Guzmán, C. 240

Martínez Carbajo, A. F. 66
Martínez Conde, M. L. 97, 523
Martínez Gómez, J. 170
Martínez Kleiser, L. 68
Martínez Llopis, M. 435
Martínez Martín, J. A. 209, 223
Martínez-Novillo González, A. 441
Martínez Reverte, J. 40
Martínez Ruiz, J. see Azorín García, F.
Mas Hernández, R. 17
Mas Mayoral, C. 26
Masats, R. 1
Matilla Tascón, A. 449
Mayoral Lobato, J. 245
Mazzini, F. 282
Medina, I. 40
Mejías Alonso, A. 170
Melcón, R. 443
Mélida Labaig, J. 439
Melón Ovalle, D. 187
Membrez, N. J. H. 410-12
Mena, J. M. de 427, 429
Mena, M. 373
Méndez Gutiérrez del Valle, R. 225
Mendoza de Lozoya, A. 189
Menéndez Pidal, R. 94
Mesonero Romanos, R. de 118, 330, 433
Mesones, J. de 257
Meza, R. 300
Michael, I. see Serafin, D.
Middleton, T. 413, 417
Miguel, A. de 138
Miguel Rodríguez, J. C. de 145
Millares Carló, A. 527
Miller, S. L. 179
Mirande, T. M. 332
Molero, J. 227, 311
Molina Campuzano, M. 66
Mollá, J. 414
Moncy Gullón, A. 338
Moneo Santamaría, F. 63
Montero, Esther 281
Montero, Eugenia 385
Montero, V. 41
Montero Alonso, J. 57, 428, 444

Montero Padilla, J. 57
Montero Vallejo, M. 57, 97
Montiel, I. 521
Montoliú Camps, P. 84, 430
Montoya, J. M. 146
Montoya Tamaño, M. A. 241
Monzón de Cáceres, A. 237
Moore, L. 423
Morales Vallespín, M. I. 453
Morales y Marín, J. L. 510
Morcillo, M. de los A. 431
Moreno Mangada, E. 467
Moya Rodríguez, A. 238
Muñoz, M. 285
Muñoz Fernández, A. 154, 170
Muñoz Molina, A. 333
Muñoz Muñoz, J. 195

N

Nadal Ortega, M. L. 194
Navarrete Martínez, E. 360
Navascués Palacio, P. 281, 295
Naylon, J. 264
Neal, W. K. 226
Neira de Mosquera, A. 430
Nelson, C. 133
Nicholson, D. 46
Nielfa Cristóbal, G. 218
Noble, A. G. 230, 261
Noel, C. C. 119
Noone, M. J. 397
Noriega, A. 256
Norman, J. 334
Núñez Pérez, M. G. 170

O

O'Hagan, A. R. 265
Olaechea Labayen, J. B. 15

Oliva Escribano, J. L. 519, 523
Olivares, J. 369
Olivares, P. 369
Oliveira Cezar, C. 351
Oliver Asín, J. 94
Olivera Poll, A. 16, 302
Ontañón, F. 4
Optiz, H. 451
Ormell, C. 304
Orso, S. N. 386
Ortega, S. 435
Otamendi, M. 234
Otero Carvajal, E. 109, 120, 461

P

Palacios Antón, J. A. 137
Palau y Dulcet, A. 520
Pallucchini, A. 376
Pamias Morato, J. 37
Parajón, M. 335
Pardo Canalís, E. 336
Parra Supervía, F. 253, 262
Pattison, W. T. 316
Paz, R. 521
Peinado, A. 181
Pellicer, L. 269
Peñasco de la Puente, H. 68
Pendleton, G. 261
Pereda, C. 246
Pereña, F. 181
Pérez, J. L. 392
Pérez de Ayala, R. 337
Pérez Firmat, G. 331
Pérez Galdós, B. 64, 338-39, 433
Pérez Pastor, C. 522
Pérez Reverte, A. 340
Pérez-Sánchez, A. E. 354
Pérez Sanz, J. J. 233
Pérez Vidal, J. 339
Perlman, J. E. 171
Piera, A. 1
Pincheson, E. 212
Piñeiro, N. 204
Polt, J. H. R. 320
Ponte Chamorro, F. J. 120, 141

# Index of Titles

## A

El abastecimiento de aguas a Madrid 195

ABC 329, 463, 468, 475

Los accesos ferroviarios a Madrid: su impacto en la geografía urbana de la ciudad 234

Acciones e intenciones de mujeres en la vida religiosa de los siglos XV y XVI 170

Actualidad Económica 479

El aeropuerto de Madrid Barajas: estudio geográfico 229

Age of gold, age of iron: Renaissance Spain and symbols of monarchy: the imperial legacy of Charles V and Philip II. Royal castles, palace-monasteries, princely houses 388

El agua en la higiene del Madrid de los Austrias 195

Air quality in the greater Madrid area: monitoring campaign in November 1990 256

Alcaldes de Madrid 202

Alfoz: Madrid, Territorio, Economía y Sociedad 502

Almagro, estudio geográfico de un barrio de Madrid 165

Almodóvar on Almodóvar 423

La Almudena y su significación en la vida y en la cultura madrileñas 150

Amar en Madrid 345

Amores y amoríos en Madrid 428

Anales Cervantinos 319

Anales del Instituto de Estudios Madrileños 85

Anales de la Universidad de Madrid 507

Anales Galdosianos 338

Análisis geográfico y representación del mosaico social de Madrid 165

Analysis of the 1985 General Plan for Madrid 265

Anatomy of Madrid in Luis Martín-Santos's 'Tiempo de silencio' 331

Los anfibios y reptiles de Madrid 284

Another man's wife 329

Antecedentes del Canal de Isabel II 266

El antiguo Madrid . . . 118

Anuario Bibliográfico 531

Anuario de prehistoria madrileña 77

Anuario Económico y Financiero 208

Anuario Estadístico de la Comunidad de Madrid 248

Aproximación al arte de la Comunidad de Madrid 347

Aproximación a la escultura religiosa contemporánea en Madrid 391

Aproximación a la geografía de la Comunidad de Madrid 15

Aproximación a las instituciones de la Comunidad de Madrid 200

Aproximación a los servicios sociales 194

Apuntes para un catálogo de periódicos madrileños desde el año 1661 al 1870 466

Aquellas tertulias de Madrid 433

Los árboles de Madrid 287

Arboles del Retiro 287

Arboles singulares de Madrid 287

Arquitectura doméstica moderna en Madrid 530

Arquitectura madrileña del siglo XVII 295

Arquitectura y arquitectos madrileños del siglo XIX 295

Arquitectura y clases sociales en el Madrid del siglo XIX 295

Art Libraries Journal 448

'Artículo de costumbres' in the periodicals of Madrid 1700-1808 343

Artículos de costumbres 343

Artículos literarios 343

Artistas en Madrid: años 80 359

Arturo Soria y la Ciudad Lineal 275

Artwise Madrid: the museum map 363

As 469, 475

Así fue la defensa de Madrid 125

El Ateneo científico, literario y artístico de Madrid (1835-1885) 352

# Index of Subjects

240

History *contd.*
gun-making 226
Habsburgs 92, 100-07, 195, 322
Herrera, Juan de (architect) 105
Holy Week 150
hospitals 121, 187, 512
hotels 121
housing 120
Hugo, Victor (novelist) 324
Ibarra y Marín, Joaquín (printer) 458
Ibarruri, Dolores (La Pasionaria) (communist leader) 125, 134
illiteracy 462
Inclusa (hospital) 186
*El Independiente* (newspaper) 463
industry 130, 225-26
Inquisition 151
Institución Libre de Enseñanza 306
Instituto de Estudios Madrileños (Institute of Madrid Studies) 137
Instituto Nacional de Estadística (INE) (National Statistics Institute) 251
Instituto Nacional de Industria (INI) (National Institute of Industry) 224
Isabella II (1833-68) 74, 303, 315, 318, 330, 338, 353, 360, 372
Jesuits 122, 153
Jews 143
Juvara, Filippo (architect) 64
labour 241, 243
press 462
language 97
Largo Caballero, Francisco (politician) 127
Larra, Mariano José de

(writer) 315, 341, 343, 415, 433
Lavapiés (district) 143, 332, 344
legends 427, 429
Ley de Prensa (1966 Press Law) 463
Lhardy (restaurant) 439
libraries 449
literature 85, 87, 115, 314-16, 318-19, 327, 330, 332, 338-39, 341, 344, 433
Civil War 327
Generation of 1898 327
local elections (1931) 205
local government 101, 117, 121
López de Hoyos, Juan (writer) 529
Madrid (Autonomous Community) 93
Madrid (name) 83, 94
Madrid (province) 93
Madrid School
painting 354-55, 361
philosophy 296
Manzanares (river) 344
markets 121
Martín-Santos, Luis (novelist) 332
Martínez del Mazo, Juan Bautista (painter) 355
masked balls 121
mayors 202
mediaeval 83, 92, 97-99, 145, 154, 425
women 99
medicine 187, 512
mentideros (gossip-shops) 69, 427
Mesonero Romanos, Ramón (writer) 60, 315, 330, 341, 374, 433
Metro system 69, 123, 238
Miaja Menant, José (General) 125

migration 99
military bases (US) 137
Miramar (palace) 384
Mola, Emilio (General) 129
Molina, Tirso de (playwright) 330
monasteries 121
Moratín, Leandro Fernández de (writer) 315, 341
Mudéjar community 145
Mulot, Jean Baptiste (gardener) 283
Museo del Prado 73, 89, 121, 378, 380
museums 89
music 85, 93, 393, 397, 399-400
National Confederation of Labour (CNT) 135
Negrín López, Juan (prime minister) 125
New Castile 106
newspaper libraries 454
newspapers 463, 466
nobility 109, 121
novels 327, 330, 337-38
Olivares, Gaspar de Guzmán, Count Duke of 383
Olmo, Lauro (playwright) 409
O'Neill, Eugene (playwright) 406
opera 394
Ortega y Gasset, José (writer) 296, 485
painting and painters 73, 354, 359-62, 368, 371
palaces 384
Palacio Real (Royal Palace) 89, 357, 384-85, 390, 399
El Pardo (palace) 384
Parque del Retiro 121, 280
Paseo de la Castellana 335
Paseo del Prado 119

241

# Map of the Madrid Metro

This map is reproduced with the permission of the Madrid Transport Consortium.

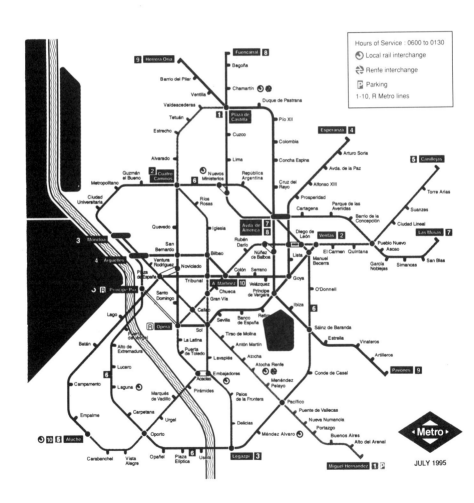

Hours of Service : 0600 to 0130
- Local rail interchange
- Renfe interchange
- Parking
- 1-10, R Metro lines

JULY 1995

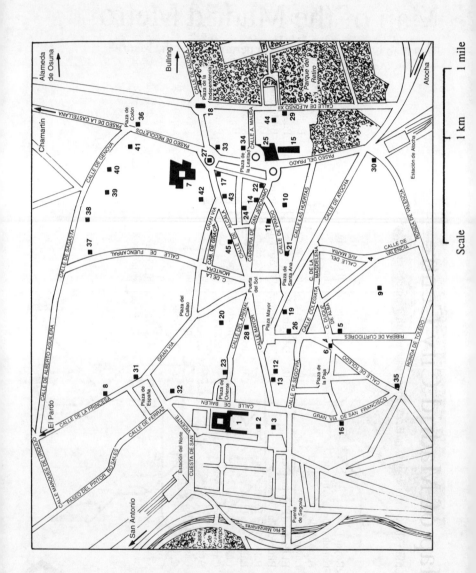

Map of the Madrid Metro

# Map of Madrid City Centre

This map shows museums, palaces, theatres and other places of interest.

1 Royal Palace
2 Catedral de la Almudena
3 Arab Wall
4 Lavapiés
5 El Rastro (Flea market)
6 Plaza de la Cebada
7 Palacio de Buenavista (Alba)
8 Palacio de Liria
9 La Corrala
10 Casa de Lope de Vega
11 Ateneo
12 Casa de Cisneros
13 Casa de la Villa (Town Hall)
14 Congreso de Diputados
15 Museo del Prado

16 San Francisco el Grande
17 Banco de España
18 Puerta de Alcalá
19 Palacio de Santa Cruz
20 Descalzas Reales
21 Teatro Español (Corral del Príncipe)
22 Museo Thyssen-Bornemisza
23 Teatro Real
24 Teatro de la Zarzuela
25 Ritz Hotel
26 Catedral de San Isidro
27 Cibeles Fountain
28 San Ginés
29 Casón del Buen Retiro
30 Museo Nacional Centro de
   Arte Reina Sofía

31 Edificio España
32 Palacio del Senado
33 Palacio de Comunicaciones
34 Bolsa (Stock Exchange)
35 Puerta de Toledo
36 Biblioteca Nacional
37 Museo Municipal
38 Museo Romántico
39 Palacio Longoria
40 Palacio de Justicia
41 Teatro María Guerrero
42 Casa de las Siete Chimeneas
43 Círculo de Bellas Artes
44 Museo del Ejército
45 Real Academia de Bellas
   Artes San Fernando

# ALSO FROM CLIO PRESS

## INTERNATIONAL ORGANIZATIONS SERIES

Each volume in the International Organizations Series is either devoted to one specific organization, or to a number of different organizations operating in a particular region, or engaged in a specific field of activity. The scope of the series is wide-ranging and includes intergovernmental organizations, international non-governmental organizations, and national bodies dealing with international issues. The series is aimed mainly at the English-speaker and each volume provides a selective, annotated, critical bibliography of the organization, or organizations, concerned. The bibliographies cover books, articles, pamphlets, directories, databases and theses and, wherever possible, attention is focused on material about the organizations rather than on the organizations' own publications. Notwithstanding this, the most important official publications, and guides to those publications, will be included. The views expressed in individual volumes, however, are not necessarily those of the publishers.

## VOLUMES IN THE SERIES

1  *European Communities*,
   John Paxton
2  *Arab Regional Organizations*,
   Frank A. Clements
3  *Comecon: The Rise and Fall of an
   International Socialist
   Organization*, Jenny Brine
4  *International Monetary Fund*,
   Anne C. M. Salda
5  *The Commonwealth*, Patricia M.
   Larby and Harry Hannam
6  *The French Secret Services*, Martyn
   Cornick and Peter Morris

7  *Organization of African Unity*,
   Gordon Harris
8  *North Atlantic Treaty Organization*,
   Phil Williams
9  *World Bank*, Anne C. M. Salda
10 *United Nations System*, Joseph P.
   Baratta
11 *Organization of American States*,
   David Sheinin
12 *The British Secret Services*, Philip
   H. J. Davies
13 *The Israeli Secret Services*, Frank
   A. Clements